BREAKING
IN

JOURNEYS TO LEADERSHIP SERIES

The Journeys to Leadership series is about successful women who have reached the pinnacle of their careers. It features stories about extraordinary women who have found paths to success—whether it is leading a college or university, becoming successful scholars in science and engineering, or thriving in some other male-dominated arena.

Available

Answering the Call
African American Women in Higher Education Leadership
Beverly L. Bower and Mimi Wolverton

Latinas in the Workplace
An Emerging Leadership Force
Esther Elena López-Mulnix, Mimi Wolverton, and Salwa A. Zaki

Women at the Top
What Women University and College Presidents Say About Effective Leadership
Mimi Wolverton, Beverly L. Bower, and Adrienne E. Hyle

BREAKING IN

WOMEN'S ACCOUNTS OF HOW CHOICES SHAPE STEM CAREERS

Ann Wolverton, Lisa Nagaoka, and
Mimi Wolverton

Foreword by *Donna J. Dean*

STERLING, VIRGINIA

COPYRIGHT © 2015 BY STYLUS PUBLISHING, LLC.

Published by Stylus Publishing, LLC
22883 Quicksilver Drive
Sterling, Virginia 20166-2102

Library of Congress Cataloging-in-Publication Data
The CIP data for this book has been applied for.

13-digit ISBN: 978-1-57922-428-8 (cloth)
13-digit ISBN: 978-1-57922-429-5 (paper)
13-digit ISBN: 978-1-62036-245-7 ((library networkable e-edition)
13-digit ISBN: 978-1-62036-246-4 (consumer e-edition)

Printed in the United States of America

All first editions printed on acid-free paper
that meets the American National Standards Institute
Z39-48 Standard.

Bulk Purchases

Quantity discounts are available for use in workshops and for
staff development.
Call 1-800-232-0223

First Edition, 2015

10   9   8   7   6   5   4   3   2   1

To the eight women who graciously shared their stories of careers, challenges, and choices, and to the countless others whose untold stories echo those featured in this book

Contents

Contents

Foreword

In 1974 in the preface to my PhD dissertation, along with the usual thanks to my PhD adviser, thesis committee, and family, I included the words "to those many people who, either purposely or unknowingly, made my twenty-one-year journey through education more arduous and difficult than it should have been because they failed to recognize that ambition and intellect are not sex-linked characteristics." Unfortunately, these words still ring true forty years later.

Today, in the culture and context of women's advancement and satisfaction with careers in science, technology, engineering, and mathematics (STEM), the data show that many challenges and obstacles remain, as highlighted in Chapter 1 and expanded on in later chapters, particularly 11 and 12. Chapter 11 adds a somber note as it reports the responses of eight anonymous young women to a survey that is a compilation of the issues the women featured in this book identified as challenges and obstructions that keep women out of STEM PhD programs and consequently out of the researcher and faculty ranks at our national laboratories and research universities.

Acquiring analytical skills and applying those skills to intriguing problems are the hallmarks of education, advanced training, and professional advancement in one's chosen STEM field. As scientists and engineers, we are taught the importance of generating and evaluating data from an objective, dispassionate perspective. No arduous accumulation of objective data buttresses my contention behind my carefully articulated statement in my dissertation preface, but rather a deeply felt courage to repeatedly tell myself, "You can do it!" The recollections and experiences of the eight women of *Breaking In* resonate very strongly with my own career passages.

We want young women of all backgrounds to know that the STEM fields can be fully open to them and that these professions can be compatible with all the other areas of life that are important. Is this going to be easy, or will every woman's pathway be smooth? Assuredly not, but the shared perspectives in this book are valuable in affirming that there is no perfect life or career and that even the most successful female scientists and engineers have surmounted obstacles and faced setbacks throughout their careers. These women generously and openly share their experiences, positive and negative. They each speak of pivotal people who supported their interests, particularly at times when they were the most discouraged or confused. They often found these individuals in their mentoring relationships or professional networks or through serendipitous encounters.

Never before has STEM been so exciting with unlimited opportunities to make a difference. The women profiled here describe how they developed essential conflict-handling skills; an understanding of the organizational cultures, customs, and structures in their workplaces; and a recognition of how their own beliefs, attitudes, and values influenced their decision making. Each chose her battles carefully, was tolerant of her own missteps, kept her sense of humor, practiced good stress management techniques, and let her own deeply felt principles guide her choices.

It is a rare STEM professional who has not heard the quip, "Anecdotes don't make data." But analysis of such data does not reveal the most evocative stories of challenges faced and obstacles surmounted. Most compelling are the narratives of people like these eight outstanding women who describe their own journeys of discovery, mistakes made, and difficult choices. They are saying to every reader of this book, "You can do it too" and "Tell your stories to others," to which I add that life is too short not to do and share what you love. Be open to the possibilities that will come your way unexpectedly.

Donna J. Dean
Executive Consultant, Association for Women in Science (www.awis.org)
Career Consultant, American Chemical Society (www.acs.org)
National President, Association for Women in Science, 2006–2007
Senior Federal Executive (retired), National Institutes of Health

Preface

Journeys to Leadership is a book series that captures the experiences of women who have moved into prominence in their professions. The books in this series present the individual and unique voices of women leaders as they discuss their values and the events that have shaped them as leaders in their fields. *Breaking In* is no exception.

The first three books in the series—*Women at the Top, Answering the Call,* and *Latinas in the Workplace*—relate the life experiences of women who by virtue of their expertise and position are considered leaders. *Women at the Top* and *Answering the Call* look at college and university presidents and women in key policy positions. *Latinas in the Workplace* features women in K–12 and higher education, medicine, manufacturing, consulting, and construction. Twenty-four women—nine Latina, eight African American, one Native American, and six White. Some married, others not, a mix of old and young. Many are firsts in the positions they currently or previously held.

Breaking In departs slightly from the previous books in the series. It showcases the stories of eight successful women in science, technology, engineering, and mathematics. Four of them have made their careers at research universities as faculty; the others chose to move into industry or policy positions outside the academy. Unlike the women featured in the earlier books, these scientists and engineers do not necessarily hold positions of official authority (e.g., president or chief executive officer). Nevertheless, it seemed a logical extension of the legacy created by the first twenty-four to broaden the meaning of leadership and explore the experiences of these women who, like their counterparts in the other books, inhabit professional worlds where they are greatly outnumbered by men.

Mimi Wolverton
Series Editor
Journeys to Leadership

Acknowledgments

A special thanks to John von Knorring, our publisher, for his suggestion that we tell the stories of women in science and engineering. It set us on a path that culminated in *Breaking In*. Thanks to Stylus's production staff for helping bring this book to fruition. Thanks too to the young women who contributed to this effort anonymously. You know who you are. And to Donna Dean for adding a thought-provoking foreword.

one

THE REALITIES OF
BREAKING IN

WOMEN IN THE UNITED STATES have made great strides in establishing parity with their male counterparts in terms of educational attainment. According to the U.S. Census, in 2012 more women than men over the age of twenty-five held bachelor's degrees (or higher) in the United States. Among those aged twenty-five to thirty-five years old, about 38 percent of women held bachelor's degrees or higher compared to 31 percent of men in the same age bracket. At the PhD level, the National Science Foundation (2014a) reports that women earned about the same number of PhDs as men in the United States in 2010. However, this good news disguises continuing challenges of gender parity in science, technology, engineering, and mathematics (STEM). The number of women in STEM disciplines continues to lag significantly behind that of men. Although women and men in the United States earn about the same number of college degrees, women still will earn fewer than 25 percent of the PhDs in engineering, computer science, and physics, and they are underrepresented in almost all STEM careers.

As undergraduates, women are less likely to major in a STEM field and more likely to switch to a non-STEM field before degree completion. And although women earned 41 percent of PhDs in the STEM disciplines in 2010 (up from 11 percent in 1972), they received only about 30 percent of PhDs awarded in the physical sciences and mathematics and about 20 percent of PhDs garnered in computer science and engineering for that year (National Science Foundation, 2014a).

Within academia and industry, women make up an even smaller proportion of the positions in STEM fields. In academia, women held about 29 percent of tenured or tenure-track positions in STEM departments in 2010, with women filling 19 percent of full professorships. To compound matters, the extent to which women are represented varies widely by STEM discipline. For instance, although women represented more than a quarter of tenured professors in the life sciences in 2010, they constituted a much smaller proportion of tenured professor positions in computer and information sciences (14 percent) and engineering (11 percent). Female participation in the nonacademic STEM workforce mirror the patterns seen in academia. Although women made up 40 percent of the professional workforce in the life and biological sciences, only 20 percent of computer scientists and mathematicians and 12 percent of engineers in 2010 were women.

Why does this matter? For the United States to continue to compete in the global marketplace, it must tap into as much of its creative and intellectual capital as possible. Study findings show that the degree to which a country graduates and hires engineers and scientists is in direct correlation to various measures of long-term economic growth (Murphy, Shleifer, & Vishny, 1991; Ochoa, 1996). And at least by some measures, the United States is falling behind. The Organisation for Economic Co-operation and Development (OECD) ranks the United States twenty-third out of thirty countries, graduating fewer people between the ages of twenty-five and thirty-four years in the STEM disciplines per 100,000 employed than the OECD average in 2009.

In terms of gender parity, almost every OECD country graduates women in lower proportions to men in the STEM fields. The exception is Turkey, where nearly 60 percent of the graduates in STEM fields are women. The United States ranks in the middle of the pack, along with Germany, Australia, and Sweden, suggesting the United States is not alone among economically advanced countries in its need to confront and deal with disproportionately low numbers of women completing advanced STEM degrees (OECD, 2011).[1] Data compiled

---

1. OECD expands the traditional definition of *STEM disciplines* to include manufacturing and processing, architecture, and construction.

by the National Science Foundation support these findings, showing that the United States graduates a proportion of women with STEM PhDs similar to the proportion in Canada, Australia, and the United Kingdom, including analogous variation across disciplines. Why do women choose not to enter STEM disciplines? A decade ago much of the conversation focused on differences in math and science test scores among men and women. Lawrence Summers, as president of Harvard University, reinvigorated a public debate on the issue in 2005, when he speculated that one reason women enter the sciences at lower rates is innate differences in mathematical ability. Summers's high-profile comments spurred a burst of research examining the factors that affect the number of women in STEM fields. Initially, research examined the validity of the innate abilities argument, including cross-country variation. Findings exposed the difficulty in attempts to parse nature from nurture. For example, in several former Soviet republics, women and men obtain undergraduate and doctoral degrees in many STEM disciplines at nearly equal rates (e.g., Bulgaria, Romania).

More recently, researchers and commentators have focused on a wider array of possible explanations for the shortage of women with advanced degrees in STEM disciplines, including how unintentional or unconscious bias can influence women's decisions to participate in the STEM fields at every educational stage; how biases sometimes reveal themselves during the job interview process, tenure, and promotion and affect collaborative opportunities; and how conflicts in work-life balance affect career choices. For example, Kane and Mertz (2012) discovered that sociocultural factors, and in particular gender equality in terms of labor participation and pay, exhibit greater explanatory power than innate ability. Ann-Marie Slaughter (2012) discusses a generational shift in the perception that women *can have it all*, suggesting that the feminist ideal of the '60s and '70s that women can have both family and full-blown career has been replaced by a desire for flexibility in the workplace to prioritize family. (See also Association for Women in Science [2012], which reports the findings of a 2011 study that supports the observations of the women interviewed in *Breaking In*.)

A longitudinal study by Glass, Sassler, Levitte, and Michelmore (2013) compared retention of women in STEM fields with that of women in other fields. The researchers identified several ominous trends: STEM women were more likely to leave their jobs; the disparity in retention is almost entirely attributable to STEM women switching out of STEM fields but not out of the labor force; women are more likely to leave STEM fields if they have an advanced degree (a phenomenon that doesn't affect women in other fields); although age and higher job satisfaction reduce the number of professional women leaving other fields, they have little or no impact in STEM fields; and finally, marriage and child rearing are more likely to push women out of STEM careers and into other non-STEM-related ones (although they are somewhat less likely to leave the field if their spouse is also employed in STEM). The authors suspect attitudes and expectations, which perpetuate traditional beliefs about the competencies of STEM women, may underlie some of these behaviors (Stansbury, 2013).

The bottom-line message from all this research is that the choices women make when entering and remaining in a STEM discipline are complex. In *Breaking In*, we wanted to develop a deeper understanding of why women are drawn to STEM disciplines, what challenges they face, why they decide to remain in academia or move to the private or government sectors, and what can be done to encourage more women to specialize in science, mathematics, and engineering. So we asked.

We used a qualitative case study approach to collect in-depth information directly from women with STEM careers. The stories captured in the first three books in the Journeys to Leadership series convinced us that the subtleties revealed as women talk about their professional and personal experiences bring to life their struggles and triumphs, the decisions they make, and the reasoning behind them more clearly than any other approach to research. We purposefully selected participants for their ability to inform the study (Lincoln & Guba, 1985; Merriam, 1998; Yin, 2003). We recruited women established in their professions who vary in age and geographic location. All eight women highlighted in this book have PhDs in a physical science, mathematics, engineering, or computer science, STEM disciplines in which women are particularly underrepresented.

We interviewed equal numbers of women in and outside academia because of the noticeable absence of women from the faculty ranks of research universities; many opt for alternative career paths. Cynthia Barnhart, Susan Blessing, Teresa D. Golden, and Bonnie F. Jacobs hold faculty positions at research universities; Linda S. Birnbaum, Sharon Hays, Angela Hessler, and Radia Perlman have achieved success in industry or government. Several of them started professional careers in one job market and later moved to another. Content analysis of their stories allowed us to look for common threads and patterns in their responses as well as differences across organizational types (Babbie, 2001; Miles & Huberman, 1994; Yin, 2003).

We developed and piloted a semistructured interview protocol before the interviews (Lincoln & Guba, 1985; Miles & Huberman, 1984; Yin, 2003). We conducted the interviews using a combination of face-to-face, telephone, and e-mail exchanges that took two to four hours to complete. All were tape-recorded, transcribed, and edited to remove repetition and enhance clarity. Content analysis was used to systematically categorize information in the transcripts with regard to themes and patterns of responses to ensure consistency and validity. Additional information pertaining to each participant and her organization was gathered via work-related documents, résumés and curricula vitae, newspaper articles, and the Internet and combined with the transcripts. Once the cases were written, we reviewed them, and each case was shared with its respective participant for accuracy.

Writing *Breaking In* proved to be a challenging journey. Not only are there few women at the PhD level in many of the hard sciences, computer science, mathematics, and certain areas of engineering, we also found some of them reluctant to speak about their experiences. In reality we interviewed ten women—the eight women featured in the book, a professor in mathematics, and a computer scientist in the private sector (STEM disciplines in which the fewest women participate)—and we were told the story of an eleventh woman within one of these stories.

All of the latter three women are highly regarded in their fields and readily entered the interview process. In fact, they were excited about the book and their participation in it. The eleventh woman, who served as a mentor to one of the others, even commented on how important the book is. Once they read the drafts of their stories, however, they decided to withdraw from the project. They realized they couldn't publicly relate their experiences because they either feared professional reprisal or were reluctant to embarrass others (all male). As one of these women put it, "I just can't see how to tell my story without offending people I don't wish to offend." One of the women also noted that reading her story in print brought to the surface the shame, guilt, and anger she continues to associate with her experiences.

We originally thought we should also include women from multiple racial and ethnic backgrounds. One of the women who withdrew was a member of an underrepresented group. Her story was complicated with layers of gender-based bias intertwined with outright prejudicial behaviors directly related to her racial/ethnic standing. In hindsight, our forced selection of White women provided us with the opportunity to engage in a cleaner analysis of their stories. The patterns that exist do so because of gender, nothing else.

We attempted to vary the age of the participants, but the withdrawal of the two women made this difficult because they were younger. In the end, the participants skew toward women who have been in the workforce for several decades. Although they sometimes reference prejudicial behavior, none does so as forcefully as the women who withdrew from the study. And to compound the situation further, as the remaining eight women read drafts of their stories, several amended them to conceal the identities of relatives and friends or to protect themselves professionally by softening language and omitting commentary.

Take this into account as you read because, left unsaid, the conclusion might be drawn that we as a society have largely moved beyond prejudicial behaviors and beliefs that perpetuate disparities based on gender to a more egalitarian community that values women's potential and real contributions as highly as it does those of men, and that indeed such misconduct is generational and lies behind us.

Although it is understated in the narratives in this book, evidence clearly points to the opposite and colors women's choices, whether intentionally or unintentionally made. For this reason, we went back to several of the eight women with a survey to ask them to indicate the top reasons their disciplines have trouble recruiting and retaining women along the pipeline (primary school through career stages), whether they think these challenges are specific to their field or apply to STEM disciplines generally, and the most important ways to improve retention. We also asked several untenured or recently tenured women in STEM faculty positions to anonymously respond to the survey. Combined, their responses allowed us to place the specific experiences of the eight women we interviewed within today's context.

In the past, bias toward women in STEM disciplines occurred as overt sexism, as experienced by Bonnie Jacobs and Linda Birnbaum, two of our older participants. Today, such behaviors can still rear their ugly heads—comments about unattractive women being attracted to neuroscience (Jaschik, 2012a) and complaints about "overt assgrabbery" at scientific meetings that are routinely dismissed by male counterparts as uncommon or imagined (see Isis the Scientist [2012] and Stemwedel [n.d.] for further examples). Unintentional or unconscious bias is more difficult to identify than outright prejudicial behavior because it manifests itself in everyday occurrences, such as the discounting or dismissal of ideas that come from women, the crediting of their ideas to male counterparts, and extensive networking among male students and young professionals that can give men mentoring and informational advantages—actions we tend to take for granted. A study in the *Proceedings of the National Academy of Sciences of the United States of America* confirms acculturated bias against female students on the part of men and (sorry to say) women scientists (Jaschik, 2012c). A later study suggests funding inequities across male and female scientists affect productivity and publishing rates (Jaschik, 2012b). These subtler forms of bias can result in inattention to and lack of support for female students in particular and women in STEM disciplines in general. As Susan Blessing points out in chapter 4, the competitive environment and a lack of positive feedback in academic settings "can be tough, and it could be more difficult for women. . . . Many people can't handle 'not nice.'"

Family and work-life issues permeate the choices of the eight women we interviewed. While they are quite cognizant of the trade-offs they are making, the dominance of work-life issues highlights the possibility that unconscious biases are embedded within particular institutions and the academic system itself. Jacobs, Golden, and Barnhart postponed careers or changed locations in attempts to gain work-family balance. Hessler enjoyed university life at Grand Valley State University but moved to the private sector to find balance. She loves her job but casts it as a choice not to think about work at night or when she is getting the kids ready for bed. Birnbaum recalls, "I can't say my moving into government was a decision that I didn't want academia . . . [but] given my previous university and college teaching experience, I thought it would be difficult to be an academic and a mother." Blessing notes that many couples have opted to live in different towns or even states to pursue academic careers; she doesn't know what she would have done if her husband had decided he wanted to stay in Chicago when she took a job at Florida State University.

The first American woman in space, Sally Ride, passed away in 2012. She made hard choices all her life. A gifted athlete, she chose to pursue a PhD in astrophysics. She shied away from media because commentators ribbed her about needing to match her purse to the space shuttle. She refused to profit from her name, choosing instead to write children's books that extol the excitement of science. She enjoyed life and had fun. She believed she was lucky. She had much in common with the eight women whose stories you are about to read. They also made hard choices in their pursuit of careers in STEM fields, whether in academia or in industry or government, and continue to make them as they grapple with the complexities of balancing work and family life. They have succeeded and are enthusiastic about their work despite overt or subtle forms of biases they've encountered. They have fun. They are a hearty bunch whose stories inspire us and we hope will inspire you.

AUTHORS' NOTE

As a mother, daughter, and daughter-in-law team of writers, we were particularly drawn to the subject of this book because our career choices have led us into male-dominated STEM fields and work environments.

Ann Wolverton graduated from the University of Texas at Austin (UT) in 1999 with a PhD in economics. Her 1993 entering class consisted of roughly 30 students, four of whom were women; no tenure-track women were on UT's economics faculty at the time. Most of the women who started the program finished it. As Ann puts it, "We were a stubborn bunch." Ann served two terms (2007 and 2009) on the Council of Economic Advisers to the President as the senior economist for environment and natural resources. She currently works as an economist for the federal government.

Lisa Nagaoka graduated from the University of Washington's PhD anthropology program in 2000, specializing in archaeology. During much of her time there, there was a lone female professor on Washington's faculty, and she was the only archaeology professor with children. Interestingly, at one time the archaeology graduate student population was mostly female, two women to every man. The attrition rate for women, however, was twice that of their male counterparts. Lisa has established herself as an international expert in zooarchaeology with a focus on human-environment interactions. Today, she is the sole tenured woman faculty member in the geography department at the University of North Texas.

Mimi Wolverton graduated from Northern Illinois University in 1967 with an undergraduate degree in mathematics and a minor in geology. She encountered no women on the faculty in either department. That year, women in STEM disciplines accounted for 8 percent of PhDs and less than 25 percent of baccalaureate degrees. After having worked a number of years in heavy construction (definitely a male-dominated field), she earned an MBA and a PhD in education leadership and policy studies at Arizona State University and spent several years in academia, retiring in 2007 as a full professor.

NOTES ABOUT CHAPTER RESOURCES

Most of the data reported in this chapter are taken from the National Science Foundation. See also reports from the Association of Women in Science (www.awis.org) and the 2012 National Coalition for Women and Girls in Education report, *Title IX at 40: Working to Ensure Gender Equality in Education* (www.ncwge.org/PDF/TitleIXat40.pdf).

While we omitted in-text references (we believe they intrude on the story being told), we provide a brief bibliographical note at the end of Chapters 2 through 9 that highlights the main sources used in telling that particular story.

REFERENCES

Association for Women in Science. (2012). *The work-life integrations overload: Thousands of scientists weigh in on outmoded work environments, unfriendly policies.* Retrieved from http://www.awis.org/associations/9417/files/AWIS_Work_Life_Balance_Executive_Summary.pdf

Babbie, E. (2001). *The practice of social research* (9th ed.). Belmont, CA: Wadsworth/Thomson Learning.

Glass, J. L., Sassler, S., Levitte, Y., & Michelmore, K. M. (2013). What's so special about STEM? A comparison of women's retention in STEM and professional occupations. *Social Forces, 92*(2), 723–726. doi:10.1093/sf/sot092

Isis the Scientist. (2012). What we learn when professorly d00ds take to Facebook. [Web log post]. Retrieved from http://isisthescientist.com/2012/10/18/what-we-learn-when-professorly-d00ds-take-to-facebook/

Jaschik, S. (2012a). *Furor over male scientist's Facebook post about female scientists.* Retrieved from http://www.insidehighered.com/news/2012/10/19/furor-over-male-scientists-facebook-post-about-female-scientists

Jaschik, S. (2012b). *Smoking gun or sexism?* Retrieved from http://www.insidehighered.com/news/2012/09/21/study-offers-new-evidence-scientists-are-biased-against-women

Jaschik, S. (2012c). *Study suggests resource inequities may impact publishing records of women in science.* Retrieved from http://www.insidehighered.com/news/2012/12/13/study-suggests-resource-inequities-may-impact-publishing-records-women-science

Kane, J., & Mertz, J. (2012). Debunking myths about gender and mathematics performance. *Notices of the AMS, 59*(1), 10–21.

Lincoln, Y. S., & Guba, E. G. (1985). *Naturalistic inquiry.* Newbury Park, CA: Sage.

Merriam, S. B. (1998). *Qualitative research and case study applications in education.* San Francisco, CA: Jossey-Bass.

Miles, M. B., & Huberman, A. M. (1994). *Qualitative data analysis* (2nd ed.). Thousand Oaks, CA: Sage.

Murphy, K., Shleifer, A., & Vishny, R. (1991). The allocation of talent: Implications for growth. *Quarterly Journal of Economics, 106*(2), 503–530.

National Science Foundation. (2014a). *Doctoral recipients from U.S. universities.* Retrieved from http://www.nsf.gov/statistics/sed/digest/2012/nsf14305.pdf

National Science Foundation. (2014b). *Women, minorities, and persons with disabilities in science and engineering.* Retrieved from http://www.nsf.gov/statistics/wmpd/2013/sex.cfm

Ochoa, O. (1996). *Growth, trade and endogenous technology: A study of OECD manufacturing.* New York, NY: St. Martin's Press.

Organisation for Economic Co-operation and Development. (2011). *Education at a glance 2011: OECD indicators.* Paris, France: Author.

Slaughter, A.-M. (2012, July/August). Why women still can't have it all. *Atlantic Monthly.* Retrieved from http://www.theatlantic.com/magazine/archive/2012/07/why-women-still-cant-have-it-all/309020/

Stansbury, A. (2013). *Women and STEM occupations: Retention rates and reasons for leaving.* Retrieved from http://journalistsresource.org/studies/society/gender-society/women-stem-occupations-retention-rates

Stemwedel, J. D. (n.d.). *Adventures in ethics and science* [Web log]. Retrieved from http://ethicsandscience.scientopia.org

Yin, R. K. (2003). *Case study research: Design and methods.* Thousand Oaks, CA: Sage.

two

FASCINATION, FUN, AND FLEXIBILITY

Cynthia Barnhart

"I GRADUATED FROM THE UNIVERSITY OF VERMONT in 1981 with a degree in civil engineering. Although I eventually ended up in academia, I began in the private sector. As an undergraduate, I knew that although I liked the problem-solving elements of design, if I had to design structures like bridges I would go crazy because of the rigid step-by-step approach I'd need to take. So I looked for a job with more flexibility.

"I ended up going to work for Bechtel. At the time, Bechtel was the construction manager for the subway system in Washington, D.C., and I was hired as a planning and scheduling engineer. My work differed from classical engineering, involved me in the transportation field, and had a little bit to do with the concept of optimization, which I'd been introduced to as an undergraduate and found fascinating.

"I oversaw the construction companies engaged in the subway project to ensure they stayed on schedule. I followed the construction schedule, assessed what they had done, and figured out what they should be paid. Here I was, a twenty-one-year-old woman (hard hat, steel-toed boots, and all) walking into a payment meeting with construction

---

Barnhart is a professor of civil and environmental engineering and engineering systems, associate dean of engineering, Ford Professor of Engineering, and director of Transportation@MIT at the Massachusetts Institute of Technology in Cambridge.

company owners (these are big companies!) saying, 'We're not paying the amount you requested' [laughing]. And they'd say, 'But we've done the work.' And I'd answer, 'No, you haven't.' It was fun. But it also, after a fairly short time, lost its luster.

"I understood the job rather quickly, and there were no new challenges, nothing more to learn. It was not the career trajectory I wanted. I was told I could become the first woman resident engineer. A resident engineer is the person in charge of the project. But to think of being a resident engineer as the pinnacle of my career just didn't sound exciting.

"I worked for Bechtel between 1981 and 1984, and my view of engineering in the field gained through that experience influenced my decision to go back to school. After about a year—maybe even more quickly—I knew I didn't want to do this the rest of my life.

"When I went back to school I never once thought about returning to the private sector. I found academia attractive for several reasons. First, my perception was—and it's proved to be true—that you really don't have a boss in academia. I learned at Bechtel that when you have a boss, and you don't believe that he knows what he's doing, it's painful. I decided it would be better if I didn't have anyone telling me what to do. Second, the very nature of the work intrigued me. It's about learning, being creative, formulating new ideas, and interacting with students. I love working with students. I think I always wanted to teach. When I was a first grader, I wanted to be a first grade teacher, and with every passing year, I wanted to be a teacher in the grade I was in. When I got to college, I wanted to teach there too. I wanted to be a professor.

"And third, there's a degree of flexibility. I determine what I want to do (particularly in terms of research), and I can change what I want to do. The academy also provides more of an opportunity to balance your professional and personal lives, but you have to work at it. I don't know anyone who really believes she knows how to obtain that balance [laughing]. But the chance to try means a lot to me. When my kids had activities—even when I was interim dean—I could attend. When my daughter Julia had a field hockey game at three o'clock in the afternoon, I went. It almost always meant that at nine or ten or eleven o'clock at night, I was paying for it, but it was a trade-off I was happy to make because I could be a part of my daughters' lives. If I hadn't had that type of flexibility, I'm not sure I would've been able to work. I would have wanted to work, but I might've made the hard choice of quitting.

"There was an emphasis on hard work in our family growing up in Barre, Vermont, a certainty that through hard work you can do whatever you want, and a belief that education can help you succeed. Neither of my parents went to college, but they made sure my siblings and I did (I have a sister, who is a year older than I am, and a brother, who is a year younger). All of us graduated from the University of Vermont.

"My parents grew up in Vermont; and in the case of my mother, her parents were born in Vermont, but their parents were immigrant farmers from Spain. My grandmother used to call us when we were young and give us Spanish lessons and quiz us on our spelling words for the week. She never went past the eighth grade but valued education. My father owned a catering business. He was smart, hardworking, and careful with his money. He saved enough to buy several apartment buildings, which he managed and maintained. My mother was the principal's secretary at our high school. She always knew what we were up to [laughing].

"*Success* was defined primarily in terms of financial well-being. Our parents worked hard to achieve the middle-class life; making money was important. In many respects, the desire to better ourselves financially drove our career choices. Both of my siblings hold MBAs. My sister and her family live in Vermont, where she works for a nonprofit. My brother recently moved from Switzerland to Connecticut. He's president of an aerospace company.

"School was always pretty easy for me. I didn't know growing up what particular field I would choose, but I always liked math. And everybody said, 'You'll get a good job with math.' I ended up in engineering even though I didn't know much about it. As an undergraduate, I found it rather boring. The first two years of engineering programs typically focus on fundamentals. Once you get to the upper level, you begin to see how it all comes together and how it applies. Even so, I didn't find it all that exciting. However, I had too much time invested in it, so I stuck with it. That ingrained hard-work-and-you-don't-quit family ethic just kicked in.

"I remember when I was accepted to graduate school, my father gave me a Charlie Brown poster. Charlie was running, and on the bottom it said, 'I'm going for it.' That's who I am. I'm going for it. I don't always know why, but once I'm going, I'm going [laughing]. I've always been that way.

"I went back for my master's and PhD at the Massachusetts Institute of Technology [MIT]. Initially, I thought about switching to business or law, either of which I actually preferred to engineering, but money was an issue. My parents paid for our undergraduate educations, but my siblings and I were on our own for graduate school. I thought that if I went to law or business school, I'd have to pay a lot of money; but if I got my PhD in engineering, the university would pay me. That was my motivation [laughing]. I received a research assistantship for the duration of my studies, which covered tuition and provided a monthly stipend. This is pretty common in engineering. Most PhD students are funded through either research or teaching assistantships.

"I married my husband, Mark Baribeau, a year after I had graduated from the University of Vermont. We were living in Washington, D.C., and wanted to return to New England. So MIT made perfect sense. In addition, I liked the creativity involved in operations research, which entails mathematically representing a physical system and optimizing its efficiency and effectiveness. (I had first been exposed to operations research as an undergraduate at the University of Vermont.) MIT's programs offered the flexibility to acquire this type of expertise and apply it in an engineering system—for me that system was and still is transportation.

"Graduate school provided me with perspective about my own strengths and weaknesses. I learned that there are many people who are smarter, who are better trained, but also that success is not perfectly correlated with these attributes. I learned the power of hard work and perseverance. I learned I really love exploration and discovery in the form of research, in addition to teaching. And I learned how much fun it is to work with others who think differently and who can teach me something. It opened up my world. Interacting with MIT's international students opened it further.

"I think the biggest difference as a woman in engineering is that you are noticed and remembered because you are one of only a few. I recall that a fellow graduate student once remarked to our adviser, 'She is good looking, and smart!' Apparently, he was unaccustomed to this combination. Women constituted 10, maybe 15, percent of my graduate school class. I was the only woman who completed a PhD in my field in the year that I finished. Another woman finished her PhD about eighteen months later. One woman finished her master's and another woman who had originally thought of pursuing a PhD decided to stop after her master's. Proportionately I think the success rate for men and women was about the same.

"In 1988, right after graduation, I took an assistant professorship in the School of Industrial and Systems Engineering at the Georgia Institute of Technology [Georgia Tech]. Mark and I commuted for the next four years. When I became pregnant, we decided that a long-distance relationship, two careers, and a baby on the way didn't mix well. I approached MIT and was offered a position as an assistant professor in the Department of Civil and Environmental Engineering. That was 1992, the year our oldest daughter, Olivia, was born.

"I didn't really have a mentor in graduate school, though there were some faculty who served as good role models. And my uncle, Richard Richardson, was a professor and a great role model. As a junior faculty member, I had excellent mentors at Georgia Tech and MIT. They didn't inform my career choice—it was too late for that—but they provided me with excellent training, and we collaborated on a number of projects. One of the mentors once said to me, 'I don't know why I keep giving you advice, you never take it.' He was right. I'm not good at taking advice. But I do seek it because I like to hear how others think about a question I'm pondering. I use mentors to make sure I'm not missing crucial information and insights. Then I make my own decision about what's right for me.

"At MIT, Professor Amedeo Odoni, in particular, stands out in my mind. He taught me how to write papers and get them through the review process. He helped me understand the political intricacies that faculty here must navigate. He is an incredibly insightful, dedicated man.

"I believe I possess qualities that make me a good faculty member. First, I interact well with people—students and colleagues. Faculty members often advise students. Sometimes the advice they give suits themselves but isn't necessarily what the student being advised is asking for. I try to understand the person who is asking for the advice and put myself in his or her shoes. I believe it makes me an effective adviser and a good mentor.

"Mentors serve different roles for different people. As a mentor, I tell my students or junior faculty, 'Here's my opinion, but my advice to you is to ignore most advice you get.' Each of us has distinct priorities determined by life events. So different solutions fit different people.

"When I interact with colleagues, I tend to be upbeat. Many of them complain or make unrealistic requests. As dean I was sometimes amazed. I'd look at them and think, 'Wow! Are you kidding?' [laughing]. They totally fail to see the bigger picture. I try to think about where they're coming from and how what they want fits into the bigger MIT schema. I work with many smart, accomplished, and sometimes insecure people. The combination can lead to myopic, demanding, and defensive behavior. That's not how I want to be described.

"Second, I am organized. As a student I went to class and worked on my research project. As a faculty member I have multiple projects, supervise numerous students, teach one or more courses a semester, write proposals, serve on committees, and participate in my professional organizations—lots of balls in the air at the same time. Managing my time effectively requires a specific set of skills, which weren't quite as critical to me as a student. If I had not successfully negotiated that transition and acquired the skills I needed, I would not have survived.

"Currently, I'm in an administrative role nobody trained me for. I ended up in administration because when I'm given a task, I follow through, and I'm willing to be a good citizen. If I'm asked, I say yes, and then I do it.

"For instance, I have been the director of the Transportation@MIT initiative since 2008. We're trying to leverage what we have at MIT to bring together people with expertise relevant to transportation and make a difference. We surveyed faculty asking whether they engaged in research germane to transportation. We identified nearly 250 MIT faculty members who said their work was either directly associated with or pertinent to transportation. Although I've been affiliated with transportation at MIT for twenty-five years, I had no idea that we would have such a response. In fact, I didn't even know most of the faculty. We really hadn't taken advantage of what we have at MIT to address critical transportation issues.

"The Transportation@MIT initiative cuts across three different schools—engineering, management, and architecture and planning—and involves over 200 faculty. We all speak different languages. We have different value systems too. But, we recognize that to effect change we need a comprehensive approach—technology alone won't do it.

Uninformed policy isn't useful either. We want to be the first university that comes to mind when Congress is debating a transportation policy issue.

"Recently, I organized a group to write a proposal for $40 million over five years, which was granted by Singapore, to work on future urban mobility. I was interim dean (for the last half of 2010 and the first couple of months of 2011), associate dean (since 2007), and director of Transportation@MIT at the same time and kept my research going. When you get the work done, you get identified as a go-to person.

"Although I have good interpersonal and organizational skills, I don't possess others that would make me a better administrator. I tend to work toward consensus, but sometimes as a leader I know that if you can't come to an agreement, you simply have to move the agenda forward. For me, there's a great deal of angst associated with people who are upset about a decision and fighting against me. Some individuals can forget about it, but I lose sleep over those situations. Being able to let go would be a good skill to have. I'm also unwilling to reduce my research agenda. I wouldn't accept the position of associate dean if I couldn't do research. I teach less as associate dean; I am willing to make that trade-off, but I am not willing to give up research.[1]

"My greatest rewards come from working with my students on research. I love working with my students. I love learning from them. We have extremely smart students at MIT. 'This is so much fun!' I probably say that once a week. It never occurs to me to say, 'Wow, isn't this great!' when I am at an administrative retreat [laughing]. Since I am a female faculty member, students sometimes look at me as a curiosity, but usually they are intrigued, not negative or hostile. And women students clearly appreciate having women faculty.

---

1. Barnhart has received numerous awards that attest to her excellence as a researcher: the Franz Edelman Prize for Achievement in Operations and Management Sciences, INFORMS Best Paper Award in Transportation and Logistics, the Advancement of Women in Operations Research and Management Science Award, the Mitsui Faculty Development Chair, the General Electric Foundation's Junior Faculty Career Award, and the National Science Foundation's Presidential Young Investigator Award. She also holds an endowed position, the Ford Professor of Engineering, and is the first woman associate dean in the school.

"Ever since my graduate school days, I've wanted to work in an environment that exposes me to a dynamic international experience. I have that now. For instance, a few weeks ago I was in China serving on the international review board of Tsinghua University, which is China's technical university. Members of the panel from all over the world were there to work together, gain an understanding of the university's educational programs, and meet students. I thoroughly enjoyed it. I like attending conferences, learning from and interacting with my international colleagues. It's a wonderful professorial perk. Our daughters have been world travelers since birth because they have been dragged along. When Olivia was five, I told her that we were going to a conference in Italy. To this day, I remember her response: 'Italy, again?' I thought, 'Oh my, how times have changed. I was never even on a plane until I was in college.'

"It's too difficult to do everything you want to do with your life and your work. When our girls were younger, I had to be extremely disciplined. That meant, honestly, for at least ten, maybe fifteen years, I didn't know how to turn on the TV in my own house. I came home, I played and worked with the kids, I got them to bed, I went into my office at home, I worked until midnight or one or two o'clock, and then I repeated the same routine the next day.

"Of course, there was leisure, but it revolved around the girls and their activities. When our oldest daughter was ski racing, we spent weekends in Vermont at races and skiing. At one point, I told my husband, 'This leisure is killing me.' When we were gone all weekend, household chores like laundry and grocery shopping went undone. Today, I know how to turn on the TV [laughing]. Now I can sit down and have a glass of wine with my husband. So it's more relaxed.

"Sometimes I think, 'Wouldn't it be great if an academic could have a part-time appointment when family priorities are at their peak?' When our girls were small, I had neighborhood friends who were doctors and lawyers, in the same situation as I was with youngsters at home. They met the school bus every day at two-thirty. I couldn't do that. I've often wondered why we cling to the notion that if you are not full-time, you're not a real faculty member. I think it has to do with the fact that men have always dominated my field. Their lives were different, especially when their wives were at home. Even now, when the topic of child care arises, most faculty members I work with believe you aren't serious about your career if you don't want [to] or can't work full-time. "All that said, I feel that being a female faculty member in engineering has been an advantage, not a disadvantage. I have never experienced bias or discrimination. In fact, male colleagues have been very supportive, and often the most supportive and sympathetic were the ones I least expected to be. My male colleagues would say, 'I don't know how you do it—juggling family and career is such a challenge.' They asked me questions about how I organized my time and so on. I discovered these men often had daughters who were trying to manage careers and families simultaneously. They were aware of the inherent challenges and supportive of women who were trying to make it work.

"In some respects nothing has changed for women in my field. In fact, stress levels seem to have risen for both men and women. The bar just keeps going up. The tenure hurdle is harder than ever to get over. At a recent retreat, we talked about how faculty value flexibility. One colleague jokingly commented, 'A faculty member has flexibility to work whatever eighteen hours a day he or she wants.' And someone added, 'True. But when it gets to the point that you can work whatever twenty-four hours a day you want, you don't have much flexibility.'

"So while in theory flexibility exists, in practice flexibility is actually being sapped away, and we are becoming overly constrained. As administrators we have at least begun to ask: Must everyone at MIT be in a full-time slot? Does everybody have to be on the same track? Can we define faculty appointments less rigidly? What about a three-quarter time, tenure-track position? The belief still lingers that you must be tenure track or you're nothing. The situation will eventually change, but I certainly haven't seen it in the top-tier universities. The University of California system recently conducted a study on work-life balance for women and men faculty. The report recommends job sharing and more flexible appointments. They seem to be more progressive than most, but I don't know whether their efforts have resulted in attracting women into their STEM faculty ranks.

"Historically, between 7 and 9 percent of the science and engineering faculties at MIT have been women. These figures remained constant for over twenty years until 1995. In 1995, 7 percent of the science faculty was women (fifteen tenured and seven junior faculty plus two women who held joint appointments in engineering). Engineering's corresponding numbers included twenty-four women (about 9 percent).

"The institute made tremendous strides in increasing the number of women faculty in both the sciences and engineering after the 1999 and 2002 reports on the status of women at MIT. Both studies were initiated and meticulously carried out by women faculty. Data were generated and analyzed, and both studies produced essentially the same findings—systematic bias and unconscious discrimination against women faculty existed at MIT. The institute took action to remedy the situation.

"In 2011, fifty-two women made up 19 percent of the science faculty and 12 percent of its tenured faculty. Currently about 16 percent (sixty) of the engineering faculty members are women, and women constitute 15 percent of the school's tenured faculty.

"One of my responsibilities as associate dean is to chair the committee of faculty search chairs. Chairs of each search committee in the school are members of this oversight group. We share best practices for identifying women and underrepresented minorities and ways to get them to apply for open faculty positions at MIT. We know that we cannot sit back and wait for underrepresented minority candidates to apply because they are too few in number, and top-notch candidates are too highly sought after. In fact, quite often a candidate is simultaneously interviewing for positions in several departments within our school, let alone at other institutions. The year before last, we hired ten women and eight men in the School of Engineering. Hiring more women than men—that was a first. This year the pool is thinner. At most, 10 percent of our hires will be women.

"Our success rate in keeping women once we have hired them is the same, or maybe even a little better, than the rate for men. But changing department composition and dynamics is a slow process, and it differs across fields within engineering. For instance, it's very difficult to attract women into fields like computer science and mechanical engineering. We see the same patterns in our undergraduate population. Forty percent of the undergrads at MIT are women, but most don't go into these fields, even though departments try hard to attract them. For us, the pipeline is definitely a choking point—it's truly discouraging.

"In contrast to the climate at MIT, Georgia Tech's environment, at least when I was there, was not as positive. Women faculty meetings constituted forums for registering complaints. The women at Georgia Tech did not have a high level of confidence that the administration was on their side. When I moved to MIT, I expected more of the same. Was I ever wrong!

"The administration's reaction to the first status report created a very positive atmosphere for women at MIT. We identified issues—low numbers, high attrition rates, little representation in administrative and senior committee positions. We clearly articulated what we wanted and why. And the administrators—the president and deans—supported us. They gave us the resources we needed to fix the problem. That was the attitude. It wasn't about complaining. It was about fixing. This approach has served the women at MIT well and is still the modus operandi here.

"Today, MIT has an associate provost for faculty equity—actually two individuals share the title. An associate provost heads a committee charged with the task of scrutinizing policies to ensure they are supporting women and are fair. For example, one of the policies put in place as a result of the status reports had to do with family leave. This particular policy allows women or men to take a semester off from committee duties and teaching if he or she is the primary caregiver for a newborn or an adopted child. Initially, the majority of faculty members taking advantage of this policy were men, whether or not they were the primary caregivers. This gave men who were not primary caregivers an advantage in advancing their research. Hence, an unintended consequence of the policy is that it exacerbates existing inequities and gives some men a competitive advantage. Now we have to figure out how to change the policy or the way in which it is implemented.

"In 2011 MIT conducted a third Status of Women Study in the sciences and engineering schools as a follow-up to the original status reports. As part of this study, all the women in the two schools were interviewed. Some of the women had participated in the previous studies. They were amazed at the difference in morale and attitude. Most of the women interviewed now said, 'It's great. Love it here. We have numerous opportunities to be important at MIT, to play roles in administration and on committees. We have access to everything we want.' They are happy. They are supported. Most of the issues that surfaced in the latest report are gender neutral—men face them too. However, child care continues to disproportionately affect women faculty. For instance, we don't offer enough on-campus child care opportunities, and the services that are available are ridiculously expensive. Many faculty members simply cannot afford to enroll their children in MIT's day care.

"I believe my career trajectory at MIT was easier than for many. People were supportive. I had children. If I needed to leave, I left. I always got home in time for our babysitter to leave by 6:00. If 5:15 rolled around and I was still at work, someone was likely to ask, 'Cindy, don't you have to go?'

"I did have a huge advantage. My husband works in money management, which gave us an income to hire in-home help. We had a nanny when the girls were little. It's so much easier to walk out the door leaving your kids in their pajamas than to get them fed and dressed. Little things can make a big difference.

"It's a difference I took for granted until one of my graduate students took a faculty position. She was married and had a child. Her husband was a political writer who was working on a book and not employed in a salaried position. Hers was the sole income. She told me how stressful it was. They were always running and always late. To illustrate her dilemma, she told me about trying to wrap a gift in the Toys'R'Us parking lot for the birthday party they were late for. I said, 'Well, this is what we always do. I tell our nanny, 'There's a birthday party tomorrow. Do you mind taking the kids to get a gift at a store downtown? They'll wrap it for you.' And our nanny agrees and says, 'Sure, we'll go shopping.'

"As I was relating this story to my student, she looked incredulously at me and said, 'First of all, I can't afford to go to the store that wraps the gift for you. And second, I don't have a nanny.' It stopped me short. I realized that the mechanisms I'd put in place to help me require money, and without it, you have a much harder job.

"In engineering, about 25 percent of the graduate students are women at MIT. Although our undergraduate female population has significantly increased relative to a decade ago (34 percent of engineering undergraduate students were women in 2001), there has not been much of a change in the percent of female graduate students.

"Even when we get women into our programs, there are leaks along the student pipeline. And if we get them through their PhDs, many don't take academic positions. They often don't find the academic lifestyle attractive. When I talk to my students about their next steps, many say, 'I don't want to live like you.' I say, 'What do you mean? I love my job!' 'Yes, but you work all the time.' Students often tell me I am their model of how to find work-family balance, but at the same time they see that achieving balance is hard and intense. There's enormous pressure associated with the lifestyle. In the end, they say, 'Gee, why do I want that?' And on top of it all, they won't get paid that much to do the job, certainly not the same as if they elect to go into management, consulting, or to Wall Street, all viable options for our engineering PhDs.

"A new trend at MIT, engineering post-docs, compounds the problem. The sciences have a long-standing culture of post-docs, but that culture has only recently been adopted widely in engineering. The result is that as a doctoral student, your quality of life goes down because a post-doc adds an extra two or more years before you move into the faculty ranks as an assistant professor. And those years are spent at a low salary. In the sciences, I believe that the National Institutes of Health has set the minimum salary at $38,000. It's a bit higher in engineering—maybe $50,000. But still, can you imagine being a PhD engineer in your late twenties or early thirties, making $38,000 or $50,000 a year, having a family, living in a city, say, San Francisco or New York? It doesn't work. As a post-doc in Boston, for instance, it would be difficult finding a decent place to live, let alone raise a family. And if you put off having a family, it might mean closing off that option. These are highly trained individuals who are asking themselves, Why should I do this when I can work in industry and make a real salary and move on with my life?

"Once a newly minted PhD has completed a post-doc and moves into a faculty position, the work really begins. The time commitment explodes exponentially and becomes all consuming. Researching and producing a body of published work that pushes the envelope and has an impact on the field is a must. You can be excellent in all other aspects of the job, but without a viable research portfolio, you will not get tenure. If you are a great researcher but a horrible teacher, you might be denied tenure. If you are an incredible teacher but don't do research, you will definitely be denied tenure. You can probably have an inadequate service record but be a great researcher and an average teacher and get tenure. If you have a great service record, it will be noted but someone will most likely say, 'Well, you seem to be saying yes too often' [laughing]. Which, by the way, women tend to do.

"So many people put their life decisions, like having a baby, on hold until after the whole tenure process is complete. And now they, especially women who are more senior than I, regret that choice because they forfeited an entire dimension of life.

"Even though we have increased our numbers, the reality is not many girls go into engineering. Young people want to make a difference in the world, and they don't see engineering as a place where they can do it. We have failed miserably in marketing this profession because engineering certainly can find and is at the heart of developing solutions to some of society's most challenging problems. But it's just not understood that way by the public.

"When I talk with my daughters' friends about engineering, most of them don't know what it is. They've never heard of it. They don't have engineering in their high school curriculum. So, it's difficult explaining what engineers do. They think it's nerdy. It's important that we get the message out to kids at the grade school and high school levels that math and science hold the solutions to societal problems. We have to raise awareness and change the image of engineering. There's a commercial about a car not being your father's Oldsmobile. It's like that. This is not your father's engineering with pens in a pocket protector in your shirt and a calculator on your belt.

"Here at MIT, we try to excite school-age girls about engineering. The STEM program targets middle school girls and boys. This program has three components: a five-week summer institute; a nine-month mentoring program that pairs middle school students with MIT undergraduates pursuing degrees in math, science, and engineering; and a series of seminars that focus on succeeding in an academic environment and applying to private high schools and colleges. The Saturday Engineering Enrichment and Discovery (SEED) Academy helps high-school-age students bring their foundational math and science skills up to speed over a seven-semester sequence that also acquaints them with how engineering and technology interface with today's society.

"The Minority Introduction to Engineering and Science program is a six-week summer academic enrichment program for promising high school juniors and seniors who are interested in studying science, engineering, and entrepreneurship. And the Women's Technology Program (WTP) encourages young women with strong math, science, and analytical abilities to pursue studies in engineering and computer science. WTP is a four-week summer residential experience for rising high school seniors. Instructors include female MIT graduate students, MIT faculty, and engineers from industry.

"Our professional organization also works to attract young people into the operations research branch of engineering. When I was president of our professional society, INFORMS [and its subgroup, the Women in Operations Research/Management Science Forum], I put in place a 'Doing Good With Good OR' (OR is short for operations research) competition for college-age students. The idea is to begin to raise the level of awareness of how these kinds of technologies can be used to benefit society. Students compete in teams and apply OR to different important societal problems. They work in health care on problems such as designing radiation treatments for cancer patients or matching kidneys or livers with patients. They design logistical responses to natural disasters. They develop ways to provide clean water to people in third world and developing countries. The experience broadens their perspectives and piques their interest.

"But my own girls? Olivia is a sophomore at Colby College in Maine. Julia is seventeen and a junior at Wellesley High School. Neither of them has shown the slightest interest in engineering. Just the opposite. There's a trade-off when it comes to parental advising. I tell them one thing, and they tend to do another [laughing]. But interestingly, Olivia, who expressed complete disinterest in taking the technical math route and started her freshman year thinking she would be an international studies/government major has now declared her major as economics, which of course is math intensive. She told me that her economics teacher (a woman) suggested she major in economics and minor in math. Olivia looked at her and said, 'Have you been talking to my parents?' My reaction—'I have to call this woman. I love her already.'"

BIBLIOGRAPHICAL NOTE

Materials for this chapter were gathered through intensive author-initiated interviews and e-mail correspondence and from Barnhart's curriculum vitae and personal biography. Additionally, the following documents were consulted: MIT's School of Engineering's Special Programs (http://engineering.mit.edu/education/special_programs/); the school's website (http://engineering.mit.edu/); the 2011 Status of Women Report (http://web.mit.edu/newsoffice/images/documents/women-report-2011.pdf); and an interview with Barnhart conducted by Toby A. Smith, July 20, 2010, as part of the MIT Infinite History Project commemorating MIT's 150th anniversary (http://mit150.mit.edu/infinite-history/faculty).

three

A CURIOUS MIND

Linda S. Birnbaum

"I CAME INTO SCIENCE, in part, because science made me different. Not many girls were interested in science in the early 1960s, so I stood out. I also give credit to a teacher I had in junior high school, Mrs. Lazzari. She was the cheerleading coach, and I was a cheerleader. She was young and peppy and blonde—I wasn't blonde, but I was peppy, and she taught biology. I could like science, and it was okay because I could be like my biology teacher, who was well liked and exuded all the characteristics teenage girls need to feel comfortable about.

"That junior high school experience had a very big impact on me. I entered the state science fair. My dad helped me build a papier-mâché model of the brain. We wired it so that when you pushed a button, different areas lit up. I didn't win a prize, but I was hooked.

"The following year I designed and completed a project on the impact of thyroid hormones on growth and behavior. My parents encouraged me to write a letter to local drug companies asking for rats, cages, and food. Unbelievably, a pharmaceutical firm about a half an hour away from where we lived in northern New Jersey agreed to give me everything I needed. I had forty rats in the basement. Some I treated with excess thyroid hormones, others with an inhibitor that

---

Birnbaum is director of the National Institute of Environmental Health Sciences and the National Toxicology Program at Research Triangle Park in North Carolina.

blocks thyroid hormones. I then measured the weight of the rats and observed their activity and their growth over time.

"I won the New Jersey science fair that year and was sent as the New Jersey delegate to a youth conference on the atom that was held in Chicago a couple of months later. I met the head of the Atomic Energy Commission and all of these other bright teenagers who were interested in science. There were a few other women, but mainly guys, and that was okay with me. These early forays into science made me feel very confident.

"I was always curious, and my parents, both first-generation college graduates, encouraged me to pursue my interests—to experiment. So I explored and quickly found out I'm not very artistic, but I was fascinated by history, enjoyed music, and liked bugs. And I was a good student. In first grade I told my teacher I knew everything, and they moved me to second grade [laughing].

"By the time I started college in 1964, I knew I was interested in biology and lab work. I still loved history and enjoyed many of the humanities courses I took. But every time I had to write a paper for one of those classes, I'd go running back to the lab because I didn't want to spend my time writing. Little did I know that as a scientist, what you really have to do is write well.[1]

"My husband and I married in 1967 right after we graduated from the University of Rochester. We'd been together since my junior year in high school. I went through college in three years because I wanted to marry him. We knew we wanted to attend graduate school, so we applied to six universities; for me, it was six different kinds of biology departments. We decided where to go to graduate school based on where we both got in and where we both got the most money, fellowships, or assistantships.

"That's how we ended up at the University of Illinois in Champaign. I was initially in the cell biology program but switched into microbiology because my adviser was in the Microbiology Department. I laugh because, if I remember rightly, I only took one micro course in my whole PhD career. Even though my degree is in microbiology, most

---

1. Since 1971 Birnbaum has written over 300 peer-reviewed journal articles, more than thirty book chapters, and nearly 500 research abstracts.

of my classes were in biochemistry, physical chemistry, and molecular biology.

"In college I did well, and I had a couple of professors who were excellent mentors. They were male. I can't remember ever having a woman as a mentor in college or graduate school. In fact, I think all my professors were men. When I was getting close to finishing, one of the faculty members was awarded a sabbatical for the following semester. The department needed someone to teach an introductory course in molecular genetics and asked me. The only catch was that I had to finish my PhD before I could teach the course. I pushed hard and completed my thesis the same month I turned twenty-five. The last semester before graduation, spring 1972—while my husband was finishing his thesis in mathematics—I taught the course. It was great.

"We were starting a family and decided that my husband would find a job, and I would look for something to do once we got settled. He took a faculty position at Amherst College in Massachusetts, and I was able to get a post-doc at the University of Massachusetts, which was in the same town. We stayed in Massachusetts for two years, and then my husband took a position at Hamilton College in upstate New York. That move presented a bit of a challenge.

"When we first went to Hamilton, I had a one-year visiting professorship replacing a faculty member who had taken a sabbatical. I taught biology. At the time Hamilton was organized as two separate schools—one for women, the other for men. I taught in the women's school. In the 1970s many colleges phased out their women's schools by merging them into the men's schools and becoming coed. Hamilton was one of them, which is why it became complicated.

"The Hamilton faculty [in the men's school] could not accept the idea that a Hamilton wife—me—could also be a Hamilton faculty member. They wouldn't even consider me for a regular faculty appointment. So after that first year, I was on the job market again. Hamilton is just outside Utica. The State University of New York had a branch campus in Utica, but no open teaching slots. In terms of faculty positions, Syracuse University was another option, but Syracuse was a good forty miles away, which was quite a drive, especially in winter. There was, however, a medical research institute on the grounds of the Masonic Geriatric Home in Utica, which was dedicated to trying to understand the biology of aging. They offered me my second post-doc.

"When I accepted the position at the Masonic Medical Research Laboratory, I made a transition from gene research into the area of pharmacology and drug metabolism. We hypothesized that some of the increase in cancer with age might be related to altered metabolism. I wrote a grant to fund much of the research. We looked at metabolic changes that occur with aging using rats and mice as animal models. All my PhD work had focused on bacteria and viruses. I was getting into bigger organisms. I was back to rats.

"At the time, we used PCBs [polychlorinated biphenyls], a commercial mixture that dramatically increases drug metabolism, and sometimes phenobarbital and other chemicals such as dioxins to increase drug metabolism capability. When I started working with these substances and began to learn that they are not such nice chemicals, I moved into toxicology. I became board certified in 1982.

"After about four years, my husband and I asked ourselves, 'Do we really want to live in upstate New York the rest of our lives?' It's the Rust Belt. The economy was poor; Utica and the entire surrounding area were losing population. We didn't see a future there for our children, who were three and a half and six years old at the time. And the weather got to us. We decided to leave.

"I'd followed my husband twice, and it was his turn to follow me, so I began looking around. I can't say my moving into government was a decision that I didn't want academia. In fact, I applied for academic as well as government jobs. Several academic institutions expressed an interest in me, but when I spoke to people at the National Institute of Environmental Health Sciences [NIEHS] and discovered that it functioned as a pseudo-academic environment, I was intrigued. Given my previous university and college teaching experience, I thought it would be difficult to be an academic and a mother. I wanted flexibility. I wanted to conduct research, and at NIEHS I'd have that opportunity. And quite honestly, one of my sisters (I have two younger sisters, both lawyers, and a severely developmentally disabled brother, also younger) and her husband and their family lived near the Research Triangle Park in North Carolina, where NIEHS is located. Being near them was a huge draw for me. My kids could be near their cousins. I have no regrets. I've loved being a government employee. I believe I'm responsible to nobody but the American people. I'm idealistic that way.

"I was hired in the fall of 1979 as a senior staff fellow (in effect, a very advanced post-doc) in NIEHS's newly created National Toxicology Program [NTP], which was also affiliated with the National Cancer Institute at the time. My first assignment was to work on a dioxin-like compound and try to understand how the body handled it.

"A year later, my fellowship was converted to permanent status, and I earned tenure at NIEHS in the early 1980s. I spent ten years in NTP, rising through the ranks and ending my first stint there as the chemical disposition group leader. In 1989 I was offered the experimental toxicology division director position at the Environmental Protection Agency [EPA] Health Effects Research Laboratory, which was located two miles down the road. Here was an opportunity to make a major career advancement without having to move my family.

"The director of NIEHS wanted to know what he could offer to keep me. In terms of pay grade, I was a GS-14 (the second highest level in the federal government civil service pay scale). I don't think there was a GS-15 woman at NIEHS, and there might've been only one other GS-14 woman, and she did not have children. So promotion and pay were on my list, but I also had other conditions that involved creating a new or refurbishing an existing lab. Unfortunately, a new lab wasn't an option at the time. I was ready to try something different anyway. I think change is good for people.

"When I took the EPA division director job, thirty-five or forty federal employees and a similar number of on-site contractors reported to me. I stayed at the EPA for almost nineteen years, most of the time as head of experimental toxicology, the EPA's largest health research division. I spent a year as the acting laboratory director for the health division and another running the human studies division, which actually conducted clinical research and epidemiology studies. That division was located on the grounds of the University of North Carolina's hospital. We exposed people to air pollutants and wanted to be in a setting where we had plenty of additional medical help available. My toxicology division eventually grew to around seventy-five federal employees and about thirty students and post-docs. It was a very productive, very successful division, focusing on air and water pollution issues and the effects of environmental chemicals on the immune system.

"My last two years at EPA, I actually stepped down from the division director position and moved into running a cross-EPA effort, dealing with problems in Libby, Montana. The whole town is a Superfund site [the government's hazardous waste cleanup program] because of mining vermiculite that was highly contaminated with asbestos. We needed to understand the health impacts on the people in the region—the exposure levels, the health effects of that exposure. I coordinated and helped run an effort that involved several EPA offices—Region 8 regulators in Montana; the Washington, D.C., office that set the regulatory limits; the risk assessment office from D.C.; and the Health and Environmental Effects Research Laboratory. It was an exciting opportunity.

"I didn't plan to apply for my current position as head of the NIEHS when it came up in 2009. I was happy where I was; it was exciting. And I actually thought, 'I've been in the government for almost thirty years. Maybe I should retire and try something new.' I had even begun negotiating for a position at Duke University. I've had adjunct appointments at Duke and the University of North Carolina for nearly the entire time I've been in North Carolina. The link to these two universities has been great because it's enabled me to have graduate students and post-docs in my laboratory.

"When the position was posted, I received numerous calls from people in and outside NIEHS suggesting that I apply because I'd be a good institute director. My husband, whom I assumed would say, 'Honey, I thought you were going to slow down a little,' instead said, 'You have to put your name in. Your whole career has been building to this.' So after a great deal of head scratching, soul-searching, and thinking about it, I applied. I found that it's great to apply for a job when you're not sure you even want it. Less pressure, more time to think—the application process was long and involved. By the time I went through the final series of interviews, I'd decided if they offered me the job I would take it. They did, and I did.

"We have two major programs in the institutes—intra- and extramural. The intramural program has two components. I'd describe one component as a standard National Institutes of Health [NIH] research program focused on basic biomedical and clinical research. The other component deals with toxicology. The extramural program handles grant applications. Its employees analyze research proposals and award funds to individuals and entities outside NIEHS. The people in this unit have a tremendously broad understanding of science.

"In the 1980s I was one of only two or three women who were tenured at NIEHS. Today, the intramural program, of which I am a part, is still dominated by men. There are several younger women who are either in the tenure track or have recently earned tenure, but the number is small. My epidemiology group has a couple of tenured women. My new head of the extramural program is a woman, and we have more women in the extramural than in the intramural program. Some women have gone into the extramural program because they feel they can control their hours better. I'm also the head of the NTP, a cross– Health and Human Services effort that involves part of the Centers for Disease Control and part of the Food and Drug Administration. I have several women in that program, but not in the highest leadership roles.

"We've started to build a leadership cadre of women within NIEHS. My new executive officer is a woman. That makes three women, including me, in top leadership positions. My deputy in the intramural program and the leadership in both the NTP and the clinical section are men. But when you go down a layer or two, the numbers of women drop off even more precipitously. We're working on that situation.

"I really love most of what I do. I love the interactions with people. I love the opportunities and the ability to make a difference in environmental health. I love mentoring others and all the learning. I love being able to get people together to talk about an issue or a problem and move forward, maybe in a new and enriching direction. I'm a pretty happy camper most of the time.

"I don't care for some of the administrative and management aspects of my job. We have so much paperwork. We thought computers would solve that problem, but they just create more work. You need twenty signatures sometimes to get work done. The paperwork alone creates unnecessary burdens. We also get frustrated because we want to shout out the exciting discoveries we make and what they mean, but we are part of the president's administration, so we often must be careful about what we say. I've had to learn that when I speak, I'm seen as a senior government official, and what I say is taken very seriously by the public and Congress.

"If I had to describe myself, I'd say I'm energetic (You need a lot of energy! [laughing]), inquisitive, flexible, and willing to compromise, and I take advantage of opportunities. I'm also collaborative by nature, which I believe is very appropriate. Many scientists are introverts. I'm not. So collaboration is very important to me. But I've had to seek it out. For me this is where post-doctoral mentoring comes in. Some scientists have post-docs and want them tied to the bench, doing what they (the scientists) want them (the students) to do, as opposed to trying to expand their students' horizons. They want post-docs who know exactly how to do X, Y, or Z and that's what they expect them to do. Such an experience can be isolating. I like post-docs to spread their wings and fly—to take a new direction, to depart from what they did as graduate students. We're working very hard at NIEHS to develop better mentoring of our students and post-docs.[2]

"I've always been willing to share the glory, and I've been fortunate to have some wonderful students and post-docs, many of them I still see, some of whom I continue to collaborate with.[3] I've been very supportive of my people, and I think that feeds back to help me.

"There certainly were, and probably are today, women who climbed the ladder and then pulled it up after them instead of reaching back. Women who said (and say), 'I made it on my own, so should you.' But it seems to me that more people now realize that it's important to help those coming up behind us.

"Over the course of my career, I can't say that I've experienced blatant discrimination. I had what I call 'uncomfortable times.' In the 1970s, when I was starting out, I truly believe that in general, to succeed, a woman had to be better than a guy. There was no doubt about that. In graduate school there were a couple other women graduate students, and we banded together, and one or two women faculty members were very helpful. We just toughed it out. I remember when I first enrolled at the University of Illinois, I wanted to work in a specific lab, but I was quickly informed that the lab's director didn't like women in

---

2. Birnbaum has served or is currently serving on PhD committees as a research adviser or a postdoctoral adviser for more than forty students at the University of North Carolina, Duke University, Harvard University, and the Universities of Utrecht and Wageningen in the Netherlands.

3. All but twenty of her journal articles are coauthored.

his lab because if they weren't married, they might get married, and if they were married, they might have children. So I said to myself, 'Okay, I don't think I'm going to work in his lab.'

"I had a somewhat similar experience at the Masonic lab. The director was a world-famous scientist. He said that all the women could sit on his lap and give him a big, juicy kiss at the Christmas party. I refused, which created quite a stir. If he had been good looking I might've considered it [laughing].

"My initial job offer at NIEHS was scaled back because I had been balancing the demands of raising two children and building a scientific career. Originally I had been recruited for a regular position. Over the couple of years that I had my two babies my publication record was not as strong as it might've been if I hadn't had children. I had actually worked part-time for five years. The search committee members knew my record because it was included in my application packet, but they still interviewed me for the permanent position. Then they used my publication record as an excuse to offer me the senior staff fellow position, which was temporary, instead. I was worried the bias would surface again when I went up for tenure. For investigators at NIH, the tenure process is relatively similar to the one faculty at research universities experience. It's a rigorous, stringent academic procedure with committees at multiple levels, eventually going up to the NIH. Had I told them that I was pregnant with our third child before the tenure decision came through, I believe I would not have been awarded tenure.

"If you're a woman, and you can keep a career going at a little slower rate and still have a little time for yourself—that's optimal. I earned my PhD in 1972 and tenure nine years later. That's not an unreasonable amount of time, if you consider I was a post-doc, having kids, and working part-time. As a working mother, I didn't think my husband or children should suffer; what suffered (and it was self-imposed) was personal time. There was never time to go out to lunch with friends; there wasn't time to play tennis or just wander around a store. It was pretty much go-go-go all the time. I think I'm pretty typical.

"When our children were young, occasionally I stayed late but it was rare. I didn't take work home at night. I couldn't. I'd get home at six o'clock, and it was time to make dinner, read a story, give a bath, and get the kids to bed. Our youngest is seven years younger than our middle child, who is two years younger than our eldest. I didn't start traveling until our youngest was in high school. I went to one or two meetings per year prior to that. In contrast, between 2006 and 2011, I gave over fifty invited addresses and workshops in fifteen states, Washington, D.C., and eight countries outside the United States.

"I've done well.[4] My greatest asset is my husband. I could not have done this without the kind of supportive partner I have. We made compromises, and we've had to be flexible. It can't be a one-way street. For instance, when we moved to North Carolina, he gave up a job he loved in artificial intelligence (he'd tired of academic life). Here in North Carolina, he developed computer software for a small education firm and later moved into computer consulting. He's now retired but keeps busy by teaching a Jewish history course, taking university classes, volunteering, and taking care of me.

"I've always tried to put my family first. Family keeps me grounded. I'm so proud of our children. They've grown up well. Our son is a physician who helps run a family practice residency program along with a health clinic. Early in his career, he worked as a physician on the Navajo Reservation for four years. His wife is also a physician. They are the parents of our two grandchildren. Our oldest daughter is an attorney. She works for the Department of Social Services, where one of her primary responsibilities is to move children out of abusive homes. She and her husband, who is a disabled war veteran from his second tour in Iraq, are expecting their first child. I told my staff that for any work we take on for the spring, they could be on their own. I may not be there [laughing].

"Our youngest daughter lives in New York City and is an actor. She's worked in off-Broadway and off-off Broadway shows, regional theater, television, and commercials. Although she holds a master's in fine arts in acting, she has always loved science. In fact, when she was in graduate school, she had to interview someone and then act out the results of the interview. She interviewed a good friend of ours who is a biophysicist. None of our kids have become research scientists (she's the closest).

"It would be very difficult to be a single woman with children trying to work with the kind of intensity these jobs take. I've often said

---

4. Birnbaum has received over twenty-five achievement awards.

that if you see a working mother, you'll find that she's not doing a lot of coffee klatching during the day. She's pretty much in there working or talking about work with others. She can't afford to spend time off topic. She's efficient, if she's successful.

"I encourage some of the young women in my division to consider part-time work if they can afford it. But many of them are afraid to go part-time because they believe doing so will hurt them. Our country hasn't worked out a good system. Extending the tenure decision by a year or two isn't always adequate. 'Stopping the clock' poses issues as well. Sometimes it means you have to step out of the tenure line, and that's problematic. The reality for women in faculty or pseudo-academic positions like mine is that the years in their careers when they need to be working to develop tenure are the same ones in which they should be having babies, if they're going to have children. I have a couple of young women who are recently or soon to be tenured, and they've figured out ways to make it work. But I also have a young tenure-track woman who is having great difficulty combining being a mother with doing her work.

"If you're in a Scandinavian country, not only does the woman get a guaranteed year off after a baby is born, a man can get a guaranteed year off too. In our country, whoop-de-do. If you are lucky, you can get thirteen weeks of leave with a guarantee of your job back when you return, but you're not paid for it in most cases. We haven't accepted the fact that the workforce has women who are going to be having children. Maybe, when men can have children, the situation will change. It may be a while [laughing].

"In all seriousness, this situation puts us in sticky predicament. In many science areas we aren't attracting enough women. For these disciplines, we need to do more to encourage girls and women to enter the field. Mentoring and providing positive role models are steps in the right direction.

"In science areas where we are doing better at attracting women, a pipeline problem still exists. In the biological sciences, we have more women than men entering, and increasing numbers of women are going into engineering, physics, and chemistry. The problems happen not so much in college and graduate school but after the post-doc stage; that's when the numbers really decrease. It might mean the post-doctoral system is out of kilter, or it could be the balance issue, because it's hard to find a palatable mix of work, family, and self. It takes so much energy. People choose to take a far less strenuous direction and enjoy life.

"And, of course, there is still a glass ceiling. The woman still has to be better than the man, at least at the higher levels. But the glass ceiling now has holes in it. We have broken through; nonetheless, the career advancement system in place continues to hamper our progress.

"And, in general, we in this country take a myopic view of just what constitutes the PhD job market. The whole job environment has changed dramatically, making retaining both men and women more challenging. Traditionally, advanced degree programs prepared graduates to assume faculty positions. Today, there just isn't room in academia for the number of PhDs we're graduating. But there are many other professions that require advanced knowledge. Parts of government are not that dissimilar from academia. (Parts are, of course.) The same holds true for industry, public interest groups, and the communications arena. I think there's a broader spectrum of people realizing that there are different directions a career can take. One doesn't need to go into academia to do interesting, intellectually satisfying work.

"I also truly believe that it's helpful for women to have role models. Having a woman role model or mentor isn't a requirement. But it helps when women see women in positions of responsibility. If all you see are White males, it's difficult to imagine how you're going to fit into that environment. For instance, guys like to go sit at the bar or play ball and talk about work. I don't like to do that. I had to learn to work around those types of challenges.

"Professional organizations also provide great opportunities to network and interact with people you might otherwise not regularly see. Over the years, I've been very involved with the Society of Toxicology, first as a council member and later in the presidential chain and eventually as president. I was also the chair of the Toxicology Section of the American Society for Pharmacology and Experimental Therapeutics many years ago when I conducted my aging work and was vice president of the American Aging Association during the same period. I've been vice president of the International Union of Toxicology. All those connections work for me.

"In the end though, some of the best advice I can give anyone is to have fun every day. If you're not enjoying what you do, think about doing something else. Be flexible. Be willing to compromise. Work hard. But realize, life is more than just your work."

BIBLIOGRAPHICAL NOTE

Linda Birnbaum's story derives from extensive phone and e-mail interviews. Her curriculum vitae provided additional details. For those interested in learning more about NIEHS, go to www.niehs.nih.gov.

four

THE CONSUMMATE
PROFESSOR

Susan Blessing

"I'M AT AN ODD JUNCTURE in my career as a particle physicist. In 1981, as an undergraduate at the Illinois Institute of Technology [IIT], I began working in the summers at the Fermi National Accelerator Laboratory [Fermilab], near Chicago. I lived thirty miles and two blocks from Fermilab [laughing]. It was fun. I worked there as an undergrad and during my first year in graduate school. Then I returned as a post-doc, in 1989, and have worked there on what's known as the DZero experiment ever since.

"DZero is a proton/antiproton collider experiment where we search for new phenomena—quarks, the top quark (which we discovered in 1995), W bosons, glueballs—don't you love our jargon! The experiment runs at Fermilab because universities simply don't have the capacity. The analysis work, however, can be done from anywhere. All you need is a computer and access. We also generate what's called Monte Carlo events off-site wherever excess computing time exists. These simulations predict how the actual events will look in the DZero Detector.

"We do analysis here at Florida State University [FSU] and, in theory, run simulations if the university has spare capacity. The downside

Blessing is the Nancy Marcus Professor of Physics and director of the Women in Math, Science, and Engineering Program at Florida State University in Tallahassee.

to working off-site is that you miss the in-the-hall conversations. An incredible amount of knowledge gets transferred person to person. Even though attempts are made and instructions given to document every detail of the experiment, it doesn't always happen. I see a weird effect during analysis, and don't know if others have observed it, or if I have designed a faulty program and my software is screwed up.

"The Fermilab Tevatron collider has been shut down. And the experiments at the Large Hadron Collider at the European Organization for Nuclear Research [CERN], in Geneva, Switzerland, have superseded DZero. But because the CERN accelerator produces proton-proton collisions, we can examine certain phenomena better at Fermilab than at CERN.

"As a consequence, I will continue on the DZero experiment until its conclusion, and I want to continue working at Fermilab, but I haven't decided what I want to do in the future. This is definitely a drawback as far as my career goes. I should know what I want to do, and I should be working on it already. My research time is greatly constrained by university-related responsibilities and activities, which creates a dilemma for me. To remain totally active in research, I would have to give up many university activities that I enjoy and think are important.

"I came to FSU in 1994. Before then, I was affiliated with Northwestern University for five years as a post-doc working on DZero and for some reason was fairly unhappy. Was it because I no longer liked the work, or was it the people, or what? I didn't know. I was hesitant to take the position at FSU until my husband observed, 'How many professor position offers are you going to get? When will you have another chance like this?' He added, 'If you don't like it, we can always leave.' I realize now what I didn't like about being just a researcher had to do with engaging in research to the exclusion of anything else. I really like being a professor, the teaching, the service, and the research. I like the variety. I get to interact with students, and I find I'm much more interested in undergraduate education than I ever imagined I would be. I hadn't taught in grad school; I didn't think I wanted to teach. But it's fun—most of the time [laughing].

"I am a first-generation college goer. In high school I liked math, but it seemed impractical so I never thought of pursuing a career in mathematics. (I no longer view math as impractical.) I took honors physics my junior year. In one class period, Mr. Rychlowski divided us into groups, each group with a separate lab setup. The 'prize' everyone wanted was to conduct the Millikan oil drop experiment. He split us up according to what we thought we wanted to study in college. And when I said physics, the expression on his face was priceless. Total shock. Did he think, 'My God, she's so horrible at it, why on earth would she want to study it?' Or was it because I was female? Or was he just surprised that he had inspired anybody to study physics? I never figured it out. I didn't get to do the Millikan oil drop experiment either [laughing].

"Most of the math-science-y kids in my class went into engineering because, when you got out, you could find a good, well-paying job. To be in engineering, you had to pick a field. And I didn't want to choose because I found most topics interesting. You can apply physics to just about everything you do. When [British physicist and Nobel laureate] J. J. [Sir Joseph John] Thomson discovered the electron, a member of Parliament asked, 'What good is this?' The response was, 'I don't know, but I'm sure you're going to find some way to tax it.' What good is the electron? Well, iPhones, computers, cars, and electricity all depend on the physics involved in his discovery. So majoring in physics meant I didn't have to pick. Eventually I had to select a subfield for my dissertation and then work in that field. But in the meantime I could learn about all sorts of phenomena.

"I went to IIT. I don't remember where else I applied, and I don't really remember why I wanted to go to IIT. It wasn't far from home, and IIT gave me quite a bit of money, so it was cheaper to go there than it would have been to go to the University of Illinois. And it was smaller, which seemed better at the time. Now that I'm a professor at a large university, I see huge advantages to being at a big institution. But there are also disadvantages. It really depends on the student. For me, IIT worked out. I got my degree, I got involved in research as an undergraduate, and I met my husband. He's an architect. I was never interested in dating a physicist. That just seemed too close.

"There weren't many female undergraduate students at IIT in anything. I was certainly the only woman in physics. In hindsight, as a place to study physics, IIT probably wasn't the best choice because there were so few students. IIT's two primary units have always been its engineering school and a very famous architecture school. When I was there, chemistry, physics, and biology were separate departments. Now they've been combined into one. That tells you the level of importance placed on the sciences even back when I attended. It's definitely a service department. The department does award degrees, and the faculty engage in research, but compared to the engineering faculty, it's not much.

"I graduated after three and a half years. I went to see my adviser my first semester at IIT, and he told me I couldn't graduate early. I hate being told I can't do something, so I just went off and did it. Now that I'm the adviser and my students want to finish early, I discourage them from doing it [laughing].

"Research Experiences for Undergraduates programs sponsored by the National Science Foundation didn't exist when I was an undergraduate, but Argonne National Laboratory [in Chicago] had a program that ran during the school year, and I managed to get a position for the spring semester after I had graduated and stayed on through the following summer. I had applied for graduate school but had set my sights a bit too high and didn't get accepted where I applied.

"Joe [Joseph S.] Chalmers, from the University of Louisville, was on sabbatical at Argonne at the same time I was. He convinced me to apply to Indiana University even though it was very late, and he made phone calls on my behalf. I visited, and they offered me a position as a research assistant as a graduate student. That's how I ended up at Indiana. I really got lucky. I don't know what I would have done otherwise.

"As an undergraduate, I worked on a biophysics experiment doing X-ray diffraction, and the guy I worked with thought I shouldn't pursue high-energy physics. Not that I wasn't capable of it, but it was a very hard life, especially for a woman, because the experiments are always remote and involve extensive travel. He strongly recommended materials science, at the time known as solid-state physics; now it's called condensed matter physics. When I got to Argonne, I changed my mind and wanted to do materials, but then it sounded so boring I backed off. At that point, I became part of the 1 percent that causes 99 percent of the trouble [laughing]. I made a big fuss and went back to high-energy physics. It just seemed more interesting.

"At Indiana I focused on experimental elementary particle physics and graduated in 1989. Unlike in some disciplines in which students make arrangements to study under specific faculty, in physics people usually don't. I'm certainly not going to commit to a student before he or she actually comes here and takes a year's worth of classes. When students choose FSU, they attend a seminar series during which all the research groups give presentations about their work. Students select their advisers later in their studies on the basis of the understanding they gain from these seminars.

"I had two advisers at Indiana. The first one fired me. He was on sabbatical at CERN, and I was taking shifts in the middle of the night at Brookhaven National Laboratory on Long Island, New York. He kept sending me e-mails telling me what to do, and I basically told him off in an e-mail [laughing].

"My second adviser, Daria Zieminska, is a research scientist. She had a pretty hands-off approach. I either went to her with my questions, or I worked on my own. I have followed her example with my students. They have to be fairly independent. I'm happy to talk to them, but I don't seek them out most of the time. I'm too busy to micromanage them.

"Indiana's program was fairly large. There was one other woman in my specialty. I don't know what happened to her. She was a product of a small school; had carried a triple major in math, chemistry, and physics; and was constantly told how fabulous she was. When she got into graduate school, she found her background was totally inadequate. To complicate matters, she married during graduate school, and I believe she was pregnant when I left. There was another woman in my class who majored in nuclear physics. She is now a professor. Those are the only two women I can think of who were in my class.

"Because I was high-energy and most of the others focused on solid-state physics, I didn't really bond with the other people in my cohort. In addition, I held a research assistantship from the onset because I'd had research experience as an undergraduate. The others had teaching assistantships and congregated in a central office dedicated to that purpose. My office was in a completely separate area of the building. I saw them in class, but that's it. It was a bit of a drawback because I missed out on doing homework and exchanging concerns and ideas with the group. There were older graduate students in my office area, but I wasn't bold enough to talk with them about homework.

"It took me five and a half years to finish. I graduated in December, and Kevin and I were married at the end of May. Throughout grad school, we had a long-distance relationship. I was at Indiana and then Brookhaven; he worked in Chicago.

"I received quite a few post-doc offers, and Kevin was willing to move anywhere except California. Actually he was willing to move to California if we were going to stay there. Obtaining an architecture license in California is an extremely time-consuming process, so if we were just going to be there for a few years, he didn't want to go. Because I knew eventually we would be moving, taking the job at Northwestern seemed like the most sensible choice. It allowed him to stay at the firm he was with in Chicago.

"The position I now hold came up out of sequence in July with a start date in January. I could spend another year at Northwestern, so I hadn't anticipated going on the market until fall. I had collaborated with Sharon Hagopian, an FSU staff physicist, at Fermilab, and two other FSU faculty, Vasken Hagopian and Horst Wahl, at Brookhaven. Vasken contacted me about the position and encouraged me to apply. When I interviewed, FSU paid for Kevin to come with me. (I always think it's easier to be up front about family issues that affect our decisions.)

"Physics departments are organized around research groups. At the time I interviewed, nuclear was the largest group and all male. (I've been here going on twenty years, and there has never been a woman in the group.) It was my first job interview, and I was late for my meeting with the nuclear group (not my fault!). I walked into the room, and there was this long table with all the nuclear physicists sitting around it. They left me a seat at the head of the table. Do you have any idea how intimidating it is to look down a really long table surrounded by guys?

"They start asking questions, we're talking, and I'm thinking, 'This is going well.' Suddenly the guy to my left (a really senior faculty member) asks me how moving to Tallahassee will affect my golf game. I had absolutely no idea what he was talking about. I'm thinking, 'My golf game?' Finally I managed to spit out, 'I don't play golf, so there's not going to be any effect at all.' And then, he pointed at my hand. I bicycle, and bicycle gloves had oval openings, so I had an oval tan line. He had interpreted my tan as a tan from golf. After that, I was flustered and didn't do particularly well. When members of the high-energy group said they wanted to hire me, the nuclear group objected, so the high-energy group paid to bring me back down. I spoke with several of the nuclear people individually, and the process went much better.

"The position was to have been funded for the first three years by money funneled through the Superconducting Super Collider [SSC] project. Between my interview and the time the job offer was to be made, the SSC was canceled. FSU had the money for the first year, and coincidentally, a faculty member resigned from the high-energy physics group. Instead of leaving the position open until the following hiring season, the faculty made the case for hiring me, and the dean gave them the go-ahead. I accepted the week before Thanksgiving. The timing and their willingness to reinterview me was a stroke of luck for me. With the demise of the SSC, there were suddenly hundreds of people on the job market, and what are the chances I would've gotten the job had they been hiring six months later?

"Kevin was fine with moving to Tallahassee. In Chicago he worked for a large internationally known firm on big fancy projects. Tallahassee was a step down. But he felt he'd had his shot, and now it was my turn. It was nice. Now he works for himself and says he's completely spoiled and would be a lousy employee. Fortunately his boss doesn't really care [laughing].

"At the moment, there are only two women in the department. The other one is also a full professor. She does theoretical particle physics, and her office is directly across from mine. For a little while, there were four women in the department, but the other two moved to other institutions.

"When we want to hire, there aren't many women applicants. For instance, we started an astrophysics group and had two openings. We didn't interview a woman for either position. No women came anywhere near the top of the interview list. A really good woman applied for a position in the condensed matter group, but her specialty wasn't exactly what that group wanted. The condensed matter people tried to argue for an additional hire, not because she was qualified, but because she is a woman. I found the reasoning annoying. Similarly, we interviewed a woman in high-energy physics several years ago. We didn't offer her the job because two members of the group claimed they couldn't work with her. One of the two was a young guy, and I really regret not saying, 'Well, then I guess you'll have to leave.'

"We also had two people leave the high-energy group recently, a theorist and an experimentalist. We interviewed a woman who was quite good for the theory position. But the argument was made that her expertise too closely mirrored that of faculty already in the program.

"Most students start a PhD program either thinking they will become professors or having not thought about it at all. In some ways, going into graduate school is an easier path than looking for a job. As a consequence, about half the students we take in leave before they complete the PhD, and I think that's pretty common. Another, perhaps more disturbing, pattern I see has to do with women. Women sometimes come into a program with a boyfriend or husband or meet one in the program. If the boyfriend doesn't make it through the qualifying exam and leaves with a master's degree, the woman leaves too, even though she does qualify. She leaves because the boyfriend or husband can't do it. Not a good reason, but it is a real one.

"Those students who do graduate complete one or two post-docs before entering the academic job market. It's not too difficult to find a post-doc, at least in high-energy physics, because there's so much work to be done at the Large Hadron Collider at CERN, but the next step is quite a bit harder.

"Students who want to become academics often take university post-docs, see what being an academic entails, and decide no way. Workload and compensation can both be issues. And although they see the amount of autonomy faculty have (which very few jobs offer these days), they tend to undervalue it. Some of our foreign students want university faculty positions but have difficulty getting them because of language deficiencies, even though they are extremely talented. We try to help them improve their communication and presentation skills, but it's challenging.

"Women physicists who choose to pursue faculty posts at research universities encounter a further complication. A large percentage of them marry physicists; if they don't marry physicists, they very likely marry other academics. Of course, the same number of male physicists marry physicists [laughing]. But because there are so few of them, the dual-career issue is more problematic for women. The other woman in our department, Laura, is not married to a physicist; her husband is a math professor. When she came to FSU, she didn't tell us about her husband. We didn't know her, and we couldn't ask. We had a hard time accommodating her husband's need for a faculty position.

"Dual careers make life complex. You're forced to make choices. I know couples where the husband's at one university and she's at an institution in another town or even across the country. It doesn't seem like much of a life to me, but they seem perfectly happy. I don't know what I would have done if Kevin had insisted on staying in Chicago.

"Once you're in a university tenure-track slot, stopping the clock, parental leave, and spousal hires help. When Dominick was born (he's now a teenager), I wrote a memo to the dean saying I planned to use sick leave and come back in the spring semester. Another faculty member who had a light teaching load took over my class for the remainder of the semester. It was all handled through goodwill. I probably should not have come back to work so soon. But I thought I had to be a 'super-person.' It would've been better if I had taken the semester off. At FSU we now have these policies in place officially, but I wonder, do people on the promotion and tenure committees look at the person with the stopped-tenure clock and say, 'Well, it's been eight years, and she really hasn't done that much,' and then vote no?

"To be honest, the academic job market is crappy. We have a large department (forty or so), and people retire or move on. We haven't hired anyone in three years because of the state budget. We need to hire. Departments at other universities have the same problem. Some graduates who hope to remain in academia end up taking positions at nonresearch four-year institutions, frequently with the intention of remaining affiliated with DZero. They teach three or four classes a semester and are expected to have a research program that involves undergraduates. How do people do this? I teach one and a half classes a semester because I direct the Women in Math, Science, and Engineering [WIMSE] Program. And I'm too busy! Even community colleges hire PhDs now because they can. These folks almost always teach to the exclusion of conducting research—there simply isn't time.

"If you don't stay in academia, the next closest research option lies at a national lab. And then there's industry. Industry is an extremely viable alternative. PhD physicists apply the skills they learn as physicists, but not necessarily the physics, to industry problems. If you do high-energy physics, you end up with a great deal of experience in 'computing' and 'problem solving,' which are two of the buzzwords in skill sets these days. We've had graduate students go into the financial sector and other fields, particularly medicine, that use visualization. The last guy who graduated in the group wants to join the Navy SEALs, his dream job, which he'll probably get. It's too bad. He's a good physicist.

"In general, the unemployment rate among PhD physicists is around 2 percent. I don't know of anyone who hasn't gotten a job. Careers, however, don't always go as planned. Here I am at FSU. I thought I might be working at a national lab by this time.

"No matter where a woman physicist takes a job, to succeed she must be smart and relatively thick-skinned. The culture of physics is different from the culture of the population as a whole. You have to be willing to work within a male-dominated environment. Men without women (or only one or two) around are different from men with women around. They behave differently. At Brookhaven, we worked in what were called porta-camps, essentially trailers. The walls of the techs' trailer were plastered with pictures from *Hustler*. I complained and was told, 'Just don't go back there.' Today, I would complain more. Of course now they wouldn't have pictures of *Hustler* hanging up [laughing].

"My attitude in school and when I entered the workplace was 'It's mostly men; I have to learn to deal with the men.' I've come to realize, however, it's not just about academics. It's about knowing other women who work in environments similar to mine. I certainly know other women physicists; I have one across the hall. That's good. But I don't have long-term friends from undergraduate school. I just don't know that many women. There's not that many around.

"The culture has and will continue to gradually change as more women enter the field. I am a member of the American Physical Society Committee on the Status of Women in Physics. I never expected so much of my career would be devoted to working to improve the work climate for women and confronting environmental culture issues. I truly believe if we improve the climate for women, we improve the climate for everybody.

"As physicists, we're expected to work independently, without a significant amount of direction, and at the same time function within a group. We're expected to compete on the one hand and cooperate on the other. People attack you, and you must be able to stand there, defend your work, and not collapse. Guys tend to be much more challenging, and their communication style differs. It's not so much meanness as it is about socialization into the culture of being in science. It's an odd combination that school does not prepare us for. Students are given far too much direction. 'Do this, this, and this, and you will succeed.' The real world offers no such rubric.

"I told Ashley, an undergraduate who works for me, 'You have to learn when to ask a question and when to figure it out for yourself.' As a consequence, she tends to not ask often enough [laughing]. In contrast, Alicia, also an undergraduate physics major, works with another professor who tells her exactly what to do. I think Ashley is actually learning more than Alicia is, but she's also making much slower progress. We also fail to provide enough feedback—especially positive feedback. The culture can be tough, and it could be more difficult for women because learning the reality of their academic status is not 'nice.' Many people can't handle 'not nice.' I try not to be mean, but if you aren't doing well in class, you're not doing well. If you get a job where everybody, including your boss, is always nice, and suddenly you get fired, it's very likely because you didn't do the job properly. I try not to be harsh, but I am realistic, and sometimes students don't appreciate it. But honestly, would they rather I say, 'Your 2.2 GPA is okay,' and have them think they're going to the Massachusetts Institute of Technology for graduate school? There's no way!

"We, as a society, also send messages about 'proper' women's roles. The other day, Samantha (my graduate assistant for WIMSE) mentioned a study about the depiction of women in TV shows. The study concluded that women today are represented by behavioral models that harken to the 1950s and 1960s—Harriet Nelson [on *The Adventures of Ozzie and Harriet*] and Jane Wyatt's Margaret Anderson on *Father Knows Best*. In contrast, TV shows in the 1970s and 1980s portrayed women in traditional male roles, strong and more independent—*Cagney and Lacy*, *Laverne and Shirley*. Today? Take *The Big Bang Theory*. We've attracted more male physics majors since its first airing but not women. I think it's because girls and young women look at these nerdy guys and think, 'I'm not like that.' They are nerdy guys. And, of course, the neighbor is this beautiful blonde woman who is a waitress/actress. One female character, a neurobiologist, is so nerdy she's not 'normal.'

"In another study, teenage girls were divided up according to whether they had or did not have science or math aptitude. Aptitude was identified by whether one of their favorite classes was a math or science class. Both groups viewed videos of women participating in math or scientific activities. Following each video, the girls were asked if they thought they would be interested in engaging in the same activity. For the girls with a perceived science aptitude, it didn't matter how attractive the person giving the presentation was, but for those in the non-science-oriented group, the chance they would choose science was much lower if they saw the attractive woman giving the science presentation than if they saw a nerdy one giving the same presentation

"We also seem to inadvertently drive girls and young women away from STEM disciplines by placing an inordinate emphasis on service work. Not that helping people is bad. But, for example, we have a program called Bright Futures in Florida. If a high schooler ranks in the top X percent of his or her class and scores above a predetermined point on the ACT or SAT, the student receives free tuition at a state university or partial tuition at an in-state private school. The catch is recipients must complete 300 hours of service to fulfill a further eligibility requirement. As a consequence, schools push engaging in service over taking additional math classes. I'd be happier if recipients had to take four years of math and science and English to qualify for this scholarship.

"For STEM disciplines, math is a defining element. If a student takes all the math classes offered in high school and decides not to pursue a subject that involves math in college, he or she can stop taking math. But if that person avoids taking math in high school and then realizes, 'Gosh, I need math,' it's extremely difficult to go back because each successive math level builds on the ones that preceded it. If you haven't been exposed to physics in high school, you're less likely to major in it in college, but I would rather have a student who comes in with calculus than with high school physics. If you know math, I can teach you physics; but if you're weak in math, I can't teach you physics.

"No one seems to realize how important math is. I'm glad people study ecology. But even they need some math—statistics and calculus for modeling. We need people to develop drugs. They need math. Students seem to study biology because it's 'science without math,' but it really isn't. Biologists use math. If I ruled the world, people would take more math and science classes. My son has had two years of high school math in middle school, and he's going into third-year math as a freshman. He'll end up dual-enrolled at either the local community college or here at FSU to take math classes. But he will take four years of math [laughing].

"I sometimes wonder if elementary school teachers are afraid of science and math and transfer this fear to their students. In middle and high school, we find an overabundance of biology teachers who are told to teach chemistry or physics. They don't like it, and they don't understand it. They simply keep a chapter ahead of the students. Such attitudes and actions don't kindle interest in the sciences.

"In an effort to ensure education quality, Florida also engages in standardized testing, which depends to some degree on memorization. We get students who have done well in school but flounder in college because they lack critical thinking skills.

"Students well versed in mathematics, however, are good problem solvers because they have developed those critical thinking skills, and they are more apt to be able to deal with ambiguity at a younger age. Open-ended work really disturbs eighteen-year-olds. For them every problem must have a concrete solution. But that's not the world we live in. In WIMSE we introduce the students to Fermi problems. These are estimation problems (named after the renowned physicist Enrico Fermi). The classic question is, How many piano tuners are there in the city of Chicago?

"When I first introduce Fermi problems, do I ever get complaints! There's uneasiness. They stress out. 'What is the answer?' 'Did I do this right?' I walk them through the logic of gathering facts and making and testing assumptions. For instance, in the case of piano tuners, you start by asking, How many people own pianos? How often does a piano need to be tuned? How long does it take to tune a piano? How many pianos can you tune in a day? And so forth. By the second semester the students are a little bit more accepting. In reality kids need to face situations in which multiple or even no answers exist, and they need to do it when they are young.

"To compound matters, once students enter college, Florida stipulates the number of credit hours we can require students to have for graduation. It's truly problematic with transfer students because they've already earned sixty credits, giving them no room for extras. I understand the desire for monetary efficiency, but in physics it can be catastrophic. Transfer students come in as juniors, but they're not qualified to take the junior-level physics classes, which makes it almost impossible for them to finish in the recommended two years, especially if they want to go to graduate school. The state claims we have seamless integration between community colleges and universities in Florida. It may work for an English major, but it doesn't work in the sciences because community colleges don't offer the courses students should take as sophomores. I feel bad for them because the state promotes community colleges as a less expensive equivalent to coming straight to FSU.

"When I arrived at FSU, enrollments were small but adequate. Women? Not many. I never figured we would generate large enrollments. I get it when the state asks, 'If you graduated fewer than five students in the past five years, why are you here?' It turns out that over half of all undergraduate physics degrees are awarded from very small programs, which means physics is in jeopardy in many places. Our program is sizable, but as 'a senior woman in physics,' I am still concerned about how few women are entering physics or science in general.

"For over ten years, FSU has underwritten the WIMSE program in an attempt to attract and retain women in the STEM disciplines. I've been WIMSE's director since 2005. WIMSE is a living-learning community housed in one of FSU's coed dorms. Each week, first-year WIMSE students gather for a yearlong, one-credit WIMSE colloquium. Students must also take two math and two science classes their freshman year. The program fosters team building, STEM learning, and hands-on experiences. Faculty partners open their research labs to our students. Guest speakers share their experiences in STEM careers. We schedule fun activities, like pottery painting and bowling, to help build community. We work with the Career Center on résumés. I push research at every possible moment, constantly.

"Students with a wide range of academic skills apply. We do not look primarily at their test scores. GPAs carry a little more weight because they indicate a willingness to work hard. I'd rather have a hard worker than a smart person who never had to work. In general, we do not get applications from the very best students. We get applications from very good students. Perhaps the best students think they don't need the support. I know I never would have participated in the WIMSE program when I was eighteen.

"Many of our program applicants want to help people. In the application we ask, Why did you pick your major? Why do you want to be part of WIMSE? Their answers tell us a great deal. If an applicant says, 'I want to be a doctor, so I'm going to study biology. WIMSE will be good for me.' We don't accept her into the program because WIMSE is a research program. In contrast, if a student starts out with, 'I always loved to play with insects, and I really like biology, so I'm going to be a doctor,' then there's hope because everybody knows doctors, but how many people have met a research biologist? I always consider it a great success when I get them to go to graduate school instead of medical school. I'm really pleased with myself.

"We use the True Colors program as part of the WIMSE colloquium to identify how people interact with each other. It's eye opening. The coding is simple. If you are green, you are curious (most professors are green); blue, you worry about people's feelings and believe a hug is worth a million words; orange correlates with adventurous; and gold correlates with organized. It's fun. This is WIMSE, right? And there are way more blue people than you would expect. Blues reason that if you just get the Palestinians and the Israelis together in a room with a plate of warm chocolate chip cookies, everything will be fine. They get their feelings hurt easily, and then they don't tell you their feelings are hurt.

"The graduate assistants for the program have been enrolled in the higher education administration program in the College of Education, which primarily trains individuals for positions in university student affairs units. They have worked out well because they're more student-affairs-y than I am. Way more touchy-feely. No matter how friendly I try to be, apparently I'm not friendly enough. I think I'm really nice, and when students get to know me, they usually like me a lot. But when they don't know me well, they think I'm too pushy.

"I had a student tell me research is boring because you sit in a lab by yourself all day. I'm like, 'Oh my God, if only I could sit in a lab by myself all day.' Nobody works by himself or herself. Nobody! Eventually I received an application for an REP [research experience program] from her, and I asked her why she had changed her mind. She said, 'I came to school for opportunities, and here is somebody I respect trying to shove an opportunity down my throat. I need to give it a try' [laughing].

"After their first semester, WIMSE students can participate in the REP, which gives them the opportunity to participate in current research in their chosen field. I have university funds to pay students to do research. Sometimes they need a bribe, and money works. Professors like to take on these younger students even though they lack experience because they don't have to pay them. A win-win for everyone. There were two or three people doing research the first semester I became WIMSE's director, and we're in the upper thirties now.[1] When students retake the True Colors test after they've engaged in the research component of the program, guess what—they're green.

"Currently, I accept thirty-three incoming students into WIMSE because that happens to be how many beds there are in the wing of the dorm where our living-learning community is housed. I get fifty-some thousand dollars a year from the university. I pay a graduate assistant, the kids to do research, and for supplies and the like. I've asked for additional university money because we've been so successful.

"A big part of WIMSE for me has to do with ensuring that students bond, that they know people, even if they don't work in exactly the same discipline. They're all on the same career timeline. Every student will be able to talk to somebody she knew when she was eighteen who's also now in graduate school. And she can talk to another woman who's also looking for a job as an assistant professor. We're trying to do a better job staying in touch with students who have graduated, both in the

---

1. In 2011 Blessing received the Ross Oglesby Award from Garnet and Gold Key Leadership Honorary, a student organization, which goes to a faculty or staff member who has served students and the university with exemplary commitment and integrity for a decade or more.

department and in WIMSE. We've set up data collection mechanisms and created databases we can use to follow up and to help them stay in touch with each other.

"I've thought about expanding the program to include more students. But it would become a different program because I meet with the students as a group once a week and each one individually once a semester, and talk with them when they drop by. It's a considerable time commitment, but the personal interaction is critical. We'd have to have more faculty involvement. I do believe if we paid this type of attention to more of our students our graduation rate would soar. But it's very costly. It's expensive for me to know all my WIMSE students.

"Programs like WIMSE are essential. They keep girls and young women in science. Women often gravitate to helping occupations. But they think of helping individuals one at a time. I try to get the point across that science allows you to help whole populations. I once had a WIMSE student who wanted to be an ophthalmologist. She worked in biology studying zebra fish eyes. One day she came to see me. They had just made a discovery about zebra fish eyes. She was so excited because she realized that those people in the lab were the only people in the world who possessed this new knowledge, and she was one of them. I pointed out that as an ophthalmologist she could help individual people, but if she discovered a cure for river blindness, she could help many more people. She decided to go to graduate school in engineering [laughing]. I'd like to think I had some influence on her.

"All of my students in principle are science oriented; and, male and female, they all wear 'the uniform'—T-shirts and jeans mostly. I used to dress to fit in. I did not want to stand out. And when I first worked at Fermilab, I definitely did not want to look like a secretary. I dressed less femininely—the jeans and shirts. Now, I dress pretty femininely. Not frilly femininely, but I can't even remember the last time I wore a pair of pants to work. In the winter, I wear pantyhose, shoes with some heel, and skirts; and in the summer, I have bare legs and sandals and dresses or skirts. I dress better than just about everybody in the department. I want to show my students that you don't have to be the nerd. It's a conscious decision on my part. I'm bucking the 'fit in to get along' norm in favor of 'girls can be girls.'"

BIBLIOGRAPHIC NOTE

Susan Blessing's chapter brings together materials from in-depth phone and e-mail interviews and her curriculum vitae. The following Web pages were also consulted: www.physics.fsu.edu/people/personnel.asp? fn=Susan&ln=Blessing&mn=, www.hep.fsu.edu/~blessing, the WIMSE website (http://wimse.fsu.edu), and http://bridgetotomorrow.wordpress .com/2011/11/19/fsu-physics-professor-susan-blessing-wins-fsus-most -visible-award-for-service-to-students/.

five

ACADEMIA, A GOOD FIT

Teresa D. Golden

"CHEMISTRY HASN'T CHANGED MUCH IN A HUNDRED YEARS. An atom is still an atom, and bonding is still the same. No matter where you go, you get the same chemistry education. To succeed as a research chemist takes curiosity about why things happen and what's going on in the research you do. And you have to be willing to work hard, long hours because, unfortunately, experiments don't run on your time schedule.

"If I have an experiment that takes twenty-four hours, I can't make it take less time or stop and start so I can work eight to five and go home. We have electrodepositions of anticorrosion coatings on metals that go for days. Sometimes film growth may take twenty-four hours or longer. So once the experiment is set up, it must be monitored periodically to record data and make sure it is still working. When an experiment needs to be checked in the evening, night, or weekends, my graduate students and I take turns coming in to the lab to record data in a notebook. Someone has to monitor progress through the night, so we rotate the responsibility among ourselves. That's the nature of the research, whether you conduct it in academia or industry.

"In industry, however, many jobs require a chemist but not a researcher. If you're not doing research, you're doing analysis, and much of that is automated. An analyst prepares samples and sets the

---

Golden is a professor of chemistry and director of the Forensic Science Program at the University of North Texas in Denton.

experiment's parameters, but the analysis runs on its own. In many instances, cameras monitor the instruments and feed information to the chemist's home computer. The chemist can then remotely stop or start the experiment as needed without having to visit the lab. It's the rare company that engages in research. Most of them farm it out to universities.

"I decided in high school I wanted to be a chemist. My senior year, I was the only girl in my chemistry class. I loved it not because of the company I was keeping, but because chemistry was one of the few subjects that challenged me. I grew up in Odessa, Texas. Odessa is an oil town, and in the 1970s–1980s it was booming in the midst of the industry's heyday in West Texas. Money flowed into the school district. Even though we were a working-class community, we attended public schools with many of the trappings of an elite private academy. We had exceptional teachers. My elementary and middle school teachers tested my ability with extra assignments and encouraged me to do well. I attended Permian High School, where my chemistry, physics, English, and history teachers all had PhDs.

"I am a first-generation college goer. My dad had an inquisitive mind but left school in the sixth or seventh grade because he lived on a farm and needed to work. To feed his curiosity, he bought encyclopedia sets and read them every night. When I was a kid, he purchased chemistry sets and telescopes. We learned together. It was great fun.

"My mother had a head for numbers and an entrepreneurial spirit. She did accounting work and owned several businesses. She started her first business, which sold irrigation supplies and serviced parts, with the help of a small-business loan. She owned a day care facility for many years and again wrote grants to fund projects and buy supplies. Later she invested in more than a dozen rental houses and managed them. From a young age I helped her do the books.

"We lived on a farm, I went to school, I had chores, I worked. The attitude around our house was, 'Just keep doing it and eventually whatever you're trying to accomplish happens.' We pushed very hard. Today, I tell students, 'Don't complain unless you can show me you've worked hard.'

"Going to college wasn't expected. My brother never attended. But it was always assumed I would go. We started saving for college when

I was in junior high. When I applied for admission, I didn't look for specific programs. I applied to the University of Texas, Texas A&M University, and Texas Tech University. I was accepted at all three, but my mom wanted me close to home, so I went to Texas Tech, which is an easy drive from Odessa. She had a hard time letting go [laughing]. "Permian High School had a dual-track agreement with the local community college. I spent half a day at high school and the other half at the community college. I managed to get my basics out of the way before entering Tech, where I started out right away in chemistry.

"To be perfectly honest, at seventeen I didn't know much about careers in chemistry. I just knew I liked the classes, and Tech had a large chemistry department and a strong analytical program because Pernendu 'Sandy' Dasgupta was there at the time. Tech had equally renowned faculty across all its chemistry subdisciplines.

"The chemistry program was cohort based. Premed majors who hoped to continue on to medical school constituted a large segment of our cohort. Quite a few were women. We entered as a group and stayed together throughout our years in the program. I even had the same lab partner for most of the program. As chemistry majors we were segregated from the general student population. If someone from another discipline needed to take a chemistry class, he or she didn't take it with us. The cohort provided community, people to interact with on a regular basis. I wasn't one in 300. I was one of a few, and everyone was in the same boat.

"As soon as I enrolled I became involved in research, which was pretty typical at Tech. We interacted with the professors. As an undergraduate I did research with Daniel Armstrong, who is an analytical chromatographer. Chromatography is a separation science that uses instruments to separate mixtures of chemicals like pharmaceuticals, biological compounds, and so on. I started specializing in analytical chemistry and worked on determining the amount of trihalomethanes (a by-product of chlorination) in water and air using gas chromatography. I was even included as an author on a couple of papers with Armstrong. I liked that.

"I planned to go into industry when I graduated. I even interviewed with Kodak. But my undergrad adviser encouraged me to continue on to graduate school. He suggested I pursue a PhD because it would give me options. But he warned, 'Don't get it in Texas. If you want to come back to Texas, schools here like variety, so go outside the state and then come back.' I took his advice. I went next door to New Mexico. I'm not sure that's what he had in mind, but it *was* out of state [laughing].

"I actually looked widely for programs. Because I wanted to specialize in analytical chemistry, I sought out the strongest analytical chemistry programs in the Southwest. There was Florida (south but not west), New Mexico State, and Oklahoma. Florida was just too far away, and I like the southwestern atmosphere. New Mexico State had a great program; I liked the location—in the mountains. I was drawn to the culture in New Mexico. And it *was* close to home.

"In chemistry, especially in the larger programs, they encourage you to go the PhD route. Even so, the majority of students who come in settle for a master's. It's a default degree because students either don't pass the cumulative exams, get a C in a class, or fail to develop adequate research skills. I started in a class of eleven; two of us earned PhDs.

"Typically it takes four to six years to earn a PhD. I was there about four years. I had a very good experience. My adviser was Joseph Wang. I was lucky. I didn't know it at the time, but he's big in the field (he probably has 500 publications by now). I also didn't realize how important publications are, but by the time I finished my dissertation, I had eight or nine of them, which was truly beneficial. I really enjoyed working with him.

"When I was a graduate student, Dr. Wang employed about fifteen to twenty graduate and post-doc students and visiting professors in the lab. He worked with two large groups, one of post-docs and one of graduate students. I was assigned to a post-doc and received one-on-one training. It was great. I was the only woman in my group and was fortunate—I worked with really good guys. We had Middle Easterners, Europeans, Chinese, and me. I was the only American. The Middle Eastern and European students continuously fought with the Chinese students. Not about research but about politics. It was bad. They nitpicked, and the Chinese got upset, and Dr. Wang got frustrated. Finally, he said, 'No more fighting. All the Chinese stay in this lab, all of the Middle Easterners and Europeans go to the other lab. My post-doc guy was Chinese, so I said, 'I'll go with the Chinese' [laughing].

"There were a few other women in the department—I remember two, anyway—one in analytical and the other in either organic or physical chemistry [p-chem]. There was a woman professor in p-chem, but she was very close to retirement. Back fifteen years ago, those numbers were pretty much the norm. Today, many programs enroll equal numbers of men and women, but the faculty splits remain approximately the same. Women these days are encouraged to continue their education through terminal degrees. But even so, few are interested in staying in academia. They think it's too difficult.

"My own students who I think would be really good in academia don't choose it. They all tell me, 'I don't want to have to work as hard as you do.' Truthfully, I wouldn't encourage any of them to go into academia unless they are interested in working at a teaching college. I don't see the ranks of women faculty in chemistry growing. They either never try or wash out early. They go to national labs or start companies after they have gained experience in industry. We may produce more PhDs now, but I don't believe we will gain additional faculty in the near future. Even the ones who go that route have trouble; there seems to be such a huge attrition rate.

"There is a program in chemistry, COACh [Committee on the Advancement of Women Chemists] that started at the University of Oregon. It's a good program. I've attended many of its workshops. You get some good advice. My feeling, however, is that they're trying to train us how to be more like men—how to interject like a man so you get noticed, how to negotiate salary like your male colleagues do. I ask myself, 'Why can't I do it like a woman would?' I like guys, I work with them every day, but I have no desire to act like they do. I've always felt that those types of workshops don't address the real issue. The issue is institutional.

"There's a recent report about the number of women chemists on faculty. A while back there was a rise in numbers, but it's flattened out and perhaps even decreased. The author's findings demonstrate that the problem's not with women; the problem's the culture. If you value certain characteristics, then those values drive institutional decision making. If you have to be a male to get ahead, then none of the women are ever going to get ahead. There are only so many women who have very male, hard tendencies. And yes, probably a lot of us in chemistry tend toward those behaviors because we're aggressive. I'm not saying the situation is right or wrong. It's reality. The end result: If we don't value women's ways, then there's no way women are going to enter the academic job market. I just don't see it happening.

"Personally, I'm not going to spend all my time strategizing about how to 'be a man.' It's too much work. I've gotten to the age where I don't want to step out of my comfort zone. I'm comfortable with my own self [laughing].

"I left New Mexico State in my third year to take a two-year post-doc at the University of Cincinnati. My adviser pushed me to do it. 'It's a good one. Finish up your dissertation there, then come back and defend,' he said. It worked out well, but it was a pain. I had to write my dissertation at lunchtime. When I was ready to defend, my adviser was on sabbatical, and I had to wait. I don't think it's typical to take a post-doc when you are ABD [all but dissertation], but the opportunity was there, and he said, 'Jump.' So I did.

"When my position at the University of Cincinnati ended, I took a second post-doc at the University of Missouri in Rolla. Rolla is an engineering campus. I was in the material science department. The post-doc position lasted one year, and I stayed on for another five years as a research associate. I was the only woman. When I arrived, the guys were like, 'Oh, now we can't cuss because we've got a woman.' And I told them, 'I don't care if you cuss or not.' I never met with my boss behind closed doors. It was just understood, you met with the guys in an open room. The guys went in and closed the door and talked. I was always very careful.

"The ratio of men students to women was six to one. So when I taught classes, I picked up on some animosity aimed toward me. They questioned whether I knew what I was doing. There were some sexually related insinuations as well. But nothing I couldn't handle. Women in the classes always remained pretty quiet. I can't remember any females coming through the lab. There was one female post-doc, from Belgium.

"I do remember the building had only one women's bathroom, which was located next to the secretary's office. The building had three floors, and each floor had a men's bathroom. I complained because my office was on the third floor, my lab was on the second, the X-ray machine was in the basement, and the one bathroom was on the first. I told them, 'I'm tired of running up and down the stairs.' They converted one of the men's bathrooms to a women's [laughing]. Overall, Rolla was a good situation. I had a great mentor, got along well, and published a great deal. It was a good fit.

"Then a friend at the University of North Texas [UNT] called me and said, 'Hey, we have a great assistant professor opening.' There were perhaps six or seven assistant professorships open across the country that year. I was happy at Rolla but decided if I'm going to apply at one place, I might as well apply everywhere else too. Rolla offered me a job, and I received several other offers including the one from UNT, which I took.

"Actually, Rolla offered the best package. Its Chemistry Department was aging and needed new blood. But they didn't have a lab for me—they didn't even know where my office would be—so there were a lot of unknowns. When I interviewed at UNT, Ruthann Thomas was the department chair. She was very specific about where my office would be, which labs would be mine, and what my startup package would include. I started here in the fall of 1997.

"The idea of being back in Texas appealed to me. My family still lived in West Texas—my parents, sibling, and aunts and uncles. I actually have quite a few relatives in East Texas too. My parents passed away in 2000 and 2004, so coming back was a good decision because we were able to spend time together.

"The chemistry department assigned a mentor to each new faculty member. My mentor interpreted that job as stopping by once a year to tell me that I should apply for a dozen grants and publish as many papers. Then he'd leave. I was lucky. I'd worked in a lab so I knew how to run one, but I've heard new faculty confess that they don't know how to handle the managerial business aspects of setting up and running a lab. So their experience gets confounded not only by having to learn the institutional, cultural, and political aspects of being a professor but by being responsible for a lab. As it was, it took almost two years to get my lab up and running. My results didn't come quickly. And even though I had held two post-docs and a research position, my experience didn't totally prepare me for faculty life. I knew the research side, but I had been insulated completely from the academic side. I worried about getting tenure.

"At the time, the department chair and an associate dean, Jean Schaake, taught courses in the department. So there were three of us, but Ruthann and Jean were quite removed from the daily trials of faculty life. I honestly don't know if I would have made it had I not started going to lunch with Nandika D'Souza, a faculty member in material science, and Sandra Quintanilla, from physics. Other women joined us occasionally. It was very informal.

"I knew nothing about being a faculty member. I was the only junior faculty in the Chemistry Department, and some of the guys were older and no longer applied for grants and the like. Suggesting such things to me just wasn't on their radar. In contrast, Nandika would say, 'Don't forget to apply for X. You ought to do Y.' Back when I started at UNT, much of the scanning electron microscopy and materials characterization experiments (the work I did) had to be conducted in the Science Research Building [SRB], which used to house lab space for all the sciences on campus. Nandika and the other women were housed in SRB. They provided a social network for me. They passed on information.

"Analytical chemistry is a mixture between analytical and materials-type chemistry. It focuses on trace analysis and instrumentation. The analysis can cover many areas—drugs, medicinal, environmental, mining, oil and gas, and pharmaceuticals. Examples include testing for drugs in urine or blood, testing for herbicide contamination in soils, testing minerals or rocks for precious metals, testing pharmaceuticals for trace contaminants, and so on. Since analytical chemists spend so much time in the lab, they also design and build new instrumentation for their work and become experts at running many different instruments.

"My research looks at corrosion-resistant-type coatings on surfaces, and then, because I have some biology background, I also do biological studies with the UNT Health Science Center on metal contamination in bones. There is a problem obtaining good DNA results when bones in remains have been exposed to metals. So we are working with the DNA researchers to study the inhibitory effect different metal concentrations have on their DNA results. It is a good combining of my group's analytical skills with their biological research.

"About halfway through the tenure process my mom became ill and passed away. Then my dad got sick. For over a year, I drove home every Wednesday and on the weekends (three hours each way) to take care of him. It was very stressful. To complicate matters, my parents had custody of my two nephews. So I took custody of them and raised them through high school and into college. I'd always had them in the summers, from the time they were seven or eight. Even when I was in Rolla, they came and stayed with me. While I worked, they spent time with friends on local farms or went fishing. They were about fourteen and fifteen when they came to live with me permanently. They're really good kids; they didn't give me any problems. But it was not easy. Overnight I became a mom [laughing]. Now they're grown and have good jobs in the oil fields. I still see them at least once a month.

"Right after earning tenure, Jean Schaake approached me about starting the forensics program. Setting up the program required a great deal of time. It's one reason it took me so long to get promoted to full rank. Service has little or no bearing on our department's promotion criteria. Program development hurt my annual evaluations. Although I'd started a nationally recognized forensics program that draws high-quality students, my external evaluations also suffered. It cut into my research. I couldn't publish or bring in monies at the expected rate. Right before the program accreditation visits, I was spending almost ninety hours a week making sure we were ready. I felt like I had two full-time jobs.

"Ironically, I mentor the younger faculty in our department. Some of this younger group went up for full rank before I did. Their career lines were very different—primarily research and publishing. They didn't develop a new program, nor do they help administer this one.

"UNT's forensic program is one of eighteen nationally accredited undergraduate programs. It cuts across biology, chemistry, and criminal justice. Its development took several years because we had to have two graduating classes before we could apply for accreditation. We started our first class in 2005 by judicially identifying several juniors and first-semester seniors and convincing them to come into the forensic program. Doing so gave us several quick graduations. We gained our accreditation in 2008 (four years after we had started the program) and reaccreditation in 2013.

"Our program is relatively small and selective. We designed it that way. Larger programs enroll as many as 800 students, admitting over 100 freshmen yearly. But their graduation rates are abysmal. When I was investigating programs to use as models for ours, I asked the director of a large one how many students it graduated—a staggering twelve.

"We handpick our students. As a consequence, we have a very low attrition rate. We'll accept students at any time during their UNT enrollment. If we take them as freshmen, they are top high school graduates. I'll give you an example. Every one of the five high school students I interviewed this year has huge scholarships coming into next year. They have top grades, they have almost perfect SATs, they're really good students. They've taken a ton of math (including calculus) and science. And they know they want to do forensics. We graduate the same number of students as the larger programs, but we don't have to deal with the constant massive influxes of new students they encounter because of their high attrition rates. I think our way works better.

"The program has grown to over 100 students. Nationally, over 75 percent of the students in forensic programs are women; it's close to 90 percent in some programs. We have more men than most programs, but we are still close to that 75–25 split. Every time I talk to the FBI director, he tells me almost all of his applicants are women. Not that he cares, but it's an observation. I think women gravitate to the field because of its applied nature. It's concrete, you see an outcome, and you're making a difference.

"We have twenty-six internships in industry- and forensic-related fields. We easily place our students because there's so much demand right now, and we have a top-notch lab. We were really lucky with UNT's former president. She was a great friend of the program. The instrumentation that you need to run an FBI-certified lab and that is required if you want to hold a Drug Enforcement Administration [DEA] license so that students can run real drugs, not placebos (they work with DNA, blood, semen, spit, you name it), is not cheap. She raised the money for that equipment. Having the instrumentation available for students to work on is good for the program and gives the students needed hands-on experience. The acquisition of state-of-the-art instrumentation was pushed by UNT administrators to help make the program competitive. The DEA license for the program allows students to learn how to run tests and experiments with real drugs as they would in a forensics lab. Having the instrumentation is a big draw. We haven't really had any new instrumental support since Bataille [Gretchen Bataille, UNT's former president] left. Our classes are maxed out. We could easily expand the undergraduate program and develop a corresponding graduate program if we had the resources.

"All of our students work in internships, and almost 100 percent get job offers. Ninety-five percent turn them down and go on to graduate or medical school. I thought it odd that so many turned down job offers until I spoke to some of them about it. As interns they realized that the people in charge of their labs had either master's degrees or PhDs, and they wanted to be in charge, not underlings. If we had a graduate program I know many of them would continue on with us. Our sister campus, the UNT Health Science Center, just received accreditation for a graduate-level program, so we feed as many of our former students to the center as it can handle. But the program is small and specific; it focuses on DNA forensic analysis. Only the students interested in that type of work want to go there.

"We were lucky. We had the right people at the right time; everybody was willing to work together to make it happen. Faculty synergy remains good. Everybody works well together. Almost all the programs that seek accreditation fail to get it because the academic departments involved can't get along. I like our program, but quite honestly, sometimes I wonder why I did it.

"The department offers an informal internship program for our other chemistry students. I started it when I came here as a young professor. I successfully approached small companies in the area to develop the internships. I continue to manage the program. No one else wants to do it because it won't help them get full [professor]. Early on, my colleagues in the department separately told me, 'Don't worry too much about your students' futures. It will not benefit you personally.'

"I actually have more chemistry internships than I can fill. Such internships often lead to great jobs. Yet, students don't always want them, and I can't understand why. They seem to think commuting thirty miles to Fort Worth is too far. Or the internship doesn't pay enough. Or they want to work only a few hours, not full-time. I tell them, 'Are you kidding me!' When I was young, I'd work for free. I'd go to another state if that was where the job was. It's a very different perspective. I'm not saying I'm old, but I sometimes feel old.

"As I get older, all my energy goes into helping the best students, the ones who want to work. It's not mothering, I simply enjoy nurturing and mentoring students. My favorite times during the week involve meeting students in the lab. We talk about research and bat around ideas. I love that time. It's energizing, and seeing that lightbulb come on is rewarding. I like seeing students grow. I don't sense such activities are quite as important to my male colleagues.

"Academia seems to fit me. I love teaching. I love research. I like writing. I have a set time devoted to it every single morning. I lock my door, and I write every single day, except Saturday or Sunday. Well, Sunday maybe, Saturday sometimes. Even if I'm behind on other things, I still write. If you want to write well, the best advice I can give you is: Write [laughing].

"I truly like being a professor. That doesn't mean I won't start my own company or work in industry someday. I'm not against it even now, truthfully. I already do a fair amount of consulting in industry. My industry-related work includes helping industrial chemistry labs choose and purchase the right instrumentation, interpreting X-ray diffraction data for oil and gas companies, and working with the paint and coatings industry and environmental firms.

"Today, there are two other women in UNT's chemistry department. Diana Mason is retiring, and Angela Wilson, the last female we hired, plans to move out of the faculty ranks and into administration. That will leave me as the sole woman in a department of nineteen chemists. I haven't seen a woman hired recently at UNT in any of the STEM disciplines. Currently, I'm on three hiring committees, in chemistry, biology, and materials. No women are even being considered. There's one woman in biology in her fourth or fifth year. She may be the last woman hired; I am not sure.

"My suspicion is that Angela's moving away from research because women researchers don't get taken seriously. She receives more recognition for her research outside UNT. Many of us [women] suffer from the 'you're never viewed favorably at-home' syndrome. Rarely will colleagues ask me to join a research project. Perhaps they don't believe we [women] do research, or they think we're not good at it, or maybe it's easier to collaborate with other guys. I have collaborated with men. I do work with a couple of junior male faculty members on occasion, but my two big collaborations at UNT are with women.

"Collaboration is a must. It's rare to get funding as a single principal investigator [PI] unless you are extremely well-known. So, if you're expected to have multiple PIs and collaborate, and opportunities don't exist within your home department, it restricts you.

"Truthfully, chemistry's golden years were in the 1960s and 1970s. After that, funding shifted to biology and medicine. Today, an average grant size in chemistry might be $200,000 or less for a single PI. The funding rate for many agencies is about 7 or 8 percent. And most want to see multiple PIs involved. The pool of available funds just isn't that big. Physics has the same problem. And probably math does too.

"I'm pretty resourceful. I write grants for funding from several agencies, including the National Science Foundation, National Institute of Justice, Department of Energy, Department of Defense, and the Welch Foundation, a private foundation that funds chemical research.

"When you first arrive at an institution, startup packages help. A new chemistry professor gets $300,000 plus for lab startup. It would be impossible to get started otherwise. The money goes for equipment, chemicals, and supplies. Some faculty might be able to negotiate an additional personnel grant to be used for a post-doc position for the first couple of years. In contrast, a big chunk of any grant goes toward personnel. If I have a $200,000 to $300,000 grant, a third or more easily covers personnel costs (graduate students or post-docs). Labs run on students. If you happen to hit a hiatus in funding, your lab comes to a grinding halt because you can't fund students.

"For every grant I get funded, I have applied for fifteen to twenty grants. It's daunting. It's a vicious circle. You can't write papers without a lab, and you can't run a lab without grant funding, and you can't get funding if you don't publish papers. It's a real pain in the butt.

"Over the years, I've received good offers for administrative positions, but I like to do research and would have to give it up, so I stay. I haven't gone looking, but I'm thinking about it. I work too many hours. I'm not happy about it. We've had a change in top-level administration at UNT. I feel uncertain about the whole situation. And it has nothing to do with chemistry. If I do look, it will be administrative work as well as faculty positions. As a full professor in chemistry, I can move a little easier, especially if I bring funding with me, than if I were still at the associate rank. It's not just the big schools that are interested, little schools want you too because everyone wants to boost their funding. As a program director with labs under my supervision, I have appeal as an administrator.

"But I'd have to be truly serious about leaving before I applied any-where because I think playing that 'matching' game is unethical. I've been in situations where we interviewed professors for a position and found out halfway through that they're just using us to get a counter-offer. It's so frustrating because it wastes time and energy. It's not right.

"I get along well with my colleagues in my department, and I like them a lot. But at the same time I feel extremely isolated. I never hear about critical aspects of department life until it's too late. No one thinks to tell me. There could be a tornado on its way, and it wouldn't dawn on them that they needed to let me know [laughing]. I just don't feel connected. I do [my job]. Everybody does his or her job. Maybe every-body in the department feels the way I do. I don't know.

"The problem for women coming into academia is everybody's too busy to mentor. To be honest, there are probably more type A personal-ities in chemistry at research institutions than not—we're driven. Very few of us sleep. All my e-mails from colleagues arrive at one, two, three, four in the morning. I know Angela and Mohammed (both members of my department) are up all the time. We can't sleep. We tend to work late (nine or ten at night) and start early (six in the morning).

"Perhaps mentoring might work at the institutional level. For instance, every Friday from one to three o'clock, why not offer a ses-sion for all new assistant professors on grant and paper writing? I've noticed the university started a similar program at the graduate level. I've sent all of my grad students to institution-wide dissertation-writing workshops, and they've done phenomenally well. I'd love for someone to proofread my grants, but I cannot think of anyone who is less busy than I am. When I do ask coworkers on grants to review applications, they don't even look at them. I'm tempted to insert cartoons half the time because I know they are going to tell me it looks great [laughing].

"In general, I think mentorship is important for women in STEM disciplines. Good mentoring can be about passing on information about applying for a grant, or something to do with institutional poli-tics, or how to handle situation X, or why it's important to apply for Y, or when to talk to the chair about a particular issue. Good administra-tors help, and programs that advance your summer pay until a grant becomes active do wonders to reduce stress and promote healthy work environments. Little in-house grants can help the professors procure more resources. But simply meeting and talking about such ideas doesn't really benefit anyone.

"I didn't have much institution-based mentoring. I always seemed to be one year out of sequence. The National Science Foundation used to have chemistry grants for women, but it eliminated the program my first year. At UNT we now have some help for individuals to move from associate [professor] to full [professor]. This time I was one year too early. Sometimes it's a matter of luck.

"I just read a paper written by a woman psychologist at Harvard, I think, that further illustrates an insidious cultural norm that works against women. This researcher studied women and men in the STEMs and the way they approached math and science. She found that if a woman was told she was good at X and then ran into an obstacle in science or math, she immediately thought something was wrong with her, shut down, and quit. She lost momentum. But if you told a guy, 'You're really good at X,' and he ran into difficulty, he just barreled on through.

"Guido, one of my colleagues in the department, had this exact experience. He confided, 'I've had problems with every woman grad student I've had. They seem to be fine, they're going along well, and then all of a sudden, they fall apart. What's going on?' Another department member occasionally asks me, 'What should I do about this female student?' The other day, I gave him articles about working with women, which he told me he handed out to all the women students to read. I suggested, 'Shouldn't you give them to the males, too? They might eventually be bosses'[laughing]. The issue hits close to home for him. He has daughters. He worries about them. He wants them to do well.

"I'll have women come to me with a problem, and I'll say, 'I'm not worried about it. You're smart. I know you'll figure it out.' And then I think maybe I shouldn't have said that. Women seem to look for perfection. My students hesitate to admit that they aren't perfect and weren't handing in papers unless they were flawless. I finally told them, 'I don't want a perfect draft. If you give me a perfect draft, I'll return it. I want to see work in progress. I want to read: Dr. Golden, I don't know what this means, please help. Or, I started writing and my dog started barking and I lost concentration. I want everything in your draft because I can work with that.' They didn't believe me, so I gave them my drafts. I do everything in longhand first, and it's a mess. I said, 'Look at it. See how crappy it is.' Now I get real drafts from them.

"I sometimes give psychological prompts to women: 'Do whatever makes you feel good about yourself and powerful. Think positively. Come to your test in your best dress.' They tend to do a little better. For some reason, women often automatically label themselves. I want the default to be 'I can figure this out,' not 'I'm dumb.'"

BIBLIOGRAPHICAL NOTE

Golden's story stems from a series of phone, in-person, and e-mail interviews along with her curriculum vitae.

SIX

A LIFE FULL OF
SERENDIPITOUS OPTIONS

Sharon Hays

"THE FOCUS OF THIS BOOK, where highly educated women in science and engineering [discuss their] careers, struck a chord with me. In the mid-1990s I was at a tier-1 research university [Stanford] where the prevailing view among faculty was, 'You're getting your PhD; why on earth would you have a problem finding a job in academia? And if you need to find a job outside academia, it must be because you aren't good enough. Why else would you choose another career?'

"I bought into that notion for a while, but I kept hearing other graduate students say, 'Are you crazy? I'm not staying in academia.' I thought perhaps I was just talking to a select group of people. I wanted to know whether this disillusionment with the academy among both men and women was widespread or simply an anomaly. So I did a study on the graduating class in biomedical sciences to understand whether people were remaining in academia or embarking on other careers. More than 50 percent of us were either considering or already committed to nonacademic careers. That finding blew those professors away.

"But let me back up a bit. I had a fairly positive graduate school experience. I picked a thesis adviser, Paul Berg, who turned out to be

Hays is vice president of the Office of Science and Engineering, North American Public Sector, at Computer Sciences Corporation in Falls Church, Virginia.

perfect for me. I don't like people looking over my shoulder, and Paul had high expectations but was hands off. He wasn't like some other PIs [principal investigators] who wanted to see their students' lab books every week. He'd won a Nobel Prize and wasn't still fighting to get tenure like some of the more junior professors in the department; he had a broader worldview. I recognized the freedom that working under him offered. He was near the end of his research career and already very involved in activities outside the laboratory, serving on National Academies of Science panels and the like. I was actually his last graduate student.

"Even so, two years into my PhD, my research project crashed and burned; there I was, starting over. It happens often in the biomedical sciences, but it's nevertheless pretty rough to go through. I wondered, 'Am I in the right field? Am I a good enough scientist?' I certainly did some soul-searching. Quitting, however, isn't in my nature. My project failure wasn't enough to cause me to say, 'Oh my God, I don't want to do this PhD after all.'

"So I regrouped and redesigned my study. About three years later, I had research results, which I was writing up for publication. I had enough results to finish my thesis, but part of me couldn't imagine I was really that close to being done because the average length of a PhD in the biomedical sciences at the time was close to nine years. That's ridiculous. It's too long before you're actually involved in, quote unquote, independent research, have a real job, and pay into Social Security [laughing]. I was all for speeding up the process.

"About that time, in 1995, Dr. Berg could not attend a scientific meeting he'd been invited to, so he sent me in his place. Turns out this wasn't a typical biomedical sciences meeting at which thousands of people converge. This conference was a fifty-person meeting of the top scientists in the field; and believe it or not, it was held in the South of France in an old castle in Avignon.

"My talk went well because I had new results; people are always interested when you present fresh findings. Afterward, as I was listening to someone else's presentation in this beautiful building, I thought, 'This is the way it's supposed to be. I have good results; I'm writing a paper; I'm at this incredible meeting where I can interact face-to-face with these bigwigs in this field, with no filters. They're not treating me like a PI, of course, but they're including me.'

"It suddenly occurred to me. 'All of these other people are living, eating, breathing their science. It's everything to them.' They each possessed such single-mindedness about their research. And here I was. I didn't have that same kind of passion about discussing how cells repair their DNA. The phenomenon we were studying was such a tiny piece of what makes the world turn. I wasn't energized. The thrill of discovery related to that one little piece of the universe wasn't enough.

"I realized, 'This is as good as it gets, and I'm still not into it.' I decided then and there academic research was not the career path for me. It was a wonderful lightbulb moment because had I made the decision to shift away from academia under other conditions, I might have always asked, 'Did something else make me unhappy?'

"The search began: what *do* I want to do? I'd always been interested in law. I worked for a lawyer when I was in college as an undergraduate. She was an appeals attorney in the criminal system. My job involved finding precedents for arguments she needed to make. It required copious amounts of digging, reading, and synthesizing.

"I was about to get a PhD in biochemistry and had an undergraduate degree from the University of California at Berkeley in molecular biology. There was a huge demand back then for people who had molecular biology experience, especially in patent law. So I decided to apply to law school. I had a stack of law school applications on my desk, all of which had a section on extracurricular activities. I'm thinking, 'Are you kidding me? For the last five years, I've been chained to a lab bench. That's all I do [laughing]. I don't have extracurricular activities! But I need to look a little more well rounded. I know, I'll join student government activities. They're always looking for people to volunteer to represent their departments!'

"What an eye-opening experience! I met all these people who were also thinking they didn't want to be academic research scientists. That's when the idea for the survey and the report came to me. We were all taking so much blowback from the professors about being a bunch of whiners. They were saying that obviously we weren't cut out to make it in academia and that's why we were looking elsewhere. I said, 'Let's find out if that's really true. Let's do some research.'

"I surveyed students, collected and analyzed the data, and wrote a report. I sent it out to every science policy expert I could think of, which was very presumptuous in some ways. It was such a hot issue at the time. One of the women I contacted at the National Academies of Science happened to be putting together an academy convocation. Instead of research reports, convocations feature panel discussions. This convocation's topic was 'Are We Training PhD Scientists Appropriately, Given Their Career Choices?'

"I called her, which in and of itself was out of character for me. At the time, if you asked me a question, I'd give you the answer, but rarely did I raise my hand in class or initiate a dialogue. (I actually tended to come out of my shell when I was in a female-only environment. I was less likely to wait in the shadows.) I recognized that the convocation represented a fantastic platform for me to present the results of my study and that I couldn't let my shyness get in the way of a once-in-a-lifetime opportunity.

"The academy staffer had assembled a panel of eminent scientists, university presidents, and so forth. I told her that was all well and good, but shouldn't they hear what an actual graduate student thinks? Especially one who's collected data on seventy-five other graduate students. I either beat her down or won her over. The result was she included me on that panel [laughing]. I flew to Washington, D.C., participated in the discussion, and thought, 'This is cool. I like science, but this policy stuff is *really* exciting.'

"Serving on that panel gave me visibility in the science policy community and opened the door to my next career move, applying for an American Association for the Advancement of Science [AAAS] Congressional Fellowship.[1] The fellowship places PhD scientists in congressional staff positions or other policy positions in the executive branch for a year. You're thrown right into the science policy arena.

"I worked for Congressman Vern [Vernon James] Ehlers, who was a moderate Republican and at the time the only PhD scientist (a physicist) in Congress. My timing couldn't have been better, or luckier. He'd just been assigned the task of reevaluating the nation's science policy by Speaker [Newt] Gingrich. It had been fifty years since Vannevar Bush wrote his report *Science, the Endless Frontier* [Washington DC:

---

1. AAAS is a nonprofit whose main objective is advancing science and engineering around the world through education, public engagement, and communication. Among its many activities, it publishes *Science*, which has the "largest paid circulation of any general science journal" worldwide. See www.aaas.org for more information.

U.S. Government Printing Office, 1945], which served as the stimulus for the creation of the National Science Foundation and government-funded research as we know it. Involvement in that project was incredibly appealing, and so I spent about a year and a half working on it. By the time my fellowship was up, I'd caught 'Potomac fever' and decided I wanted to stay in D.C. and make science policy my career.

"The project went well, and in 1999 the U.S. House Science Committee (now called the House Science, Space, and Technology Committee) offered me a job as a committee staffer. I planned and brought to fruition congressional hearings, helped draft legislation, and analyzed a variety of scientific and policy issues. I stayed at the Science Committee for three and a half years, eventually becoming a subcommittee staff director, which involved, among other things, helping to shape the research subcommittee's agenda and steering science and technology–related bills through the legislative process. Then, in 2002 a former member of the House Science Committee who had moved to the White House Office of Science and Technology Policy [OSTP] recruited me.

"I moved up the ranks at OSTP, eventually becoming a deputy director. In that role I led strategy development for all activities related to environmental science; the physical, life, and social sciences; biological, chemical, radiological, and nuclear security science; and math and science education. In 2007 my role at OSTP expanded when I was tapped to lead the U.S. delegation to the Intergovernmental Panel on Climate Change [IPCC].[2] Climate wasn't my area of expertise by training, and I hadn't focused on it in my policy career. In fact, I regarded it as something of a 'third rail' issue: Everyone who touches it gets burned. Reluctantly, I had learned a bit about climate change in 2006 in preparation for my Senate confirmation hearing for the deputy director position. That particular subject had tripped up my predecessor, and I was determined not to suffer the same fate.

"Leading the delegation to the IPCC was a turning point in my career. It was enormously challenging, and I was thrust into a media spokesperson role that I found terrifying, but I also found the subject

2. The IPCC won the Nobel Peace Prize in 2007 along with former Vice President Al Gore "for their efforts to build up and disseminate greater knowledge about man-made climate change, and to lay the foundations for the measures that are needed to counteract such change" (see www.nobelprize.org/nobel_prizes/peace/laureates/2007/).

matter extremely compelling. It was exciting to be involved in such an important and highly visible policy debate. Today, climate change is the focus of my work in the private sector.

"I found working in the [George W.] Bush White House inspiring. There were a lot of women to look up to in the administration: Condoleezza Rice, U.S. secretary of state; Margaret Spellings, director of the Domestic Policy Council; Fran Townsend, chair of the Homeland Security Council; Dana Perino, press secretary; and others. It really hit me one day when I was attending a White House meeting, I looked around the table and realized there were some really powerful, accomplished women in the room.

"In terms of career advancement in the science policy arena, being unique helped. And here's how I was unique: I was a PhD scientist who was a Republican. There aren't many of us [laughing]. Academia is overwhelmingly Democrat. If you look at the AAAS fellows, they disproportionately work in the offices of Democrats. On top of that, I'm a woman. Like many other fields, the uppermost ranks of the science policy field have been male dominated. To this day, there has never been a female presidential science adviser. They've all been men (and the majority of them physicists). A woman in a male-dominated field automatically stands out.

"When the administration changed in 2009, I went to work for CSC [Computer Sciences Corporation], a large international company. I was hired as a vice president and created the Office of Science and Engineering in the North American Public Sector [NPS]. I lead a small group focused on providing strategic guidance to the rest of our business unit regarding the emerging market for climate change and energy solutions. My job is to ensure that CSC is positioned to be a major player in that market. To do that, I meet with other business leaders in our company to learn more about what they are doing and what their needs are. I also meet with our customers (mostly people who work in U.S. government agencies and departments) to make sure we understand their challenges and to provide them with strategic feedback. I bring to the table an understanding of what and how the government customer thinks, which is beneficial to CSC as it competes for government contracts and seeks out new opportunities.

"More recently, my group has become engaged in product development, so I have been spending quite a bit of time managing and leading that effort. It's exhilarating. We're focused on creating new products aimed at helping our customers understand and adapt to climate change. In many ways, my group functions as a small, entrepreneurial startup business that exists within a much larger company. It's very exciting.

"I'm a manager, and so my role is as much about 'managing up'— solving problems and clearing the way so that the rest of the members of my team can accomplish our goals—as anything else. I'm also a member of a couple of advisory committees and am on the board of directors of a company, so some of my time is spent contributing to those activities.[3]

"My PhD helps me in my current job as it did when I was at OSTP and on Capitol Hill. People generally respect those three letters behind your name. It opens doors. It lends credibility. Having earned a PhD also instills in you a way of looking at a problem—a way of breaking a seemingly unsolvable quandary down into answerable questions. That's an extremely useful skill—the ability to tease apart difficult problems and understand how to attack them.

"My biggest challenge right now is that I have niche expertise, gained from the work I did in government. I do not have enough of the kind of business experience that will carry me into the upper ranks of management in a big company. And CSC is a very big company. It is a global leader in providing technology-enabled solutions to the government as well as to other companies. We employ around 98,000 people, generate revenues in excess of $16 billion annually, and provide services in over ninety countries. Other leaders in the company have a very different experience set than I do; they've been working on the operational side, or they've been managing profit-and-loss units. Many of the people I work with have been working for CSC (or similar companies) for much of their career.

"I've been lucky so far in my career to engage in work that excites me. Six months ago, I had a lot of doubts about whether I had a future in a company like CSC, or whether my unusual background would

---

3. Hays is a member of the board of directors for Jefferson Science Associates, a joint venture of CSC's that is responsible for the operation of the Department of Energy's Jefferson National Laboratory in Newport News, Virginia. She chairs the Committee on Operations and Safety.

ultimately limit my ability to advance. But the current role I've carved out in product development for the climate and energy market provides me with opportunities to gain needed experience. At the same time, I get to work on something that I care deeply about. I consider myself to be a 'climate pragmatist.' I think the polarizing debates on the issue, with climate evangelists on one side and the deniers on the other are totally counterproductive. I believe that the private sector has an important role to play in addressing the global challenge of climate change, and the work my group is doing is part of the solution. That's the bigger-picture goal that makes me passionate about my work at CSC.

"I am the worst career planner. I've done almost none, mainly because I haven't had to. I've been incredibly lucky. I happen to walk in the door at the right time; I end up working for the right person who shows me that next door and helps me open it. In the past I've tended to float along from one experience to another, and while it's worked so far, it's a lot more stressful nowadays not knowing exactly where I'm going. Uncertainty was fine when I wasn't paying a big mortgage! I am married and have more responsibilities now. I might not be able to depend on serendipity in career planning anymore.

"Serendipity could be my middle name. It's been there throughout my life and affected many of my choices, even when I was young. My dad is not a scientist. He's an architect who spent most of his career managing large-scale construction projects. He often joked about how he got a D in chemistry in college and knew science wasn't for him. My sister, Karen, is two years younger than I am and generally steered pretty clear of science, like Dad. Unlike me, she is gifted in her artistic abilities. She takes after our dad in that way.

"Mom, however, had a huge influence on my decision to study science, although I didn't realize it until more recently. She has a bachelor's degree in zoology and actually wanted to be a doctor. If she'd been born a generation or even ten years later, I have no doubt she would have become one. But, after she finished college, my dad still had to finish architectural school, and so my mom needed to find a job immediately. That put an end to her med school dreams.

"Later, when I was around nine or ten, she got a job running the anatomy and physiology lab at a local community college. When her students dissected frogs or pigs, she brought home the extra specimens, and we'd carry out the experiment at home. It was great fun. One of the books on our shelves when I was a kid was *Science Experiments You Can Eat.* Those experiments were cool and made science cool.

"In high school I was actually more attracted to some of the non-science fields. I had an unusual high school experience. I attended a very good public school for two years. In fact, my parents decided to settle in Albany, California, because of its great school system. Then in 1983 my dad took a job overseas, and my sister and I ended up at an American boarding school in Europe. That school had a truly crappy science program (our laboratory equipment consisted of one or two Bunsen burners, and that was about it) but fantastic history and literature teachers.

"Perhaps because of the lack of any scientific stimulation during the latter part of my high school experience, I came out of high school thinking I was going to go into prelaw. But something was going on subconsciously because there I was, a, quote unquote, prelaw student, enrolled in freshman chemistry, which is a notorious GPA killer. Exams were graded on a curve, and it was rumored that 90 percent of the people in the class get Cs (probably a slight exaggeration). Why take it if I wasn't interested in science? I told myself I wanted to keep my options open.

"Partway through college I read an article in the *New York Times Magazine* about cancer research and was riveted. I immediately decided that's what I wanted to do—to be one of those people who tries to solve that particular health-related puzzle. I switched my major to molecular biology. My GPA went up. I loved learning about the clever experiments that the pioneers in the field of molecular biology had to design in order to understand something that they couldn't see. It was fun and fascinating.

"I lived with my uncle, John Hays, and his family the summer between my junior and senior years of college so that I could work in his lab at Oregon State University. He played a very significant role in my whole career progression because he is a molecular biologist. Working in his lab was my first hands-on foray into research. I enjoyed it and the laboratory camaraderie. My uncle even added my name as an author to a paper describing the work we did.

"When I graduated from Berkeley in 1989, I had not applied to graduate school. I didn't feel ready to make that leap. I did, however, want to work in a lab. I called my uncle and asked, 'Any ideas about what I might do?' He phoned a friend, Myron Goodman, at the University of Southern California [USC], who called me and said, 'When can you start?' [laughing]. Talk about serendipity! My 'interview' consisted of a five-minute phone conversation, but it ended up being the perfect position for me.

"In many ways I functioned like a graduate student. I wasn't just ordering supplies and cleaning up after others. I had my own research project. That opportunity led me to graduate school because it answered my questions about whether I liked research enough to pursue a graduate degree. I thought, 'I can do this for five, six, seven years, however long it takes to get a PhD.' And I figured getting a PhD couldn't hurt. It still allowed me to keep my options open, which was important because at the time I thought I might like to do field research on parrots. I had one as a pet, and I found him intriguing. (And still do. He's still alive and very much a part of our family.)

"Dr. Goodman would have loved for me to enter the molecular biology PhD program at USC and continue working in his lab, but he also encouraged me to apply to other places. He viewed Stanford's biochemistry department as *the* place; it's where all the forefathers of molecular biology were (and they had the Nobel Prizes to prove it). I applied, thinking I wouldn't get in—and then I did. That's how I ended up in graduate school at Stanford.

"When I was interviewed for the program, multiple professors asked what I wanted to do when I finished graduate school. 'What are your career goals? Where do you see yourself in five, ten years?' I knew the right answer was, 'I want to go into academia.' However, a little voice in the back of my head said, 'Maybe academia, maybe not.' Even then, I wasn't 100 percent committed to academia. I liked science, and doing experiments, and being the first person to understand something new about the universe. But . . .

"For the most part I never felt I belonged in academia. Even though half of the PhD candidates in the biomedical sciences back then were women, there was only one woman on the faculty in the department. She was married to a super big shot professor in Europe. She didn't have children. I don't say this in a disparaging way, but at least from our point of view as graduate students, she didn't appear to have much of a life outside the lab. As a consequence, there were no female role models who had lives that looked anything like the one I wanted to live.

"I wasn't married at the time, but I knew from talking to other women who wanted to have children that they saw how hard it was. Not that it couldn't be done; but the degree of sacrifice it would take, especially if there were expectations that you were going to be the primary caregiver, was daunting. To me, having kids seemed totally incompatible with the hundred-hour workweek in the lab—from morning until midnight— that was the kind of life that a career in science seemed to require.

"In a study I heard about while I was in graduate school, the woman conducting the research looked for conditions that predict or determine whether a couple is likely to share child-rearing responsibilities as opposed to the woman having the majority of the responsibilities. Her results were crystal clear. It came down to who the primary breadwinner in the family was. If it was the guy, then the woman carried more of the general household and child-rearing responsibilities even if she had a full-time job. If the woman was the primary breadwinner, and it didn't necessarily have to be by much, then all of a sudden the responsibilities shifted, and the guy typically did more. My husband and I haven't had children, so it hasn't been an issue.

"Today, it seems that more couples share the load. For instance, most of the people who work at OSTP have science PhDs, and when I worked there, many of them were women who had children. I found it impressive that these women, most of whom were younger than I, had figured out how to have careers and families at the same time. Many of my female role models and colleagues at my level or above at OSTP did not have children. To me that was normal, since it fit with my limited observations in graduate school. It wasn't until I saw the young women we hired at OSTP that I noticed this new (to me) trend. I see it as well in the private sector. I am one of the few women I've met at CSC who doesn't have children. For me, this shift was unexpected. I wonder whether it's linked to the greater pay parity for women, which has been gradually happening. I don't know whether it's happening in academia as well.

"One explanation for why we find so few women in science and engineering faculties is that we seem to disproportionately lose women every step along the path to the professoriate. In some fields, we don't attract enough women into the field to begin with, but even when we do, fewer go into post-docs, fewer take faculty positions, and even fewer become tenured. That in turn sets up a vicious cycle, in that young women entering academia have a limited set of female role models. We need to change that dynamic if we're going to get more women in senior tenure-track research positions.

"In the biomedical sciences we have seen an uptick in women entering graduate-level programs. They constitute 50 percent or more of our PhD cohorts. It's a lot different in other fields of science, where women are still a distinct minority at both the graduate and undergraduate levels. I suspect that the biomedical sciences is different not because there was better recruitment of or mentoring for women, but because there's a fair amount of spillover in the biomedical sciences from medicine. Women have accounted for 50 percent or more of med school populations for some time. Some of those students start out thinking they will go to medical school and then get hooked on research instead.

"My people skills helped me make the transition from being a research scientist into a successful career in the policy arena. I'm not an extrovert. But I'm good at reading people, and that's critical in the policy realm. Quite often you must understand what a person thinks even when that's not exactly what he or she tells you. I can work with almost anybody, and that's a huge asset too. I've seen people who have all the right skills on paper, but because they are difficult to work with, either they don't advance, or if they manage to move up in the organization, they have problems once they are in positions of authority. In certain positions in government you can get away with being incredibly arrogant, but I don't think that works in a lot of other fields, although academia may be another exception. Certainly my experience in grad school bears that out. I often had the sense that certain people were used to being the smartest ones in the room, and they didn't hesitate to make sure you knew it by asking 'gotcha' questions during group meetings.

"Being able to communicate well is another critical skill in my field. Again, it's not a skill that necessarily gets honed in a scientific research environment. While I had some professors who were entertaining speakers, many others completely lacked any such skills. We used to chuckle about some professors. In class they faced the whiteboard while talking, which meant that we couldn't hear them well, all the time scribbling down formulas in writing so small we couldn't see— zero interpersonal skills.

"On the downside, I am rather risk averse. I prefer to be the one in charge, and I don't have qualms about taking on leadership roles, but I have to force myself to accept risk, and it's always uncomfortable for me. I sometimes feel those two qualities put me at odds with myself, because often leadership involves taking risks. I worry that it hinders me.

"I also lack confidence in myself, and I sometimes underestimate my abilities. Other women tell me they feel the same way, but few men I've encountered do or at least are willing to admit they do.

"Here's a couple of good examples of what I mean. One of the professors at Stanford was an editor for a scientific journal in our field. He asked me to review a couple of papers, and I must have stammered something in regard to my ability. He said, 'Why is it that every time I ask a young woman like you to do something like this I have to convince them that they're good enough to do it? You are!'

"Flash forward fifteen years when OSTP was looking for a deputy director for science, which requires Senate confirmation. Two of my colleagues (and mentors), one man, one woman, had recommended me for the position and were encouraging me to take it. One of them was a female colleague who had recently gone through the Senate confirmation process and was the second in command in a prominent government agency. I confided in her that I was terrified about the confirmation process. She looked at me and said, 'Do you think [a male colleague of ours who was in a very similar role to the one I'd be taking on] worried about whether he was ready for it? He just went for it. You are absolutely prepared, and you should go for it too.' She continued, 'When I was nominated for my current position, I had all the same feelings. Why do we agonize over this stuff? Guys don't, or if they do, they hide it well.' This ingrained lack of confidence and fear of failure (which I still sometimes have) seems to be a frequent difference between men and women. For me personally, it contributes to my reticence when it comes to risk taking.

"I do believe that part of my reluctance to stay in academia revolved around thinking I wasn't good enough. I sometimes think, 'If I'd been a man and had the confidence that seems to come so naturally to many of them, it's entirely possible I would've gone into academia.' But I'm glad I didn't because the bottom line is that I didn't love it enough; I didn't 'eat, sleep, and breathe science,' and I think that's a necessary prerequisite to a successful academic research career.

"I like being different, and I appreciate it in other people. Some would say that my husband, Mike, and I are an example of 'opposites attract.' Mike is a captain in the Washington, D.C. Fire and Emergency Medical Services Department. We met in 1998 when I participated in a congressional ride-along night, an optional activity for congressional staffers who were interested in learning about how the D.C. fire department works. I went on a lark and was paired up with Mike, and we hit it off. Serendipitous or what! We didn't start dating right away, but we ended up together and married on New Year's Eve, 2002. We have strong interests, shared and separate, and we're both okay with not being around each other 24/7. He's comfortable with my career choices and the hours I sometimes work, and vice versa.

"I love that we're in such different fields. If there's one profession I could never in a million years do, it's being a paramedic. I'm super squeamish, and the possibility of making a mistake and actually hurting or killing somebody terrifies me. But I love hearing about his work and about the difficulties of working within the D.C. bureaucracy. I'm extremely proud of what he does. He is amazingly good at it. I would hate coming home every day to someone who works for another big company and is engaged in the same stuff I do. I can bounce ideas off Mike, but we don't talk shop, and most of the time I'm pretty darn happy that we can't. It makes life much more interesting.

"Whether a woman stays in science or enters the policy arena or business or whatever, my advice to her is, make sure you're doing something that truly interests you. It's hard to go wrong when you're enjoying living in the moment, as opposed to going through the motions because you feel you absolutely have to check the box in order to get to the next phase of your career. Life's too short. Why spend five years getting a degree just to check a box? I went to graduate school because it was fun. I didn't know exactly what I was going to do afterward, but I knew I would enjoy doing graduate-level research for the six years it would take to get a degree.

"I'm often asked, 'Should I get a PhD, even though I'm not sure what I want to do?'" My answer is always, 'Yes, as long as you like the process enough, as long as you like doing research enough, then absolutely!' The discipline of thought that it teaches you, those critical thinking skills you gain, can't hurt you.

"There have been times in my career when I was the only woman at my level within the organization. For a while I was the only female senior staffer on the House Science Committee. I'd been in that position for probably six months before I looked around the room and it occurred to me, 'I am the only woman here.' I have never sensed any gender-related discrimination. I never felt like being the lone woman in any particular organization hindered me personally, but it's certainly not ideal.

"In any field in which we don't have a solid, if not 50 percent, representation of women, we're missing out on 50 percent of the brainpower that we could be tapping into and the creative ideas that we could be exploiting.

"We need to catch young girls early if we want more women to go into science. We don't necessarily want to convince young people they want to be scientists at age five or seven or ten or whatever the magic number is. But science is one of those fields that if you don't have the right foundation, it's extremely hard to catch up. If you don't take freshman chemistry, you can't major in molecular biology. You don't have a prayer of making it through physics if you don't understand calculus. And you can't do calculus if you don't have certain underlying mathematical skills. We must reach girls at an age when the door hasn't already been shut, when they haven't tuned out algebra and geometry for so long that they can't get through college calculus and therefore are never going to major in the sciences. These are enormous problems. It seems counterintuitive, but I believe that if we are going to get more women on science, math, and engineering faculties, we need to emphasize that scientific study opens up many other career choices as well.

"Faculty at Stanford felt it was sad when so many of us chose 'alternative' careers, that it was a problem. But was it really? When you're in graduate school, you contribute to the research enterprise. (Some people refer to it as 'slave labor.' It is certainly cheap labor.) The strength of the system, though, is that graduate students bring different perspectives, an untarnished optimism, a fresh creative spirit that wanes after people have been in the field for years and years. There's a good reason to bring new young people into the research enterprise, and there is absolutely no way that they can all go into academia. There aren't enough new academic positions being created every year to make up for the sort of exponential growth you get when every PI trains between five and twenty-five graduate students. It's a mathematical impossibility.

"We don't need to worry that the whole research enterprise is going to fall apart because PhD graduates seek alternative careers. Actually, people who are successful in these other careers are some of the best ambassadors for recruiting young people into science because they demonstrate that scientific study doesn't have to lead to a career as a scientist; rather, you have many different choices and opportunities. We in the STEM disciplines do very poorly when it comes to exposing youngsters to options other than academic careers.

"There are other factors as well. Think about what's on television. How many programs are there about doctors and lawyers? Many, and the professions are glamorized. They make these professions exciting. You rarely see glamorized depictions of research scientists—*CSI* might be one of the exceptions [laughing].[4] Young kids need to understand that getting a degree in a technical field doesn't mean they have to wear a white lab coat and spend their entire career at a lab bench, looking at and interacting with test tubes. Science gives you options.

"I'm a testament to the truth of that statement. I am a scientist, but that's not my career. I've had experiences I never would have had without science. It prepared me, it stimulated my creativity, it helped separate me from the pack. It gave me tools and problem-solving skills I might otherwise have never developed. Yes, I worked hard, but science helped me advance."

---

4. It has stimulated interest and increased applications to forensic anthropology programs.

BIBLIOGRAPHICAL NOTE

Hays's chapter derives from multiple phone and e-mail interviews. Her résumé and an article in *Diversity Journal* featured in a CSC news release provided more insights (see www.csc.com/newsroom/press_release/ 36845-csc_s_dr_sharon_hays_among_women_worth_watching_in _2010). Go to www.csc.com for more information about CSC.

seven

ENJOYING A LIFE THAT FITS

Angela Hessler

"To be a good geologist, you must like uncertainty. Scientists often develop a hypothesis, design an experiment, and collect data that provide an answer or at least another testable possibility. Geologists can spend years looking at rocks to come up with a theory that, as geologists like to say, is probably wrong [laughing]. Most of our ideas can't be tested in a laboratory. It takes a certain personality to be comfortable with such ambiguity. We like the process of taking our observations, stretching our imagination to come up with a working hypothesis, and then testing that hypothesis vigorously against new data.

"Most geologists also thrive on being outside and having somewhat adventurous field experiences. We go to remote areas—we tend to work in deserts because rocks are so well exposed, but also in alpine mountains, jungles, along shorelines—which means dealing with the elements. Fieldwork, however, is not an absolute must; many earth scientists rely completely on computers. In either case, geologists must have flexible minds, deal with time and geographic scales, and be able to think in three dimensions without pictures. The imagery has to be cerebral. If you don't like to engage in such mind manipulations,

At the time of the interview, Hessler was a research geologist with Chevron Energy Technology Company in San Ramon, California.

chances are you won't like geology. In addition, I see girls and women shy away from more male-dominated fields, such as geology, for three reasons—a desire for relevance, an aversion to math, and an inability to envision having a career and a family simultaneously.

"For example, at Chevron I conduct Take Your Daughters to Work Days (I do Take Your Sons to Work Days too). I've noticed that the girls ask more questions about how my job helps people. Not that boys don't care about helping others, but girls are much more interested in how what I do contributes directly to society.

"As scientists we must emphasize how what we do informs the larger picture and ultimately affects the broader community. It's easier in fields like medicine and engineering to see a direct societal impact. In geology you work for years on a problem and begin to wonder, 'Does this matter? Who cares if this rock was deposited X many years ago?' It can seem isolating, and there's no such animal as instant gratification. But the only reason we fully understand climate change and a host of other environmental and energy issues is because geologists look for answers to when and how our planet formed, how and why it continues to change, and where our water and energy resources exist. It takes time, but the knowledge gained helps every single person on Earth in very significant ways. That's the story we as geologists, as scientists, need to tell.

"Likewise, when I speak with youngsters about my work, math frequently surfaces as a stumbling block. I mentor middle school girls from the Techbridge program, and they always ask me if I liked math when I was their age.[1] I never gloss over how much schooling they're going to need or how much math they're going to have to take. To succeed in almost any science or engineering field, you have to be willing to learn math. I try to couch the rigor of academic preparation as a fun, rewarding challenge. I stress that one doesn't have to be exceptionally good at math and science to be successful (although it helps!).

"It helps if they see math applied to real problems, to experience the power of struggling through a math problem to its end. I explain it's about valuing the pursuit of answers, learning along the way, and keeping an

---

1. Chabot Space and Science Center in Oakland, California, founded Techbridge in 2000. The program targets girls in grades five through twelve. Its mission is to promote girls' interest and skills in science, technology, and engineering through multifaceted programs. Chevron is one of its partners.

open mind. I make it clear that of all my science and math classes, I found geology to be the hardest and most frustrating, but I also found the knowledge and conceptual understanding I gained from geology to be the most enjoyable and rewarding. The reality that they can and should pursue not what comes easiest but what motivates them resonates with girls.

"As for the family-work issue, I try to describe what I do as a fun job with complications. I let them know that they can achieve a healthy work-life balance because doing so is fundamental. People need to be inspired by their jobs and driven to do the work. It's exciting to have a job you want to think about on the weekends and you want to work on at night. But that type of commitment must be cast in a positive light—as a choice not a necessity. I can choose not to think about work at night when I'm fixing dinner or getting kids to bed. I don't have to be overly stressed out by work. I continually strive for that balance because I know it can exist. I saw it growing up.

"I was born in 1973 in Columbia, Missouri, the third of four kids. My dad was a professor in the Department of Sociology at the University of Missouri–Columbia [MU]. My mom stayed at home with the four of us until my little sister started second grade in 1984. Mom then entered graduate school in history at MU, earning her master's in 1991. She started teaching at Columbia College in 1992.

"I find my mom's persistence remarkable. She dropped out of college when she and Dad married (just five courses short of graduation) but chipped away at those classes while raising my older brother and sister and officially graduated eight years later in 1972. We all followed her example. We persisted through school. My brother went into writing; my two sisters went into social studies and history education. I became the lone physical scientist in the family.

"I had a natural affinity for science at a young age. Our family took cross-country road trips. We'd drive to the mountains, and I was fascinated by everything we saw. We all had fun on those vacations, but I was the one who wanted to know how the mountains were formed, why canyons existed. I collected rocks, something most geologists do when they're younger. No one else in my family did. In fact, they all teased me about it [laughing].

"My dad encouraged my curiosity. He and I attended astronomy lectures at MU (we laughed that most of it went right over our heads) and participated in public telescope viewings. He took me to a rock quarry and told me, 'We're standing on the bottom of an ancient sea!' We looked at the fossils, and it sparked my imagination. I think it was extremely important that my parents encouraged all of us to pursue careers that we enjoyed. The goal was certainly to support ourselves, but they never advocated one pursuit over another on the basis of potential earnings.

"In my freshman year of high school, our science teacher incorporated more lessons related to earth science into our classes than did most ninth grade science teachers. He was surprised when I developed a couple of science fair projects that focused on rocks and minerals on my own and supported my efforts. I liked science and did well in my science classes. But I never imagined I could make a career out of picking up rocks [laughing]. I considered other sciences, like biology and medicine, which were more viable options. In general, my high school teachers wanted me to do well academically, but no one specifically took me aside and said, 'You should study geology.'

"In 1991 I entered the University of Notre Dame and took the Intro to Geology class. All of a sudden I realized I *could* make a career out of studying rocks. I learned that geology was much more than collecting rocks and that geologists were trying to solve all sorts of interesting problems. I loved it. I signed up to be a major right away. Freshman year, first semester, first two weeks. I left all my doors open, though. I took the most advanced science and math classes to give me the flexibility of switching to engineering or medicine if I wanted. That action proved fortuitous because the geology program became part of the engineering college after I had declared my major, and I didn't need to retake any courses to fulfill the engineering college requirements.

"As an undergraduate, I was aware that I was entering a male-dominated profession; many of my engineering-related courses had only a handful of women. But I didn't feel broadly discriminated against. Of the four Outstanding Graduating Engineering Students at Notre Dame, three of us were women, so it was difficult to feel our options were limited by our gender. The criteria by which we were judged were so objective—we took tests, we wrote papers—there were few opportunities for outright discrimination. I can't remember a time when I missed out on a big opportunity and thought it was related to my gender (although I certainly know women who have). On rare occasions I felt my work was diminished because of my gender. For instance, when I was an undergraduate, I did a research program over the summer and produced a manuscript that I wanted to get published. I showed it to my undergraduate adviser, who said, 'Oh, that's cute.' I remember thinking, 'No, it's not cute. I spent three months conducting real scientific research.'

"On the whole, the professors were great and I learned a great deal in the classroom. No one, however, talked to me about careers or planning for one. My brother was the one who pointed me toward an undergraduate research program sponsored by the National Science Foundation in Hawaii that one of his college friends had taken advantage of and valued. It was that experience that really set me on the path to a PhD.

"I arrived at Stanford University in 1995 to work with Donald Lowe on industry-related geology research. About a month in, I realized I was much more interested in his NASA-related work on the ancient Earth environment. I was nervous about changing projects, but he was enthusiastic about the change.

"As a graduate adviser, Don was our biggest critic and skeptic when it came to his students' work, but if we presented clear arguments with quality observations and data, we ultimately gained his respect. This type of relationship didn't suit everyone, but I know it made those of us who studied under him excellent critical thinkers and good communicators. As a rather reserved, fresh-out-of-undergrad PhD student, I had much to learn about communicating with a faculty adviser. I didn't provide enough updates, which resulted in misunderstandings about what I was accomplishing. As soon as it dawned on me ('I need to be better about telling him what I did the past eight weeks'), our relationship improved. It was a good learning experience. He was encouraging but not to the point of undeservedly propping us up.

"I appreciate Dr. Lowe's approach because I didn't harbor any fantasies about my abilities or the quality of my work. It can be a humbling experience and for some a confidence breaker, but when I submitted my final thesis chapter and he said, 'You are ready to do this on your own, as a faculty member,' I knew I had earned it. His final assessment of my work improved my confidence more than garnering a slew of little compliments along the way.

"I don't remember the exact number of women in the PhD program, but the male/female split seemed pretty even. A small number came for a master's, but most were aiming at the doctorate, and most graduated. It was a strong program. It was intense, but the faculty worked to get us through. A few people came close but didn't finish, and a couple of others didn't make it through their oral qualifying exams. When someone dropped out, it was a big deal, a rare occurrence.

"Stanford's program did have an unintended consequence, though. People typically entered the program thinking they wanted a research career and quite often left knowing they were more interested in teaching. I'm not sure the intensity or stress of doing research turned people off to academic research careers as much as the realization of how it diminished the teaching aspects of the job. Many of my fellow graduate students were very talented teachers and loved that aspect of academia, but teaching was simply not encouraged by the faculty and was to a great degree viewed as a distraction from doing good research. I had to convince my adviser to let me be a TA [teaching assistant] for a few classes. I wanted the experience. Today, research institutions seem to value teaching (by their best researchers) more than when I went through my program. It's no longer an either/or situation. And it appears to be more feasible now to do quality research at teaching institutions.

"Our faculty role models were experienced, accomplished, and established. We didn't have any untenured faculty role models, which made it difficult to visualize ourselves as new tenure-track faculty at research institutions. Stanford has since hired new faculty who are fresh out of graduate school. My sense is that current students see faculty positions at research institutions as viable career options.

"I had a great time at Stanford. I wasn't married. I didn't have children. I was free to work and finish my degree in a timely fashion. Fieldwork can be difficult if you have a family because it often requires extended travel and involves a great deal of uncertainty—going to the middle of China and not being able to communicate with people, for example. I spent time in Peru, Chile, South Africa, China, Hawaii, and Nevada and reveled in every adventure I had.

"Once women start families, it's harder to get away for a big field season. If you have a new baby, you're going to be much more hesitant to spend eight weeks in Mongolia. You delay. Eventually you decide, 'I loved going to Mongolia, but it's just not happening. Maybe I'll choose a more practical career.' If you get into a marriage, and your spouse doesn't understand the field component, the importance of it, and how long it needs to be, it becomes a problem. Relationships suffer. Geologists often marry each other because we understand the demands, but it can still add stress to the partnership. Now that I'm sitting here being interviewed with my six-month-old daughter on my lap and my two sons off to school, I'd probably have a slightly different take on fieldwork [laughing]. But back then I was young and free, and it was fun.

"PhDs in geology tend to find careers in industry (primarily oil but also mining and mineral extraction, and occasionally environmental consulting), at research or undergraduate universities, or with the U.S. Geological Survey [USGS]. The USGS is a large organization, but it's not hiring significant numbers of people because its employees usually stay in their positions for their entire careers. So perhaps half of Stanford's graduates went into the academy, and most of the rest into industry.

"Stanford has a particularly strong connection with the oil industry. Many people engage in dissertation projects that have industrial applications but also make it easy to slide into faculty positions. In contrast, I did a study of the Earth's surface environment using the world's oldest river deposits in South Africa, a purely academic exercise because I wasn't interested in industry at the time. Eventually I decided I should at least check it out. I interviewed for and was awarded an internship with Phillips Petroleum, which dealt with deepwater exploration in the Gulf of Mexico, the summer before I graduated. It did broaden my options.

"I'm not sure the situation would have been the same had I attended another institution. Oil companies tend to favor a small number of universities. They pay attention to the people going through their programs and interview at those schools. It limits your alternatives if you don't happen to be enrolled in one of them, especially if your dissertation research has no obvious application. Nevertheless, the gap between the number of PhDs that geology programs produce and the number of jobs available is narrower than it is in other fields. Generally, a geologist can find work. Colleges and universities might not be hiring, but industry is. Companies need to replace employees who are about to retire. It makes for a pretty secure field at the moment.

"I was one of those people who entered Stanford interested in doing groundbreaking research and left more interested in doing groundbreaking work in the classroom. It seemed more exciting, more tangible, and more rewarding than the research I was engaged in. I enjoyed my thesis project, but I was a bit burned out by the loneliness of it, and I had difficulty seeing the 'greater good' application of my work.

"Perhaps I would have had a keener interest if I'd been part of a peer group working on similar questions and validating their significance. I should have been applying for post-docs to continue research unfettered by the need to develop course materials and teach classes, but I didn't have the drive to continue the research developed in my dissertation or even to publish what I had. I did eventually rediscover my excitement and grasp the world relevance of my research, and I published most of my dissertation. I do regret its taking so long. Now I always advise people to publish as much of their dissertation as they can while in graduate school. It only gets more difficult once you have your first job.

"I loved school, and I've always loved the academic environment. Growing up in a college town with a parent academician was a good experience. I felt Dad had a nice balance in his life between work and family. He had a relatively flexible schedule. He took time off. I liked the lifestyle. I was too naive to understand how hard his job actually was. He made it look easy. Plus, my mom was primarily taking care of the home front. Once I grew up and embarked on my own academic career, I began to see. 'Yes, I have a flexible schedule, but I'm working sixty hours a week, and my apartment is a disaster' [laughing].

"When I applied for positions, I was open to going to a research university, but I was nervous about starting my career in one. I was hesitant. I didn't feel ready. It wasn't an issue of faulty mentoring. My adviser certainly encouraged me to write proposals and publish, but he didn't light any official fires under me, which seems to have been what I needed. The bright side is that I was able to focus instead on doing very careful science and writing a really solid thesis. Going into a post-doc position would have been the obvious next step to gain more research independence, but I was offered a very attractive tenure-track position at a teaching institution, which appealed to me.

"I had confidence in my teaching abilities. I had taught a geology class at Columbia College in Missouri one summer and monitored undergraduate labs at Stanford. I was comfortable with the idea of teaching at an undergrad school where I could still do research but without the added pressure I would experience at a research university.

"I started at Grand Valley State University [GVSU] in Allendale, Michigan, just outside Grand Rapids in January 2002. I loved it. I liked designing my own classes and thinking about research problems on my own. My graduate school experience had been satisfying, but once I started at GVSU, I appreciated leaving behind the constraints imposed on me as a graduate student.

"My position at GVSU revolved around a significant teaching load, twelve credit hours a semester with as many as six labs in a single day. I found repeating myself that many times in one day a little irritating. At Stanford, professors had graduate students supervise lab classes. It's good experience for a graduate student, good practice in the classroom, and good preparation for them as future faculty, but it eats up a professor's time. That was my one big disenchantment. It made it hard for me to develop research projects. I tended to put too much effort into my classes. There's an endless amount you can do, and I had a hard time limiting myself and setting aside time to think about research.

"Four times I took groups of students to Death Valley, California. Other professors thought I was crazy [laughing], but I had a blast. It was tiring and stressful but fun because most of the students at Grand Valley hadn't gone anywhere. Many of them had never been on an airplane. For them, it was an incredible adventure, and it gave me a great deal of pleasure taking them on that first big adventure.

"I loved interacting with students. I have a mind that enjoys the puzzle of trying to make complex information accessible to people who don't have the background needed to understand it. And I liked designing scientific labs around current events. Students got engaged in what we did. It was rewarding to see the students' lightbulbs turn on. I'm not big on lecturing. I don't crave being in front of people, but I managed, mostly by making my lectures interactive. I taught giant classes and I taught tiny ones and enjoyed both, but I liked the more intimate experiences of the lab classes the best.

"The department itself was a wonderful place to work. The faculty members were great, and working with them was easy. I didn't feel any of those stresses that you hear about. It wasn't just our department. There was a general, positive feeling on campus that permeated its departments. People were well rounded and pretty well balanced. The administrators knew what they wanted the institution to be, so they didn't send conflicting messages about what was expected from the faculty. There were few if any interdepartmental problems. I always felt confident about what I was doing, and those in the department were always pleased with what I did. Sure, I got frustrated by students who didn't seem to care about being in my class, but that comes with the territory, and there were plenty of high-quality students who made it all worthwhile. In four and a half years, I had only one semester when I generally didn't relish going to class.

"Even after four years, my research drive wasn't ready for 'the big time.' I published a couple of papers in well-regarded journals. I did fieldwork one summer and went back to Stanford another summer to do research at their SHRIMP [Sensitive High Resolution Ion Micro Probe] lab, conducting high-resolution age dating of samples I had collected along the coast of Peru. So I generated work, but it was hard to get it done. I found it difficult to dive into a long-term project because of the teaching load. Trying to figure out how to include undergraduates in the work tested my endurance. I was so used to the model at Stanford, where people follow one line of inquiry for years. At a place like GVSU, you need to find projects that students can work on for a couple of months because, by the time they're ready to do the research, they're almost done with school. It's a complex problem.

"It would've been easier for me to design a grant proposal in which I said, 'I'm going to send students every summer to Peru, and we're going to continue the work I started in grad school.' I did submit a proposal to do international fieldwork with undergraduates, but it went unfunded. The selection committee obviously understood the issues better than I did. It's hard to get students up to speed that fast and difficult to complete such a project when you deal with so many students on a daily basis. I had at least one new class prep every semester I was at GVSU. I never had one of those semesters where I thought, 'Okay, I taught this class already. I'll just repeat what I did last year, and I'll work a little bit more on my research.' I'm sure it would've come eventually. I mean you can't teach a new class every semester for twenty-five years. Can you?

"We didn't have graduate students at Grand Valley. I knew that going into the job, but I didn't realize I wouldn't like not having them until I didn't. Gradually I decided I'd be interested in a university that at least had a master's program—for the long haul I wanted to work with graduate students.

"I also started thinking about family life. My husband, Andrea, was in the graduate program in geology at Stanford for the first few years I was at GVSU, and our long-distance relationship worked. But by my fourth year at GVSU, he had a job at Chevron in the San Francisco Bay area, and I was pregnant. The university was amenable to finding a job for him, but because we would be in the same department, the administrators weren't willing to offer a tenure-track position, at least not right away.

"We are both sedimentologists, and we have published a couple of papers together. Even though we have separate interests in sedimentary geology as well, it would certainly be challenging for us to find academic jobs because of our overlapping expertise. Other couples in the same situation have eventually been successful, but in all the instances I know of, one member of the couple took the full tenure-track position, and the other a non-tenure-track position that could, but might not, lead to a full tenure-track position. The situation at GVSU didn't really suit Andrea professionally. He's more of a researcher, and Chevron was supporting him to do the research he really wanted to do.

"With four years of teaching under my belt, I was ready for a new experience, and it seemed better for me to make the move to the Bay Area than for Andrea to come to Michigan for a temporary position. The problem was that when I started looking for jobs, there were very few attractive academic positions. The ones that were available constituted a step backward in my career. I thought, 'I've been around universities my entire life. Maybe I should check out something different,' so I looked into industry.

"I didn't consider Chevron as an option at first. I interviewed at an alternative energy think tank and an environmental consulting firm before I applied at Chevron. When I interviewed at Chevron, I was surprised by my eagerness. The work sounded interesting, there were a number of exciting training opportunities, and my husband and I had the added benefit of being in one place, which meant no commuting for either of us. It has been much easier for us to get comparable entry-level positions in industry. That said, eventually one of our careers will advance at the expense of the other. It will be difficult for both of us to land international assignments, which can be big career boosters.

"My first job at Chevron was as a technical services team member, which means I was an expert consultant for the rest of the company. If there was a project going on anywhere in the world that needed my kind of expertise, the unit with the problem 'hired' me. For instance, when I came back from my first maternity leave, Chevron had just completed an exploration well in the middle of the North Atlantic, and I was contracted for three months to analyze the data coming from the new well, design a geologic model of the region, and consult with the team in Houston to decide where to place subsequent wells. Those kinds of projects could be as short as a few days or as long as a year or more.

"Today, I am part of the research division of the Energy Technology Company [ETC] of Chevron. I work on longer-term development and testing of new technologies and ideas. I have a great deal of autonomy to design and complete my work; it's similar to academic research in many ways, but obviously with the caveat that what I do needs to add value to the company.

"The technology is incredible. I have access to the most amazing amounts of data. I'm always learning. And I love the work-life balance. My weekends and evenings are almost entirely free from work worries. The company is quite vocal in its support of work-life balance and healthy living, and I don't feel pressure to take on more than I can accomplish. My one complaint is it takes a long time to work up to what I consider a healthy amount of vacation. A formal sabbatical system like the one in academia might prove a nice benefit for both the company and the employees.

"When I started at Chevron, I was surprised to discover that work in industry is more team oriented and less of a solo effort than at universities. It added unexpected value to my new position. It made me think about how academic institutions might benefit by bending the traditional model of hiring 'one of each kind' of geologist and instead hiring for overlap. There are two main benefits to doing so: One, you can focus on hiring the best candidate overall and let his or her research drive the department in new directions, and two, you can ease some of the research isolation felt by department personnel. It could also help with the problem of dual-career couples, where both come from the same subdiscipline.

"When I was first hired, business was good, and Chevron invested money back into its new hires in the form of training. I could take a weeklong class on some aspect of geology or engage in field training. These offerings have slowed since the economic crisis in 2008. But generally, we have the opportunity to become technical experts. If we want, we can also become business experts within a specific technical area. The company offers workshops, training, and mentoring for both types of leadership. The combination is quite powerful. It opens doors.

"We also have fairly extensive maternity leave benefits; it's a different approach from the one taken in academia. GVSU offered me a semester at home at full pay during which I still worked but at a reduced level. I actually thought it was quite a decent deal. Some of my friends at other universities who are having babies before they get tenure have gone back to the classroom the same semester. They don't feel they can be out for several months. Maybe the stakes are higher. It's harder to shift work around in an academic department. If I'm the only sedimentologist, then I feel the pressure to teach the sedimentology classes. And it's so difficult to step away from graduate advisees for very long, especially if they're preparing for qualifying exams or trying to finish.

"In my current industry job, I have long-term projects. I either wrap them up before taking a maternity leave, they get shifted to someone else, or they wait until I return. Even so, paid leave time in industry usually doesn't match what GVSU offered. It turns out that we're lucky we live in California. Chevron provides up to four weeks predelivery, full-pay, disability leave, as well as up to eight weeks full-pay, postdelivery disability. A California mandate adds another six weeks paid family leave, which can amount to no more than 50 percent of your base salary and is capped at about $1,000 per week. California also protects jobs for six months in the case of family leave (this can be for newborn care, for sick parents, and so on). So I am able to take five to six months of unpaid leave if I want or need to. Most people who work in the oil industry in other states don't have that option and need to be back at work within three months. Chevron is also good about providing people with part-time and telecommuting options. If a woman telecommutes, she can tend to her baby's needs with the help of a nanny and still be a productive employee—although I will say that not many people choose to do this on a regular basis.

"On a day-to-day basis, there is appreciable flexibility in my industry position for family responsibilities (working from home when needed, taking time for appointments, and offset scheduling—coming in late or leaving early). There is no on-site child care here or in other locations, but Chevron does provide backup care through a child care agency in Houston and San Ramon if parents need to travel.

"My husband and I work an offset schedule. He goes in early, and I cover the morning shift of getting the kids ready for school; he comes home early and picks them up and gets dinner ready. I'm home in time for dinner. It might be more difficult for academics working in the same department to establish such a routine. Meetings here rarely occur outside the core hours of 9:00 a.m. and 4:00 p.m. In academia, teaching schedules vary each semester, and meetings or events often occur outside that nine-to-four slot.

"We do not have a strict chore-sharing regimen, but it works out, and neither of us feels we are doing more than the other. I travel less for work, partly because of personal choice and partly because of the nature of my current job. It doesn't offer me many chances to go into the field. The pressure (or opportunity, as the case may be) to attend or present at professional meetings that exists in academia does not in industry, which also keeps me home.

"To be a successful faculty member, you must have a passion for passing on your expertise to other people. I know people who are incredibly smart and good at what they do. But they have no patience for students or anyone who doesn't understand, and it doesn't work. It also helps to have an incredible passion for the problems you're trying to solve because without that inspiration it gets very difficult to write proposals. To get research done, you have to be able to prioritize, manage your time, and not get too frustrated with how much there is to do because the amount of work that you can do as a faculty member is limitless.

"The same qualities lead to success in industry and consulting-related positions, but there is an added dimension in the academy. As a faculty member I dealt with more diverse types of individuals than I do as a geologist in industry. I confronted students who didn't know anything or didn't care and worked with colleagues on high-level research.

Many of my current colleagues have PhDs. I'm not working with people who have no understanding of what I'm doing.

"And there are other differences. When teaching, students might be more interested in a class if the instructor is a bit edgy and colleagues respect him or her for thinking outside the box. Although being eccentric in academia is acceptable, it's those with standardized personalities in industry who tend to go places. In industry the acceptable norm is to fit in. And there's probably more room for failure in academia—for trying new things and taking risks in the classroom or in research—than there is in the industry. In industry, roles and responsibilities are more clearly defined; there's not as much tolerance for risk, and the stakes are very high both in a financial sense and in terms of safety.

"Very rarely do people bring their children to work. I did bring my first son to two meetings when he was an infant, but beyond that I sense the lines are more divided between work and family in industry than they are in academia. When I was young, my dad took me on his research trips to interview elderly populations in rural Missouri. I sat in on and sometimes helped with the interviews. I know quite a few academic colleagues who take their children on field trips or research excursions.

"My undergraduate field camp professor, Elizabeth Miller at Stanford, brought her two children, five and eight at the time, for our eight-week trip, along with a babysitter, of course. I do not remember thinking that having the children there was disruptive or made the experience less worthwhile. Others might have; I don't know. It can be fun if it works out. The kids learn, they get exercise, they're outside, and their parents aren't sacrificing what they want to do. They're together as a family. Of course, it can be distracting for the parents, or the kids might rebel and not want to go, but the flexibility is there to do it, and parents can take advantage of the opportunity it provides to work together in the field.

"I cannot envision a comparable situation for geologists in industry. Taking children into the field is much harder to swing because in addition to concerns (even if babysitters are on hand), companies have to be worried about liability.

"No matter which environment, academic or industry, I've rarely felt my options were limited by being a woman, but I do see instances where women have to work harder to get noticed professionally. Now I'm more sensitive to seeing the bias in how women get overlooked for technical awards or consultation, in hiring, or just presenting a good idea. It's hard to put a finger on because it's not a fixed glass ceiling but more about subtle dismissiveness.

"I don't want to blame anything on gender that's not there. But in graduate school, I began to notice that after lectures and presentations, rarely would a female grad student pose a question to the speaker or to the instructor. And I also realized for the first time that there was such a thing as a stupid question. People discussed and ridiculed fellow students (behind their backs, of course) for asking certain questions. It made me hesitant to speak up, to say the least!

"I do know at Chevron, my style is different from most of my male counterparts. I'm quieter; I don't speak up at every meeting. I've heard from management that my reserve can be viewed negatively. In group situations I'm not very talkative—that's partly what it comes down to. Some of it also stems from a fear of asking a naive question. Some has to do with wondering, 'Is this really a question worth asking, or am I talking just to hear myself talk?' By the time I think it through, the meeting is over and everyone's getting up to leave [laughing]. I probably just need to be a quicker thinker.

"Organizationally, Chevron is in transition. Upper and midlevel management is definitely male dominated, and most researchers are men. The company has hired quite a few women in the last five to six years. (And we're all having babies and taking six-month leaves of absences [laughing].) But overall, there haven't been many women at Chevron or in the industry as a whole. Companies engaged in massive hiring twenty-five to thirty years ago and then pretty much stopped hiring until ten or so years ago when officials realized that those early-wave hires were on the verge of retirement. Men constitute the majority of that earlier near-retirement group. That's one reason upper management is male dominated. Although newly hired employees, especially since 2000, are more evenly distributed across gender, an adequate pool of women simply hasn't been around long enough for promotion to leadership positions. However, that doesn't fully explain the dearth of women in leadership. Chevron's eleven-member board of directors has one woman; similarly, three of eighteen corporate officers are women.

Most disappointing to me is that only one or two of the twenty-five Chevron fellows (the company's most valued technical experts) are women.

"Although women seem to be entering geology PhD programs at increasing rates, they are not pursuing academic careers, and in industry more women work part-time or quit their jobs than do men. When I started at GVSU, there were three women tenure-track faculty, none of us married or with children. Every male faculty member had a spouse at home. A few were former geologists and taught occasional classes as adjuncts but didn't work full-time. A female undergraduate geology major paying any attention would get the message that a woman needs to choose between having a tenure-track job and having a family.

"At Chevron it's not quite so clear-cut, but women are the only ones with part-time positions, and at the time of this interview, my husband is one of only two people on his all-male team with young children and a spouse working full-time.

"A number of top female executives in industry, however, serve as good role models for those women who want to successfully balance motherhood and a STEM career. The key is to find those examples of a lifestyle you want, consider it possible, and trust that even though many women seem to be scaling back their careers, it doesn't necessarily mean they are making the better decision. It's hard to change the landscape if you're not there."

BIBLIOGRAPHICAL NOTE

Hessler's story derives from extensive phone and e-mail interviews. Her résumé provided further information. Since Hessler's interview was conducted, she and her family have moved to Austin, Texas, where her husband took a position with another oil company, and Hessler left the corporate environment to try her hand at independent consultancy work.

eight

AN ARDENT ADVENTURER

Bonnie F. Jacobs

"I AM A PALEOBOTANIST with a PhD in geosciences. My graduate research was in palynology (the study of pollen) in sediment cores from northern Arizona. The pollen in these sediments, which dates to 42,000 years ago, documented a record of vegetation and climate change in that region of the Southwest. As I was completing my PhD work, I moved to East Africa with my husband (a vertebrate paleontologist) and became interested in African plant macrofossils. As a consequence, for most of my career in paleobotany, I've focused on the reconstruction of past climates in tropical Africa, past ecosystems and community ecology, and the evolution of Africa's biomes. My work and that of my students has also dealt with the evolutionary significance of particular plant groups. Field areas included Tanzania, Kenya, and primarily Ethiopia during the past twelve years.

"Our research in Ethiopia has focused on two regions—one where fossil plants date from 27 million years ago and the other where fossils are 22 million years old. A comparison of the fossils from these two sites is particularly exciting because between the two times represented by the fossils, global warming appears to have taken place, and a land connection developed between the island-continent of Afro-Arabia and

---

Jacobs was promoted to full professor (2012) in the Roy M. Huffington Department of Earth Sciences at Southern Methodist University in Dallas, Texas.

Eurasia. The fossils provide information about past temperature, rainfall, and atmospheric CO_2 concentrations. The significance of this work lies in its value as a deep-time perspective on the impacts and direction of change in the twenty-first century, given our ever-increasing concentrations of atmospheric greenhouse gases and ecosystem disturbance. If we can better understand what took place in the past regarding ecosystem changes and their causes, we might be able to apply the insights gained to the environmental events occurring today.[1]

"I've always had an interest in science. I grew up in New York City, and visiting the American Museum of Natural History and the Metropolitan Museum of Art were my favorite weekend treats. I found them fascinating. Thanks to my parents, I discovered my love of dinosaurs and mummies. Early on, I decided I'd be an archaeologist only because I didn't know the difference between archaeology and paleontology.

"I'm not sure how I ended up a scientist. But I do know that my parents encouraged my interest in science, and I grew up understanding that my sister and I would go to college. My sister, Marian, is a successful interior designer in New York with her own business. Marian and I always joke about our differences—artsy versus science. Although we are quite different, we are very close.

"We lived in a very middle-class neighborhood in Queens. All my friends, except one who went to Cornell on a scholarship, attended state colleges because we couldn't afford to go to private ones. I don't remember ever meeting with a guidance counselor in high school, not once. My parents knew I was applying, but I don't remember them being very involved in the process. I simply filled out applications and sent them in.

"The state of New York had an academic tracking system. So when I was in K–12, I was in the 'smart' classes all through elementary school. New York also had the SP [Special Progress] program. If you achieved a certain minimum score on a standardized exam in the sixth grade you were eligible to skip eighth grade or have an enriched three-year program (seventh, eighth, and ninth). I skipped eighth grade. By the end of ninth grade, I was fed up with the SP classes.

---

1. The contents of this paragraph in part come from an interview by Dawn McMullan. McMullan, D. (2011, October). Dallas big thinkers. *D Magazine*. Retrieved from www.dmagazine.com/publications/d-magazine/2011/october/dallas-big-thinkers?page=2

"I was in with very competitive students and felt a great deal of pressure to perform. I no longer wanted to be special but to blend in and take it easy. I declared to my parents that I would not be in any honors classes in high school and I developed new friends (some in regular classes and some in the three-year SP program). It was a rebellion of sorts, and a foolish one at that. Had I been less rebellious and more focused on my studies in high school, I might have started out at a higher-ranked school than the State University of New York [SUNY] at New Paltz.

"I spent my first two years at New Paltz, where I enrolled in two introductory geology classes. I enjoyed them. I tried to get into archaeology, but New Paltz didn't allow freshmen or sophomores to take the class. So I transferred to SUNY Buffalo [UB] in 1972. UB had more extensive archaeology, anthropology, and geology programs.[2] I couldn't make up my mind which way to go. Fortunately, UB offered an option where you designed your own degree. My program of study combined geology and anthropology, mainly archaeology.

"Geology and archaeology are not what you might call practical sciences like premed or engineering. My parents never pressured me to be practical. They didn't say, 'You have to get a job when you finish.' Given their backgrounds, having grown up during the Depression, you might have expected they would. In contrast, when I mentioned to my boyfriend's mother my sophomore year that I was transferring to BU and majoring in geology, she said, 'My son can't afford to do something like that. He has to support a family when he's done with school.' Her perspective upset me. What's ironic is that eventually he ended up with a degree in psychology—now what's so practical about that?

"My fear wasn't about practicalities. It had to do with transferring from a small school to a large one. To me UB was gigantic! And academically it was a step up from New Paltz. The entrance standards for freshman were higher. It was where all the 'smart kids' went. I thought, 'Oh my God, I like science and enjoy earth history, but can I really do this?' Being a girl made it especially intimidating. There were only a couple of other women in my major classes, and geology required participation in an extensive field component.

---

2.   Archaeology is often a subdiscipline housed in anthropology. The degree awarded is usually in anthropology with a focus on archaeology.

"One of the geology professors and an archaeology professor teamed up to create a new field school in Venadillo, Mexico. The prospect of combining my interests in the field excited me, so I chose to go to Venadillo instead of attending a traditional geology field camp. Looking back on it, I wish I'd gone the traditional route.

"One other girl attended the Venadillo field school. We had a pre-field-camp meeting, and the archaeology professor assigned the two of us to supporting the kitchen staff. I asked why he chose us for that job, which made him defensive. His only response was, 'Well, somebody has to do it.'

"Because my degree combined geology and archaeology, my understanding was I'd conduct fieldwork and get instruction in both disciplines. My assignment outside kitchen duty, however, turned out to be exclusively in archaeology. I did the excavation work for a male archaeology graduate student who was working on his thesis. Digging is slow, careful work, but every day he chastised me for being too slow. After two weeks in his pit, I asked when I was going to work with a geologist and was told, 'Girls shouldn't be geologists.' Finally I went to the two geology professors; they drove me out to the middle of the region being studied, handed me an aerial photo, and as they left, said, 'Find your way back.' That was my day of geology education [laughing].

"I knew I had to go to graduate school. In fields like archaeology and anthropology, the only way to pursue your intellectual interests as your life's work is through a PhD. And the only way to do that is to excel in a strong program, garner a post-doc position, and then hopefully land a faculty position. At least with geology, there are other options. You can go into industry.

"We didn't have the Internet back then, so it wasn't easy to find out about programs. Foolishly I didn't seek out the advice of faculty about where I should apply, and what I discovered on my own worried me. Most programs, whether in anthropology or geology, didn't provide students with the time to combine the two. I went ahead and applied to several programs and was accepted at the University of Wisconsin in Madison in the anthropology program.

"The summer before I was to start at Wisconsin, I worked at an archaeological site in upstate New York. Mary Kay O'Rourke, a graduate student at the University of Arizona in its palynology master's program, visited the site. The two of us decided Arizona was the perfect place for me because its geosciences program gave students the flexibility to design their own programs of study. I applied at the last minute. Mary Kay made sure my application got to the department's admissions desk. I was accepted, and in the last three weeks of the summer, I shifted gears and went to Arizona. I even had to take out a small loan to pay for school since I didn't get a teaching assistantship right away. The decision to go to Arizona changed the whole course of my life.

"The summer after I started graduate school at Arizona I was offered a teaching assistantship at UB's field school in Mexico (the same one I had attended my senior year at UB). I was assured that as a teaching assistant I could work on my master's project and that the field school would provide an assistant and limit my assistantship duties. Perhaps they were trying to make it up to me. My adviser at Arizona suggested an easier route—pick a nice little lake nearby, take a core sample, and write a report. But I wanted to do palynology work in Mexico for my thesis because the tropical setting and general absence of palynological work at low latitudes was really a draw, so I ignored his advice and took the assistantship. I completed my master's thesis fieldwork that summer. But all the same, some of the behavior I witnessed was unprofessional to say the least. One professor propositioned me; another frolicked naked in the swimming pool with equally naked undergraduate students. Not long ago, I was reminiscing with a friend who is a little older than I am about our early experiences. She doesn't tell younger people her stories anymore because they don't believe her.

"My master's adviser left Arizona and was replaced by another palynologist, Vera Markgraf, who became my PhD adviser. As I progressed through my doctoral work, my interests turned to climate change. Vera and I went to Mexico a few times to take core samples with the help of some fellow graduate students. In contrast to the data collected for my master's thesis, which examined modern pollen distribution, I needed much older core samples to study climate change, but we couldn't find lake sediments old enough to meet that requirement. I ended up examining past vegetation and climate on the Mogollon Rim in northern Arizona, still an interesting project.

"I was out in the field for a month on my own, except for a female senior in high school looking for summer work who accompanied me as my assistant. We camped out. It was great! In the fall, a fellow graduate student, Pat Fall, and I managed to take a five-meter core out of Hay Lake with a hand corer. That sample provided the main data for my dissertation. Later, a couple of male graduate students and I took a larger power corer up to the rim and completed my sample collection.

"Although women were a minority at Arizona, there were more of us than at UB. It was a much more comfortable environment. To begin with, it was a much larger program. In addition, Arizona was one of the few places in the country where you could chart your own interdisciplinary course. I was lucky, I was in with a group of people, grad students and faculty, who did and talked about interesting things. Mentors might be your faculty advisers, other faculty, graduate students who were much further along, or people who helped lead field trips into Mexico. An older graduate student got me excited about working in the tropics. Vera Markgraf served as my role model. She was driven, hardworking, and dedicated to her career and her work.

"And, of course, there was Mary Kay O'Rourke, the woman I met in New York and who was instrumental in my decision to go to Arizona. Mary Kay married Paul Martin, a professor at Arizona. She and Paul together were important to me. Paul was bright, thoughtful, and insightful, and he was great at encouraging people to pursue their dreams. He came with me to Mexico after I had completed my master's to investigate the site. He was curious about the origins of its groundwater, the way the system worked, and the reasons people could live there. He told me, 'You should pursue this line of research.' I didn't think I was capable enough. I'll never forget what he told me. He said, 'Bonnie, you can do whatever you set your mind to.' It meant a lot to me.

"Graduate school was a magical, wonderful time for me. Years later, Paul described it as 'the golden years.' I said, 'Oh, I thought it was only my golden years.' I guess it just was such a great time.

"I didn't finish writing my dissertation right away. I was dating Louis Jacobs, who is five years older than I am. He'd already finished his PhD and worked at the Museum of Northern Arizona in Flagstaff. Its board of directors decided to focus the museum's research work on the local area, but Louis conducted research in Asia, Pakistan in particular. He knew the museum would not keep all the scientists they had hired, so he went on the job market.

"The National Museums of Kenya, in Nairobi, offered him a position as the head of paleontology. He wanted to take that job; we discussed it, and the short story is we got married. Louis went to Kenya. I, with the help of Pat Fall, finished up all the extractions of my samples in the lab at Arizona and then took the residues with me to Kenya. I was terrified that I wouldn't find a microscope, that I wouldn't be able to complete the analysis. I really didn't want to go to Africa. This simply was not in my life plan. But it all worked out. We met a wonderful guy, Don Fawcett. He'd been a professor at Harvard and had moved to Kenya to work for the International Laboratory for Research on Animal Diseases. The lab had money and great equipment. He provided access to the equipment I needed, and I did all my pollen counts there.

"Richard Leakey, who headed Kenya's National Museums, where Louis worked, hired me as a part-time researcher. He asked me to write a proposal to fund a pollen lab at the museum and then set it up, which I did. I spent the few months before I returned to Arizona to write and defend my dissertation training an African student to continue building the reference collection we had started under the grant. I was in Kenya a few months ago, and the lab is still running. It felt good to see it flourishing.

"Altogether, I was in Kenya about two and a half years. We came back to the States, again for Louis's job. I wasn't quite finished with my dissertation. At a very late date (I was actually done writing), Vera Markgraf moved on, so she was no longer my dissertation chair. Owen Davis took her position and by default became the professor to sign off on my dissertation. I defended my thesis in the spring but officially graduated in December 1983 because he objected to certain aspects of my work, and I had to fix them. Louis and I moved to Dallas in August of the same year. This is not a normal person's story. I did everything the hard way [laughing].

"When Louis negotiated the terms of his contract with Southern Methodist University [SMU], I told him not to ask for anything for me. After all, I had my pride. All I wanted was a desk and some type of affiliation so I could apply for grant money. And that's exactly what I got. We started at SMU in September 1983.

"I immediately submitted two grant proposals—one to the National Science Foundation [NSF] for work on a macrofossil site in the Tugen Hills in Kenya. We had a friend, Andrew Hill, a paleoanthropologist, who had started a project at the site the first year we were in Africa, and I had become involved in it. The other was a proposal to the Mellon Foundation to engage in work that extended my PhD research area beyond Arizona to include the northern mountain region of New Mexico. I expected to be turned down by NSF but get the grant from the Mellon Foundation. Instead, I was turned down by Mellon and funded by the NFS. We returned to the Tugen Hills once before the grant kicked in for about a month in January 1984.

"I found out that the NSF grant had been funded in September 1984, the same month I had Matt, our first child. That was the beginning of my freaking out [laughing].

"At about the same time, the administrator of the anthropology department at SMU asked me to run its pollen lab and supervise students who had been working under a faculty member affiliated with the lab before she left the institution, but they didn't want to pay me—not too appealing an arrangement. As luck would have it, SMU houses the Institute for the Study of Earth and Man [ISEM]. Its purpose is to support students and faculty in interdisciplinary endeavors, especially between geology and archaeology. Jim Brooks, the president of the institute, committed funding for a part-time position. And since I was having a baby and I was flipping out, I decided on a third-time position. The ISEM supported me in that part-time post for almost seventeen years.

"When Louis and I ended up at SMU, the juggling began. And along with it, *stress!* Louis grew up in a family of five children. He was the only boy. His father was a career military man, and his mother a stay-at-home mom. In our early years of marriage I actually tried to work full-time as an adjunct (although paid part-time) to maintain an active research agenda. In fact, we brought Matt with us to Africa three times. He was seven months old the first time and learned to crawl in Nairobi. We made the same trip the next two years. But full-time work at the university meant having our son in day care, which was costly, and traveling to and from Africa proved too difficult for us all. The combination just wasn't worth it.

"So I became a stay-at-home, part-time working mom, adjusting my schedule according to Matt's and, later, our daughter's ages. I came to resent the assumption that if it was domestic, I would do it. At home almost everything is domestic. I had no idea how much time raising babies and kids takes. When I suggested that we work out a schedule in which Louis stayed home during work hours once in a while, he said, 'I won't do that.' He was tenure track back then but . . . it was hard for me to concede, and that brought some conflict. Matt was a colicky baby, and to his credit, Louis stayed up with Matt when he cried all night. As long as it wasn't during work hours.

"When Matt was about ten months old, we put him in day care where he contracted a horrible ear and eye infection, which sent him to the hospital. Louis had to have minor surgery at the same time. Soon afterward my mom came for a visit. She took one look at me and said, 'You're emaciated [an exaggeration]. Something has to give here.' I finally admitted I couldn't do it all. It was terrible. I felt like a failure. I cut back my hours (which began my part-time schedule). The decision to have a second child was a huge one because I knew I was postponing my career that much longer. I think now how nutty I was. But once I decided to have a second child, I was thrilled and couldn't wait for her arrival.

"We had Melissa when Matt was about four years old. I constantly felt there was more work that I either needed or wanted to do, more than I could possibly handle. At SMU, it was preparing for classes or trying to keep the research going. At home, the work was never ending. When at work, I felt I should be at home with our children, and when at home, I felt I should be at work.

"Years earlier, over Christmas, I temped at a department store in the tablecloth department. It was the easiest money I ever made. I just stood there and talked to the other saleslady. Once in a while, one of us had to ring up a purchase. When my life got really crazy, I daydreamed about having a job in a department store in the tablecloth department.

"When Melissa was about five years old, I decided I either had to quit academia altogether and get a regular full-time job doing something else or go after a 'real' academic job. I contemplated seeking employment with the Nature Conservancy, but conservancy properties in Texas are prairie preserves for the most part, and the work didn't excite me. I loved my projects in Africa and decided to find a way to continue.

"Luckily, in the mid-1990s, the NSF housed a program called the Career Advancement Award, not to be confused with the CAREER [Faculty Early Career Development] Award for brilliant, productive people coming out of graduate school. A Career Advancement Award was what a friend of mine and I jokingly called the 'Shameless Hussy Award.' It specifically targeted women who'd had interruptions in their careers and needed funds for research to get back on track. I applied and received one of the awards; it was just what I needed. I completed a project that did not require fieldwork. I studied modern leaves of African plant species. I figured out a relationship between leaf morphology and climate that I could then apply to fossils. I strung that project out for six years. Somehow I hung in there by the skin of my teeth.

"When Matt was little and we brought him with us to Kenya, he always stayed in Nairobi. When I returned to fieldwork, Melissa was six, and Louis and I started switching off going to the field. I went to the field, and he stayed home, and vice versa. The arrangement was hard but doable. The kids never came in the field with either of us in Africa. It just wasn't appropriate in my opinion. But we took them on field trips in Texas and New Mexico and had fun.

"In about 2000 I was ready to go on the job market. Louis and I applied for two positions at the same great institution. The search process for Louis's position moved along more rapidly than the one I had applied for. He'd been interviewed twice when, suddenly, SMU found a job for me—clearly so we would be more likely to stay. I was a target-of-opportunity hire, which allowed the university to skip the usual year-long search process. I was offered a tenure-track position, but none of my work prior to 2000 counted toward tenure. Fortunately, Louis volunteered to pick up the slack on the home front. It was now my time to work the long day-to-day hours.

"I was hired as director of the environmental science program, which was housed in the Geology Department, and told by the dean that I was getting a course release for taking on that extra burden. I found out later that my teaching load was identical to everyone else's in the department. We all taught three courses per year. I thought, 'This is just another one of those things women do. We don't negotiate.' I probably should have educated myself about faculty loads and the like prior to speaking with the dean, but I didn't feel I was in a good negotiating position (because I had not been offered a job elsewhere), and I was just so grateful to get the position at SMU.

"Because I was hired by the dean and not through a usual departmental search process, I was uncomfortable with the prospect of being inserted into a department, essentially from above. I had already been an adjunct in geology for seventeen years, so obviously they weren't eager to hire me. In a way, that's understandable. I worked part-time. Nobody really knew for sure what I was capable of.

"The dean was pretty clever. I held a regular tenure-track faculty line, but the tenure and promotion committee (my equivalent to a department) that reviewed me as I went along was made up of people from anthropology, biology, chemistry, and geology, along with the associate dean. When I had my first-year review, the committee compared my teaching load to everyone else's in the geology department and insisted the dean give me another course release. I ended up with a one-and-one teaching load. That made it easier to run the program and still focus on research and teaching.

"I grew the environmental science program, taught, conducted research, and published. In 2006 I received tenure and was promoted. The university-wide review committee members said I needed to be in a department. I've been in the Geology Department (now the Roy M. Huffington Department of Earth Sciences) ever since.

"I've been the only full-time female department member since 2001. Actually, for as long as I've been at SMU, there has never been more than one woman in a regular faculty line. My experience suggests the younger the department the better it is for women. Young men today grow up in a world different from the one I was raised in. They seem to be more accepting of having women as colleagues and are more apt to help at least to some extent at home and with child rearing. In the fall of 2012, there was one woman in a non-tenure-track line and me, and I have three younger colleagues. But most of us are from my generation and are male. In the past couple of years, we've been able to hire two more tenure-track women. Our department now has fourteen members, four women and ten men with one retiring in 2015.

"Among our students we do better. Slightly more than half of our undergraduate and one-third of our graduate students are women. I don't get the sense that we have a male-dominated student body at either level. Interestingly, more female PhD candidates study geophysics and isotope geochemistry than paleobotany (my area of expertise).

"Quite often our students go to work for the oil industry, where jobs tend to be plentiful. These firms offer interesting and challenging work. But even though competition for the few open positions is stiff, some choose academia. I come down on the side of making life satisfying, and if academia is the only way for you to do that, then go for it. We tell these students, 'You must push. You have to go, or you'll be gone.'

"Academic careers are not nine-to-five jobs. Dual careers, in particular, can take a toll on families, whether you're male or female, especially in field-oriented professions because you have to be away from home for weeks (or months) at a time. The women in my cohort at Arizona tackled many of the same issues I've faced, each in her own unique way. One went straight to an academic job and simultaneously handled having two children. She had challenges. At one point a female department chair told her that if she had a second child, she could forget about getting tenure. Can you imagine that? Another took a faculty position, but she and her husband had careers at different universities the whole time they were married. When he finally moved into a position at her university, they ended up getting divorced. They had one child. I know other women who made the decision not to have children.

"My career trajectory took numerous twists and turns as it collided with my personal life. Louis has had a stellar career in vertebrate paleontology, and I could have been a collaborator. But I made a conscious (or maybe it was unconscious) decision to differentiate my career from his because I had a feeling (or perhaps a worry) that as the wife of a prominent scientist, I'd be viewed as subordinate and not as a scientist in my own right. These past couple of years, we've spent our field seasons together at my field sites in Kenya and Ethiopia. It worked out well. It's been really nice to be away together.

"Every academic faces times when papers get rejected, funding doesn't materialize (which happens more often than not), or the perfect job goes to someone else. Science careers can be particularly nerve-racking, in part because the NSF serves as the primary funding agency for the majority of scientists. In addition, the job situation right now is especially grim. In fact, in my little backwater of science, a few years ago there was an unexpected blip in the job market when three excellent academic positions opened up for people in paleobotany. All were filled by outstanding women. Then the economy went south, and jobs everywhere dried up. This past year, another miracle job opened up—a joint, interdisciplinary position between ecology, evolutionary biology, and geology. It was perfect for any paleontologist, especially one who specializes in paleobotany. But the money evaporated along with the job. It's a hard time. It's been better the past few years.

"These are difficult encounters, and you have to have that core inside you that keeps you going. That drive, determination, and perseverance. You must love what you do. That's what it boils down to.

"Should women have to choose between family and career? It's such a hard question to answer. When I started, I didn't believe I had to make that choice, but I was also naive about what it would take. I functioned under the notion that I could do both—and I did, but not the way I thought I would.

"Today, family leave helps, but it's insufficient. We need to continue to move in a direction that makes life more tolerable for people who want to choose both family and work. Institutional policies and culture often work against creating that type of environment. For example, every new provost at every university says, 'We must increase the amount of outside funding, namely research dollars, by X amount.' We also want faculty to pay more attention to teaching. But teaching takes time away from going after grants, and going after grants takes time away from teaching and conducting research. To make matters worse, every year the research dollar pie gets smaller. So competition increases, the size of the pie decreases, and the workload swells. How is that going to work? It puts so much pressure on people who are already under a tremendous amount of strain, especially those in tenure-track positions. I don't know how we change that culture. It's a culture that challenges all parents, not just women.

"I sense that women now recognize the importance of being visible, being out there. It helps establish our worth in the eyes of both boys and girls. I talk to our female graduate students about the importance of being visible. We all, however, have limits on what we are willing to do. I don't want to be the person who appears on a local TV talk show to argue about global warming. But I am willing to promote science and talk about what I do.

"I often participate in science workshops the American Association of University Women hosts for adolescent girls. These and similar programs are important. But to some degree they are self-selecting. That is, some girls may have already turned away from STEM disciplines and will not attend the programs. Nevertheless, I hope young people who do see women scientists come to understand that 'normal' girls can grow up to be scientists. Whether this really works or not, I honestly do not know. But girls today have a lot more going for them if they are interested in STEM disciplines than we had as children. Despite the presence of stereotypes out there, people overall are more open to women being scientists than they were in the past.

"In January 2011, I contributed to a blog called *Scientist at Work: Notes From the Field* for the *New York Times*, and it was really fun! The blog is essentially a modern field journal that reports the daily progress of scientific expeditions. A person in SMU's public affairs office nominated me for a slot. The *Times* asked for and reviewed writing samples and then made its decision. Being from New York, I was excited to do it. I wrote the main piece before I left for Ethiopia; the rest I did from the field. I had one of these hookups (about the size of a laptop) that beams up to a satellite so I could connect to the Internet. I'd be out in the dark and the cold typing away. It's funny. I subscribe to the *Times*, and I don't have time to look at everything, but boy, it's amazing how many people have seen that blog! It's what prompted *D Magazine* to feature me in an issue about six cool scientists (two women) in Dallas. It's the kind of visibility women in science need.

"I'm fifty-nine. Our kids are now twenty-four and twenty-eight, so they're on their own. Matt is in medical school. Melissa graduated in sociology but likes science. Despite this, she's working at a company that does online couponing, which she enjoys. But I don't think that's her final destination. She's still figuring things out for herself.

"To a certain extent, she's like me. I've always followed the path that interested me most—not the one that was necessarily the most practical. In ten years I hope I'm retired, still healthy, and have married kids with grandkids. I don't tell them that of course. I honestly don't know how many more years I'll do fieldwork in Africa. The conditions can be tough, and it's getting harder and harder. But even if I no longer go to Africa, I'm not going to stop thinking. I'd like to write a book. I'd love to tell our stories in a humorous and educational way. I've had so many adventures. I've been very lucky."

BIBLIOGRAPHICAL NOTE

Jacobs's chapter is the culmination of in-depth interviews and e-mail exchanges. In addition, her curriculum vitae, the article in *D Magazine* (www.dmagazine.com/Home/D_Magazine/2011/Dallas_Big_Thinkers .aspx), and her blog on the *New York Times* website (http://scientist atwork.blogs.nytimes.com) were also consulted.

nine

JUST HAPPENED TO BE IN THE RIGHT PLACE AT THE RIGHT TIME, AND INCREDIBLY BRIGHT

Radia Perlman

"I OWE MY PHD TO SMOKERS [LAUGHING]. Let me explain. Although I enjoyed my work at Digital Equipment Corporation in Littleton, Massachusetts, I always had a horrible cold. I had the loudest sneeze you can imagine and carried a large box of tissues everywhere I went. When I sat in a meeting, the pile of dirty tissues grew higher and higher. It was incredibly undignified. I assumed it was because I had two young kids. I wasn't getting enough sleep, and I was doing way too much.

"I'd stay home, rest up for a few days, go back to work, and get the cold again. Eventually I went to a doctor. I told him, 'I know I'm not taking care of myself. The situation isn't going to change. Just give me something to help me get rid of this cold.' He asked, 'How long have you had it?'

'Three years.'

'Well, I have news for you. It's not a cold. It's allergies.'

Perlman is a fellow and director of Network and Security Protocol Research at Intel Laboratories in Redmond, Washington. She works remotely with people in various locations, including California, Oregon, and Israel.

"I realized I must be reacting to cigarette smoke. No one in my family smoked; nobody I came into contact with in college smoked. I'd never been around cigarette smoke until I joined Digital. The company was housed in a large building with cubicles instead of individual offices, and people smoked like chimneys. I went to personnel, and the staff offered to make sure no smokers sat in the cubicles adjacent to mine, but since the room was one big cavern, that remedy wouldn't help. I told my colleagues, 'I think I'm going to have to quit. I'm tired of always being sick.' And they said, 'Be patient. Digital's working on the smoking problem.'

"I discovered Digital had a great program that sent a select number of employees to graduate school for two years, full salary, all expenses paid. Taking advantage of this option resulted in my second attempt at graduate school. I never liked beginning an activity and then failing to complete it. But being ABD [all but dissertation] since 1980, when I started at Digital, had never provided enough reason to return to MIT [Massachusetts Institute of Technology]. Cigarette smoke, however, did. Instead of math (my first program of study), I went into computer science and finished in the allotted two years. When I arrived back at Digital, PhD in hand, the company had solved the smoking issue by banning it in the building [laughing].

"But let's go back to why I dropped out of graduate school the first time around. At that time I thought everybody else was there because they were smart, and I'd only gotten in because I studied hard. I didn't realize everyone feels that way. I finished my course work but had no idea how to fulfill the thesis requirement, or even how to find an adviser. I couldn't imagine doing original research. It seemed like a task only some other species could do, not 'an ordinary person' like me.

"A friend asked, 'Are you happy in grad school?' and I replied, 'Not really.' He suggested I join his group (at a company called BBN), which happened to be developing network protocols. I decided to give it a try and loved it. It's possible I was 'born to design protocols,' but more likely at that point I'd have been happy doing most anything as long as it was reasonably interesting and I respected and liked my colleagues. I tell people who agonize over decisions like choosing between colleges or job offers, 'First, there is never enough information to make such a decision. Second, there are two kinds of people; those who will be happy with either decision, and those who will be unhappy no matter what.' I guess I'm pretty much the first type of person.

"Owing to another totally random event, I wound up solving a problem that the DECnet [Digital Equipment Corporation Network] people had been struggling with for a while. Folks at Digital were impressed, even though, like everything I've ever done, the solution was very simple, and they asked if I wanted to be in charge of designing layer 3 of DECnet, and that's how I got the job at Digital.

"Layer 3 is the distributed algorithm by which networks self-form and automatically decide how to move data. Although I think my work on routing protocols used in layer 3 is more profound, I'm more known for the spanning-tree algorithm used today in Ethernet.[1]

"Let me explain what a spanning-tree algorithm is and why anyone would want one. Ethernet was originally designed as a convenient way to interconnect a few hundred nodes within a building. It was not designed to be a complete network, just a single link within a network, requiring a layer 3 protocol, such as IP [Internet Protocol], to tie the links together. People somehow got confused and thought Ethernet was a replacement for layer 3 and built protocols that only worked on a single Ethernet. Once they realized they needed to move data between Ethernets, the problem became how to implement layer 3 without endnodes, which if used would result in a system looping back into itself rather than expanding across systems. Expanding the system required a different topology. We needed a spanning tree algorithm—a way for the switches to cooperate with each other and discover which links to refrain from using to forward data.

"The solution turned out to be remarkably simple. I figured it out in one day, wrote the specification in two days, and then spent three days writing the poem *Algorhyme*; so I wound up spending more time on the poem than on writing the specs! The time writing the poem was well

---

1. Much to Perlman's chagrin, she's been dubbed the "mother of the Internet" for her role in developing this technology. As she put it, "Some reporter came up with the title, and it stuck because father of the Internet was already taken. I'm not keen on the title because many people had large roles in developing the Internet. The moniker also emphasizes gender, a subject I rarely think about." For a more In-depth discussion, see Foremski, T. (2011, April 21). Intel's Radia Perlman: Don't call her "Mother of the Internet." *Silicon Valley Watcher*. Retrieved from www.siliconvalleywatcher.com/mt/archives/2011/04/profile_of_radi.php

worth it because it's been great fun. I used it as the abstract to a professional paper. My son set it to music, and my daughter and I performed
it, along with a bunch of Italian and German arias, at a recital (my
daughter sings opera, and I was her piano accompanist). *Algorhyme* gives
you a glimpse of just how straightforward the solution was.

> *Algorhyme*
> I think that I shall never see
> a graph more lovely than a tree.
> A tree whose crucial property
> is loop-free connectivity.
> A tree that must be sure to span
> so packets can reach every LAN.
> First, the root must be selected.
> By ID, it is elected.
> Least-cost paths from root are traced,
> In the tree, these paths are placed.
> A mesh is made by folks like me,
> then bridges find a spanning tree.[2]

"Digital was at the forefront of developing networking technology,
and I could define whatever I wanted to do without having to deal with
a large standards group. Standards groups write specifications so that
multiple vendors can implement interworking products.

"If I could change one aspect of the industry, it would be the
standards organizations. It is extremely discouraging and annoying
how much politics comes into play, and how the people who are most
influential tend to be bullies. They steal ideas; they use any ruse to slow
down progress for other people; it is so unpleasant. It's like the reemer-
gence of the *Lord of the Flies*, where a bunch of adolescents rule the
roost without any consequences. It's worse in standards bodies than in
companies because if you acted that way in a company, you'd get fired.

"In an ideal world people would realize that being a leader means
nurturing those around them. My job at Digital was very different from

---

2. Perlman, R. (1985). A protocol for distributed computation of a spanning tree in
an extended LAN Poem presented at the Ninth Data Communications Symposium,
Vancouver, Canada.

working in a standards body. My charge: Come up with the right technology. Collaboration helps the design process, especially if you work alongside people who have complementary skills and see the problem from diverse perspectives. It's especially important to include implementers in the group because they can recognize the implications of a design on application. The more people who buy into an idea the more momentum the idea gains. I truly like working in groups, but when the group gets too big, it's hard to make any decisions or have decisions stick. Have you tried to pick a restaurant when you have a group of more than seven people? You'll starve before the group decides where to go [laughing]. For me, Digital happened to be exactly the right place at the right time.

"If I'd finished my PhD the first time I was in graduate school, I might've gone into academia. I probably would have enjoyed that too. I love teaching and nurturing students. But I like industry better. Academia, where you have to constantly beg for money by writing grant proposals, seems scary.

"Academics often say they want to be in a university setting because they have complete freedom over their research agendas. Such autonomy has never been a draw for me. I much prefer having problems that are real and practical with specific needs. There's just as much opportunity for innovation in industry, and the results actually get deployed in the real world rather than existing only in papers in fields populated by a few researchers who cite each others' work.

"Research is an essential part of what I do.³ If I had never had the chance to teach, I would be much more attracted to academia. But just as you can engage in research even if you're not in academia, you can also teach. I have been adjunct or affiliate faculty at MIT, Harvard, Chinese University of Hong Kong, and the University of Washington. I've written or coauthored two seminal textbooks. That's another way of teaching. And I occasionally conduct one- or two-day tutorials. Teaching these seminars has some advantages over teaching traditional university courses. The participants attend because they are truly interested in the topic, as opposed to some students in a university classroom who seem to be mostly interested in minimizing the amount of

---

3. Perlman currently holds over 100 issued technology-related patents.

work they do for a particular grade. You know, the ones who ask, 'Will that be on the test?' Since I've never been a full-time faculty member, perhaps always writing grant proposals and begging for money isn't as unpleasant as I imagine [laughing].

"After Digital, I went to work for Novell in 1993 and then Sun Microsystems in 1997. One day at Sun, a coworker said, 'Oh boy, Radia, are you in trouble!' I said, 'What?!' She showed me an article in the *Boston Globe* about a hospital network that failed for several days. The article was fascinating, detailing the impact of such a shutdown on a hospital. In the middle of the article I found the phrase 'spanning-tree algorithm.' I thought, 'Whoa! Those words don't belong in a *Boston Globe* article.'

"I tracked down the engineers at the company who had supplied the network to the hospital, and indeed it was based on spanning tree. Spanning tree is actually somewhat fragile; for a network to not completely fail, the switches must be fast enough to simultaneously look at all the incoming packets (the source and destination addresses and the data to be transported). In fact, the original specifications at Digital stated this requirement in the standards that guide the tree's use, but when IEEE [the Institute of Electrical and Electronics Engineers] assumed oversight of the standard, it removed the requirement.

"The reason the industry needed spanning tree in the first place stems from a couple of important mistakes. Because people thought Ethernet was a complete network, they removed layer 3 from their computer systems. That was the first error. The second mistake proved more problematic. The industry as a whole chose IP as the communication protocol for layer 3 rather than the protocol created by the International Organization for Standardization [ISO]. ISO's format was much better than IP's because IP's addresses are too small. Every link has to have a different block of addresses, so if a node moves, it needs to change its address, and switches must be configured to know which addresses are on which port. In contrast, ISO's protocol had much larger addresses (twenty bytes versus IP's four bytes) and a feature that allowed a fairly large cloud of links to share the same block of addresses instead of requiring each link to have its own block of addresses. The switches inside the cloud didn't need to be configured, and nodes could move within the cloud without changing their address.

The spanning-tree algorithm offsets IP's limitations somewhat—by simulating a cloud that looks, to IP, like a single link. If ISO's protocol had won the battle for being the layer 3 protocol for the Internet, spanning tree would have only been a quick fix for a couple of years until people reinstalled layer 3 on their computers.

"When I read about the hospital system failure, I decided it was time for Ethernet to evolve beyond spanning tree. I came up with the concept of TRILL [transparent interconnection of lots of links] and published a paper about it. The IETF [Internet Engineering Task Force] standards body decided to create a working group, modify it (of course! Actually, I like most of the modifications), and standardize it.

"In 2010, I moved to Intel Labs as director of network and security protocol research. Here, my job entails framing the right questions, getting people to crisply understand what they're arguing about, and thinking outside the box to come up with creative solutions.

"I find groups that should be collaborating often compete with each other, sometimes because they don't know about each other. I look for opportunities to bring such groups together Intel-wide. I find that one of the best ways to foster creativity is to create a safe environment, meaning there is no such thing as a stupid question or shame in suggesting an idea that turns out not to work. Within such a culture, not only will a design be more sound because the team can explore it from all sides, but team members grow and learn and have fun. I'm a big fan of fun.

"I try to show others in a group that it is okay to ask basic questions by asking them myself. It can take courage to admit we might not know all there is to know about a particular topic. Asking and answering basic questions often forces us to rethink our assumptions. It broadens our understanding. Sometimes these questions are very profound. And sometimes they simply provide an opportunity to teach. If I'm asked about a fundamental concept like public key cryptography, I get excited and say, 'It's cool, and I'm so glad that I have the honor of being the first person to explain it to you.'

"Unfortunately, some people are impressed by those who act pompous and condescending. Once I had a coworker who answered pretty much any question with 'If you don't know that already, you don't belong in this group.' People like that can do quite well. They give a talk, and others listen and say to themselves, 'Wow, I didn't understand him; therefore, he must be smart.' But individuals like my coworker are toxic to the team. They shut people down. Furthermore, they usually aren't all that good technically, and even if they are technically savvy, unless they can be convinced to change the way they behave, any contributions they make to the group are offset by the harm they do to the productivity of the other team members.

"I am nonthreatening. Deer hang around my yard and eat the flowers. If I go out and yell at them, they look up, see it's me, and calmly go back to munching. Airport security people take one look at me and wave me through. I don't think I could ever change that aspect of my personality, not that I'd want to. It helps me communicate effectively. I make complex concepts easy to understand. I avoid unnecessary detail, partition the problem into conceptual subproblems, avoid acronyms and other unnecessary jargon, and ignore syntax. A colleague once commented, 'I love how you can take X's fifteen-minute discourse, condense it down to one sentence, feed it back, and have him say, "That's what I said."' It's both a strength and a weakness. In the first instance, it helps people focus and learn. In the second, many people are impressed by someone who can make trivial details incomprehensible, which puts my simple-is-better approach and me at a disadvantage.

"At Intel, I don't have any particular positional authority, but I try to be as influential as possible by explaining options clearly. It could be that the amount of authority I have hinges on how much I act as if I have it [laughing]. It's a cool job. In effect they've said, 'Radia, you're an adult; you're senior enough; do what you see is useful.'[4]

"Seriously, though, not everyone should act like me. An organization needs people with complementary strengths. That's the type of 'diversity' that really matters. It's not so much about individuals with

---

4. Perlman received lifetime achievement awards from the Special Interest Group on Data Communication (SIGCOMM) in 2006 and from USENIX–The Advanced Computing Systems Association in 2010, the Women of Vision award from the Anita Borg Institute for Women and Technology in 2005, the 2004 Silicon Valley Inventor of the Year by Silicon Valley Intellectual Property Law Association, and an honorary doctorate from the Royal Institute of Sweden in 2000. She was also listed as one of the twenty most influential people in the tech industry by *Data Communications Magazine* in 1992 and 1997.

different body shapes, races, or genders. In this industry, having diversity becomes a matter of hiring people from multiple disciplines and not about having a certain percentage of women.

"Diversity as I envision it gets at the notion that we need people who look at problems differently—people who think conceptually, people who communicate clearly, others who remember all the rules for building a protocol or procedure within a certain environment, and some who can schmooze with customers. For instance, I have a bad memory for specific details, so I must get to a theory's essence in order to understand it. At school, where others could get through exams by remembering what the teacher wanted us to say, I had to derive the answer from the two or three facts I could fit in my brain. I get down to basics. In contrast, people who have good memories provide context.

"We all possess different skill sets. Success in this industry doesn't require a degree in computer science. In fact some of my most brilliant colleagues majored in pretty [unrelated] subjects (like archaeology) or have not gone to college at all. Taking a few rigorous math courses is useful in any career because math teaches you to think cleanly. You walk into a math class, and they give you crisp definitions. 'This is a frob. This is a glotz. Prove that all frobs are glotzes.' A week later you don't remember what either a frob or a glotz is, but you've been trained to think logically.

"I love to puzzle over a problem and figure it out. I try to come at a problem from multiple angles, and I sometimes ask others for their views. I enjoy those aha moments when I finally grasp a concept's meaning and experience the thrill of figuring out exactly the right problem to solve with a new, eloquently simple approach. It's exciting when I come up with an outside-the-box solution. I can't really help thinking outside the box because I can never remember where the box is supposed to be [laughing].

"Life experiences can matter too. They help shape you. I was born in Virginia but grew up in New Jersey. My parents were both civilians working for the government. My father was an engineer involved in the early development of radar. My mother was also an engineer but held the title of mathematician. She worked as a computer programmer. My parents made up the name Radia. I was actually named after my grandfather Rubin. In Jewish tradition you just need to use the first letter.

They played around with strings starting with R, and when they created Radia; they liked it because it is reminiscent of various math and science concepts (radio, radar), and it reminded them of the word *radiant.*

"I was a very odd child growing up. My sister, Serena (whose name my parents also created, having never heard the name before—it was rarer back then), was much more of a real girl. She played with dolls. I wasn't interested in dolls. I didn't build with erector sets either. I actually don't remember what I played with. She cared about the clothes she wore. I put on clothes, and she made mysterious comments like, 'They don't match.' Eventually, she wound up laying out clothes for me each night (I am four years younger than Serena, so she enjoyed taking charge). From then on, my clothes matched.

"I did like doing puzzles as a child, and homework (other than memorizing, which I absolutely hated). When the teacher assigned a report, I designed a puppet show—making costumes, composing music and lyrics, performing it. When we were assigned group projects, I'm sure the other kids were torn about whether they wanted to be in my group. On the one hand, it was going to be a lot more work than necessary. On the other hand, we'd all get As.

"I didn't have much in common with other girls in high school. I always wished I had a best friend. It sounded so romantic to me. I had some girl acquaintances, but we weren't close. And the smart boys didn't interact with me either; I tried. They had their own little community with girlfriends but not girl friends.

"I took honors math and science classes. When we didn't understand a homework problem, we'd come to class the next day and argue about whose parent was right. Someone would say, 'My father says it should be done this way,' and someone else would counter that his father knew the correct approach. And I'd chime in, 'My mother said it should be done this way.' Our teacher thought it was funny [that my mother, not my father, made the suggestion] and called it to my attention. Breaking the stereotype, I suppose.

"I never held any particular aspirations to get a PhD. In high school I thought I should go to as prestigious a college as I could. So I went to MIT. I majored in math because chemistry was out of the question. I'm so incredibly clumsy I shouldn't be trusted near any lab equipment [laughing]. And organic chemistry involves torturous memorization.

"I enjoyed writing, but I didn't like the seeming arbitrariness associated with the grade I might get. In math or physics or chemistry, if I understood the material and had confidence in my answer, I knew I'd get credit. In high school I wanted straight As, probably not one of my best aspirations because when it came to studying subjects like history I'd cram, memorizing facts I later regurgitated on an exam. Half an hour after I finished the exam, the information was completely gone from my mind.

"Math and science were always my favorite classes in high school. We had a chemistry teacher who introduced each new topic by starting out with a quiz to stretch us. I found those quizzes fascinating. Everybody else hated them. I did quite well in those classes without working particularly hard. It was lucky I didn't need to spend much time on math and science because I needed it for history. I wasted so many hours of my childhood learning historical facts [laughing].

"I guess I went the more technical route because I was well suited to it but not necessarily in the way others are. We assume that from the time they are quite young, engineers are curious about how objects work and take them apart. It never occurred to me to dismantle anything. I went to MIT without even knowing how to change a lightbulb. I assumed doing so was dangerous or at least incomprehensible. When one burned out, I'd tell my father, and a few days later it was fixed. I honestly wasn't even curious about what he did. The first time a bulb burned out in my dorm room, I wandered around saying, 'Hey, is there anyone here majoring in double-E [electrical engineering]?' And then I found somebody, and he said, 'I am, why are you asking?' 'My lightbulb burned out. What do I do?' [laughing].

"As an undergraduate I didn't interact with the professors, but I did have plenty of friends, all male. There were very few women my freshman year because the total number of women MIT could accept was limited to the number that fit in the one dorm reserved for women. Later, all the dorms went coed. I thought, 'Gee, that sounds like fun,' so I moved into a coed dorm and promptly discovered that coed meant I was the resident female.

"I seldom interacted with women after I had moved into the coed dorm. There were few enough women at MIT, but even fewer of them majored in math. There were no other women in my math classes. It didn't seem odd because, if you're the only woman, you look around and the whole class looks the same. You don't think that you look different from the rest of them. It's only when there's another woman that the group's compositional imbalance strikes you.

"I'm a child of the 1960s, I guess. I don't believe in marriage, so I have never been married. I truly believe the only legitimate reason for two adults to live together is because they want to. As a protocol person, I watch people interact, and I see the ways in which they blunder. Building healthy personal relationships entails ensuring that people relax when they're with you and building up their self-confidence, making them feel they are the smartest, nicest people in the world. I see some couples constantly tear each other down, criticizing, and wanting to monopolize their partner's time. In the end, the time they do spend together is stressful and joyless. This notion of 'I married you, so therefore, you're required to stay in love with me even though I'm no longer nice to you' causes problems in society.

"I certainly had a long-term, good relationship with the father of my children, and we're still friends. We didn't act any differently than married couples we knew. Our daughter, Dawn, was six months old when I started at Digital. She was six years old, and our son, Ray, was three when I went back to graduate school. So I was building my career while they were young. I have no idea how I juggled it all. Now I simply look at somebody who has a toddler and I get exhausted. How do you survive? I guess you just do.

"The kids were in day care centers of course, but drama always surrounds day care centers. The center decides to close because there's a dusting of snow, but you still have an important meeting. Or where do you find a babysitter because your son is sick, and you and his father both have meetings? For me, it was actually easier to be in graduate school with young children than it was to be working. Time is more flexible. Their father and I shared child care responsibilities. I did more, which seems to always be the case, but certainly I can't imagine doing it all by myself.

"I always thought the reason for any difference between girls and boys had to do with sexist parents bringing up their children to conform to certain expectations, until I had my own. Then I rethought my position. It is amazing how much of one's personality and skills are inbred, that come with the DNA or the mixture of chemicals you were steeped in while you grew inside your mother. Even though my sister and I are the offspring of the same mother, we are very different people. And my kids couldn't be more different from each other.

"Although I don't like to admit it, and of course, stereotypes are only statistical, little boys tend to play with trucks and want to build things, and little girls tend to want to interact with other kids. After watching my own two, this tendency seems to be surprisingly inherent and not dependent on 'other' parents being sexist.

"The kids are grown now. They both went to MIT. Ray works for the National Institute of Standards and Technology, a government physical science laboratory that encourages U.S. technological innovation through research and grants. He's in the cryptography group, which is great fun because occasionally I can call him up and ask him questions or collaborate with him. For instance, he wrote 'Algorhyme v.2,' which is in the TRILL specification. Dawn is currently busy with her own two little ones and attends graduate school in marketing.

"I'm often asked why there are so few women in STEM fields. Here's my take on the issue. Some women believe they won't be good at it (like my insecurity when I was in graduate school the first time); others shy away because they harbor misconceptions about STEM fields and fear they won't enjoy the work. And finally, we lose women (and men) because of the unpleasantness of dealing with aggressive, overbearing, condescending individuals.

"I fully understand why women feel unqualified. Despite always being the top math/science student throughout high school, I had a weird experience when I enrolled in my first computer programming class. It shouldn't have been any harder than anything else, right? Wrong. When I walked in, and all the others were talking about how they had built ham radios when they were seven, I panicked. They used intimidating words like *input*. I didn't know what it meant. I felt I was so far behind I was unable to learn. Self-confidence is such a necessary part of accomplishing any goal. I eventually learned but not during that class. I'm glad I had that particular experience because I grasped, probably for the first time, how panic can prevent people from learning, and the empathy I gained makes me a good teacher. I understand how capable people, once they convince themselves they can't be good at a particular task, aren't.

"To complicate matters, we limit the number of women attracted into some STEM disciplines because we have set notions of what an engineer, for example, does as a professional or is as a person. To illustrate this point, I've heard of a hiring manager at a high-tech company who asks during interviews, 'What were your hobbies when you were twelve?' If you don't say, 'I built computers out of spare parts,' he'll assume you're not a 'real' engineer. Likewise, girls sometimes view computer science as writing code, which they deem boring, and not tackling real world problems, a prospect they find exciting.

"I believe increasingly that young women are interested in engineering and science. A colleague mentors a high school girls' team for robotic competitions. She has no trouble recruiting team members, and they often win. But I'm not sure how to attract more women into computer science or how to keep them on the technical track (many women choose to go into management). Other countries often retain higher percentages of senior technical women in STEM fields. Here, the more senior the technical level, the fewer women there are, and that trend does not seem to be changing.

"Perhaps, it's the work environment that needs changing. We can make sure people feel safe enough to ask questions, ask for help, and admit they are not all knowing. Doing so will not only help retain women but make all of us more productive. We assume getting enough women in senior roles, as professors or in top management, will help. But it isn't so much that leaders must be female as that they must be the right people—approachable, nurturing, generous with credit, collaborative. There are certainly men like that, and there are certainly women who are self-promoting bullies. I'd rather we focus on building and sustaining cultures that foster creativity and productivity than concentrate solely on gender.

"In the same vein, I have mixed emotions about women-only events. Such proceedings can be fun, and even inspiring. But making it exclusionary to one gender perpetuates the myth that women are always getting favorable treatment or are incapable and need help. It's fine to have a conference that discusses issues like how to balance work and parenting. But many men have the same concerns. It might actually help the work culture to include men in these discussions. If there really are problems that women see in the workplace, don't we want men to hear these concerns?

"People often ask me how I've managed to 'succeed.' My original view of success was a job that paid me well enough to live comfortably (and I do not have expensive tastes), that was reasonably interesting, that I felt competent at, and that gave me colleagues whom I respected not only technically but as human beings and with whom I enjoyed spending time. With that definition, I was pretty much guaranteed to be a success. Truth be told, however, people are referring the success represented by my title (fellow), being reasonably well-known in the field, getting invited to give talks, being thought of as someone worthy of a chapter in a book such as this. How did that happen?

"The real answer: hard work, coincidences, and luck. I just happened to be in the right place at the right time to shape the field, and even with that, I doubt whether I'd have been known for what I'd done if I hadn't happened to write the book *Interconnections.*[5]

"Writing *Interconnections* changed my professional life. It became the book from which most people learn the field. As a consequence, I don't have to act important to be taken seriously. Writing the book was certainly educational for me, and it's fun having a book to my name. At first there was the incredible high of walking into an office and seeing my book on someone's shelf. Then I got spoiled, and if I walked into someone's office with a bunch of books, and mine was missing, I was crushed. Once I pretended to be joking while looking at a wall of network books and said, 'Hey, where's my book?' The response: 'It's at home. I'm in the middle of reading it.' Yikes!

"My favorite book anecdote, though, comes from an incident that occurred when I was in the Chicago airport for a four-hour layover, and I was too tired to do anything useful. The airport was pretty deserted and quiet. I milled around glassy eyed until I saw a group of five men sitting together talking. I thought I heard some of the right words— *bridge, router.* One of them had a book on his lap with papers on top of it. All I could see was the edge, but the color was right. I wondered, 'Could it be my book?' I walked over and sat right next to them. They stopped talking and stared at me. I realized then I was acting strangely and was kind of embarrassed. I said, 'I'm sorry, I'm just curious. What

---

5. Perlman, R. (1999). *Interconnections: Bridges, routers, switches, and internetworking protocols.* Reading, MA: Addison-Wesley.

book is that?' The person held it up. It was *Interconnections*! I said, 'I'm Radia Perlman.' In unison, they exclaimed, 'No!' and turned pale. When one of them recovered enough to speak, he explained, 'We are in a panic. We're trying to put together a customer presentation and sound like experts, and just before you showed up, one of us said, "If only the author of this book were here!"' I responded, 'No problem. Comes with the book. Wish for me and I show up [laughing]. How can I help?' We prepared their presentation, I signed their book, and it was the most fun I've ever had at an airport.

"I am a bit different from those around me, and that makes me successful too. If I were competing head-on for the number of lines of code written per day, or the ability to remember all the details of particular implementations, I would not stand out. But I'm good at things that most traditional engineers are not: looking at a problem from multiple angles and coming up with a simple solution that addresses all the issues.

"I've never been good at self-promotion, and I don't set particularly spectacular goals for myself. A person might say, 'I aim to win a Nobel Prize.' There's so much randomness to that level of recognition. Despite engaging in all the right activities and racking up impressive accomplishments, someone else might have independently discovered the same phenomenon or technical solution and published his or her findings earlier than you did. Or somehow your work just doesn't capture the attention of the awards committee. Life can be chancy. You're bound to get discouraged when you set extremely lofty, narrowly defined goals you have little control over.

"Instead, I suggest: Be the best you can, be as productive as you are able, and always keep learning. Nurture those around you; it makes you a leader. Think of life as a journey not a series of stepping-stones to the future, and take time to enjoy it."

BIBLIOGRAPHICAL NOTE

Radia Perlman's story began with an extensive telephone interview, which was then expanded on by e-mail queries. In addition, we used information from her résumé and several online sources, including "Radia Perlman" (en.wikipedia.org/wiki/Radia_Perlman); Anita Borg Institute (http://anitaborginstitute.org/about/who-we-are/radia-perlman/); and "Why IEEE Fellow Radia Perlamn Hates Technology," by Alexander Pasik (April 22, 2011, *IT World*, www.itworld.com/network ing/158579/advice-engineers-ieee-fellow-radia-perlman).

Perlman's textbooks include *Interconnections (1999, Reading, MA: Addison-Wesley)* now in its second edition; and *Network Security: Private Communication in a Public World* with C. Kaufman and M. Speciner (2002, Upper Saddle River, NJ: Prentice Hall).

ten

THE REALITIES OF CHOICE

F OR THE EIGHT WOMEN WE INTERVIEWED, interest in science began at a young age and was actively encouraged by a parent or other relation. In some cases, the women had mothers who had themselves specialized in a STEM discipline or had an active interest in it. Sharon Hays observes,

> Mom . . . had a huge influence on my decision to study science, although I didn't realize it until more recently. . . . She got a job running the anatomy and physiology lab at a local community college. When her students dissected frogs or pigs, she brought home the extra specimens, and we'd carry out the experiment at home.

Teresa Golden decided she wanted to be a chemist in high school. "I was the only girl in my chemistry class. I loved it not because of the company I was keeping, but because chemistry was one of the few subjects that challenged me."

Encouraged and excited as they might have been about science or engineering, having fulfilling careers as professional scientists has not been free from challenges. For example, the tension between work and family life is evident. Radia Perlman recalls, "I was building my career while [my children] were young. I have no idea how I juggled it all. Now I simply look at somebody who has a toddler and I get exhausted. How do you survive? I guess you just do." Bonnie Jacobs, who started her "freaking out" stage of life when she had her first child and continued to try to build her career, expresses a sentiment often heard from professional women: "When at work, I felt I should be at home with our children, and when at home, I felt I should be at work."

Some of the women we interviewed deliberately partition work and home life as a way to maintain balance, though this comes at a cost. For Linda Birnbaum,

> As a working mother, I didn't think my husband or children should suffer; what suffered (and it was self-imposed) was personal time. There was never time to go out to lunch with friends; there wasn't time to play tennis or just wander around a store. It was pretty much go-go-go all the time. I think I'm pretty typical.

Cynthia Barnhart suggests money can sometimes buy time, but this is not a realistic choice for many women.

> We had a nanny when the girls were little. It's so much easier to walk out the door leaving your kids in their pajamas than to get them fed and dressed. . . . I took [my ability to hire a nanny and the time it gave me to concentrate on my work] for granted until one of my graduate students took a faculty position. She was married and had a child. . . . Hers was the sole income. She told me how stressful it was. They were always running and always late. . . . I realized that the mechanisms I'd put in place to help me require money, and without it, you have a much harder job.

Life partners play a key role in providing many of the women we interviewed with the flexibility and support they need to pursue their careers. Linda Birnbaum declares, "My greatest asset is my husband. I could not have done this without the kind of supportive partner I have. [However] we made compromises. . . . It can't be a one-way street." These compromises take different forms. For some women, career priority shifted over time. As Bonnie Jacobs notes, "Fortunately, [my husband] Louis volunteered to pick up the slack on the home front. It was now my time to work the long day-to-day hours." Barnhart and Blessing also state that their husbands' support was key to career decisions they've made.

Academia has a reputation as being incompatible with a balanced family life, particularly pretenure. Susan Blessing observes that "students . . . see what being an academic entails, and decide no way." She continues, "Workload and compensation can both be issues. And although they see the amount of autonomy faculty have (which very few jobs offer these days), they tend to undervalue it." Linda Birnbaum also suggests few women choose academia "because it's hard to find a palatable mix of work, family, and self. It takes so much energy. People choose to take a far less strenuous direction and enjoy life." Hays, Golden, and Hessler agree.

However, Cynthia Barnhart identifies this conundrum as not just a women's issue.

> Stress levels seem to have risen for both men and women. The bar just keeps going up. The tenure hurdle is harder than ever to get over. At a recent retreat, we talked about how faculty value flexibility. One colleague jokingly commented, "A faculty member has flexibility to work whatever eighteen hours a day he or she wants." And someone added, "True. But when it gets to the point that you can work whatever twenty-four hours a day you want, you don't have much flexibility."

Demographic shifts compound these challenges. Today, most families consist of multiple wage earners. Angela Hessler felt her academic father "had a nice balance in his life between work and family," but she also observes that her mother "was primarily taking care of the home front." As she embarked on her own academic career, reality set in. "Yes, I have a flexible schedule, but I'm working sixty hours a week, and my apartment is a disaster."

Linda Birnbaum points out that women often put off having children, choosing to finish their educations and begin their careers first. As a consequence, their peak years of research productivity are more likely to coincide with child-rearing responsibilities. Even so, some women in the STEM disciplines still see academia as the best option for them. Cynthia Barnhart believes "the academy . . . provides more of an opportunity to balance your professional and personal lives, but you have to work at it." With a laugh she continues,

> I don't know anyone who really believes she knows how to obtain that balance. But the chance to try means a lot to me. When my kids

had activities . . . I could attend. . . . It almost always meant that at nine or ten or eleven o'clock at night, I was paying for it, but it was a trade-off I was happy to make because I could be a part of my daughters' lives. If I hadn't had that type of flexibility . . . I would have wanted to work, but I might've made the hard choice of quitting.

Dual-career challenges can also affect the choice between academia and the private or government sector for women with advanced STEM degrees. Many women who obtain PhDs meet their life partners in graduate school. For instance, 48 percent of women in the natural sciences and 43 percent of women engineers have partners in academia. And quite a few of these women are in the same field as their partners (e.g., 83 percent in natural sciences, 64 percent in engineering) (Schiebinger, Henderson, & Gilmartin, 2008). Angela Hessler corroborates this trend, "Geologists often marry each other because we understand the demands [of the profession], but it can still add stress to the partnership." She notes that even though she and her husband "have separate interests . . . it would certainly be challenging for us to find academic jobs because of our overlapping expertise." Susan Blessing states, "Dual careers make life complex. You're forced to make choices. I know couples where the husband's at one university and she's at an institution in another town or even across the country." Having two academics in the family can, as Bonnie Jacobs describes it, "take a toll on families, whether you're male or female, especially in field-oriented professions because you have to be away from home for weeks (or months) at a time."

All the women we interviewed commented on the options for scientists and engineers that exist outside academia. Pay and benefits are competitive if not better. Hays and Barnhart note that the length of time it takes before earning a decent salary in academia discourages women and men from continuing on that path. And it appears easier to achieve work-life balance in the private sector. Angela Hessler observes, "My weekends and evenings are almost entirely free from work worries. The company is quite vocal in its support of work-life balance and healthy living, and I don't feel pressure to take on more than I can accomplish."

A study by Petersen, Riccaboni, Stanleye, and Pammolli (2012) found that among physicists, long-term career success is associated with the ability to attract new collaboration and production opportunities.

Failure to foment collaboration and publish early is a frequent reason for the early death of a physicist's academic career. The authors argue that their findings are applicable to other disciplines in which collaboration is typical, and success is measured by publication of research. Teresa Golden confirms that in chemistry, "Collaboration is a must. It's rare to get funding as a single principal investigator [PI]. . . . So, if you're expected to have multiple PIs and collaborate, and opportunities don't exist within your home department, it restricts you." She adds a disturbing observation. "Rarely will [male] colleagues ask me to join a research project. Perhaps they don't believe we [women] do research, or they think we're not good at it, or maybe it's easier to collaborate with other guys."

Similarly, Isbell, Young, and Harcourt (2012) observe that among primatologists, the majority of whom are women (i.e., 60 percent), women tend to be overrepresented in noninvited, less prestigious poster sessions at their national conference. For sessions that were invited, female-organized sessions had nearly 60 percent women presenters while male-organized sessions had only 30 percent women presenters. Whether such incidences reflect bias or self-selection, they hold obvious implications for networking, collaborative opportunities, and ultimately, a woman's relative chance of success in an academic setting. Such tendencies breed a sense of isolation and not fitting in.

Linda Birnbaum states,

I love the interactions with people. I love the opportunities and ability to make a difference in environmental health. I love mentoring others and all the learning. I love being able to get people together to talk about an issue or a problem and move forward, maybe in a new and enriching direction.

She sounds as if she's describing life as a college professor, but she's speaking of the collegial environment that permeates the government agency where she works. Radia Perlman describes it this way: "There's just as much opportunity for innovation in industry, and the results actually get deployed in the real world rather than existing in papers in fields populated by a few researchers who cite each others' work." Sharon Hays characterizes the availability of private and government sector alternatives as a positive, noting that academia cannot possibly absorb everyone coming out of graduate school in the STEM fields.

Most of the women we interviewed were the only woman or one of a few in college classes and function in similar situations as professionals. Bonnie Jacobs recalls that as an undergraduate, "being a girl [in the sciences] made it especially intimidating." Sharon Hays said that she was often the only woman in the room. Six of the eight women describe incidents at some time in their careers that range from explicit gender discrimination (e.g., being propositioned by a professor, being told that women can't be geologists) to subtler forms of bias (e.g., a man's surprise that a young woman would be interested in studying science, having research work dismissed as "cute"). Linda Birnbaum states that she and the few other female graduate students "banded together" and "just toughed it out."

Men also played important positive roles as mentors and advisers for many of these women in their careers. Cynthia Barnhart said,

> Male colleagues have been very supportive, and often the most supportive and sympathetic were the ones I least expected to be. . . . They asked me questions about how I organized my time. . . . I discovered these men often had daughters who were trying to manage careers and families simultaneously. They were aware of the inherent challenges and supportive of women who were trying to make it work.

However, the eight women point to ways in which differences between men and women have introduced a unique set of challenges. First, they have sometimes second-guessed their abilities. Teresa Golden describes research on differences in the way women and men approach math and science when she summarized research findings. "If a woman was told she was good at X and then ran into an obstacle in science or math, she immediately thought something was wrong with her, shut down, and quit. . . . But if you told a guy, 'You're really good at X,' and he ran into difficulty, he just barreled on through." Hays and Jacobs relate experiences in which they questioned their own abilities and were chastised by others for it. Blessing, Hays, and Hessler note that they or women they know have tended not to ask questions as often in the classroom.

Second, men often behave differently with few women around. Teresa Golden mentions never meeting with a boss behind closed doors, but "the guys went in and closed the door and talked." Linda

Birnbaum reminisces, "Guys like to go sit at the bar or play ball and talk about work. I don't like to do that. I had to learn to work around those types of challenges."

In spite of the many challenges of a career in a STEM discipline, which we explore in greater depth in Chapter 12, the women we interviewed love what they do. Sharon Hays explains,

> I've had experiences I never would have had without science. It prepared me, it stimulated my creativity, it helped separate me from the pack. It gave me tools and problem-solving skills I might otherwise have never developed. Yes, I worked hard, but science helped me advance.

All eight women are comfortable with their choices to stick with academia or pursue a career outside it. In many instances, they do not seem to face the stark choice of being entirely in or outside academia. Teresa Golden observes, "Academia seems to fit me. I love teaching. I love research. . . . I truly like being a professor. That doesn't mean I won't start my own company or work in industry someday." Cynthia Barnhart states,

> When I went back to school . . . I never once thought about returning to the private sector. . . . The very nature of the work intrigued me. It's about learning, being creative, formulating new ideas, and interacting with students. . . . There's a degree of flexibility. I determine what I want to do (particularly in terms of research), and I can change what I want to do.

Radia Perlman observes, "I might've gone into academia. . . . I love teaching and nurturing students. But I like industry better." Sharon Hays wasn't energized by academic research: "The thrill of discovery related to that one little piece of the universe wasn't enough." But in moving to the government and then the private sector, she found that thrill.

Cynthia Barnhart, Linda Birnbaum, Susan Blessing, Sharon Hays, Teresa Golden, Angela Hessler, Bonnie Jacobs, and Radia Perlman are remarkably humble, crediting their success to a combination of hard work, perseverance, and luck. As Bonnie Jacobs states, "You have to have that core inside you that keeps you going. That drive, determination, and perseverance. You must love what you do." Radia Perlman observes, "I just happened to be in the right place at the right time to shape the field, and even with that, I doubt whether I'd have been known for what I'd done if I hadn't happened to write the book *Interconnections* [1999]." Sharon Hays feels similarly. Teresa Golden declares, "I was lucky."

REFERENCES

Isbell, L. A., Young, T. P., & Harcourt, A. H. (2012). Stag parties linger: Continued gender bias in a female-rich scientific discipline. *PLOS One, 7*(11), e49682.

Petersen, A., Riccaboni, M., Stanleye, H., & Pammolli, F. (2012). Persistence and uncertainty in the academic career. *Proceedings of the National Academy of Sciences, 109*(14), 5213–5218.

Perlman, R. (1999). *Interconnections: Bridges, routers, switches, and internetworking protocols.* Reading, MA: Addison-Wesley

Schiebinger, L., Henderson, A. D., & Gilmartin, S. K. (2008). *Dual career couples: What universities need to know.* Stanford, CA: Michelle R. Clayman Institute for Gender Research. Retrieved from http://gender.stanford.edu/dual-career-research-report

eleven

IS THE PAST THE PRESENT?

THE WOMEN IN THIS STUDY ARE CLEARLY well established in their careers and accomplished in their disciplines. Both enterprises take time. All of them have been working at least ten years and several for closer to thirty. Collectively, over the course of their careers to date, they identified multiple factors that deter women in STEM disciplines from seeking academic positions at research universities and, in many instances, careers in these fields at all.

Chief among these reasons are the general perceptions of STEM disciplines as geeky (among girls) or unrelated to solving complex but applied societal problems (among college- and career-age women) and a lack of mentoring and female role models. These reasons are closely followed in any list by the difficulty in balancing work and personal responsibilities and the need to work hard for recognition of research contributions.

To determine whether their observations hold currency in today's work environment or whether they reflect past situations, we compiled a list of items related to the question that has been raised throughout this book: Do present experiences of STEM women mirror those of the women featured in this book? In all, we organized the following twelve items into three life-stage categories—elementary through high school, undergraduate through PhD, and career years.

1. Perceptions of STEM as geeky, boring, abstract, and not concerned with helping others
2. Lack of mentoring, which includes parental support; girls' encouragement to pursue other interests; mentoring by others at all three stages; and lack of access to career-building information
3. Lack of role models—lack of exposure to women in STEM disciplines at younger ages and of role models in STEM disciplines and in institutional leadership once at a university
4. Lack of math skills
5. Unrealistic portrayal of women scientists in the media
6. Isolation—being one of a few women—and girls' desire to fit in at a young age
7. Family-work balance—the nature of the work, particularly as it relates to long hours and extended fieldwork in some disciplines, and the need for two academic careers in the same city (often in the same specialization)
8. Lack of confidence, which entails needing to be 100 percent sure of something before you feel qualified
9. Better-paying options outside academia
10. Disrespect on the part of male colleagues, which includes lack of recognition of work or research and lack of credit for ideas (we also included outright discrimination as part of this item, but disrespect was the common thread in all replies)
11. Extensive expectation for service—includes women being pushed into administrative positions and away from research
12. Stress related to the work required for tenure

Several of these items appear in each life-stage category, giving us a total of thirty-two items.

We then invited untenured or recently tenured women and one nonacademic scientist from a STEM discipline to anonymously rate whether each of these items is relevant in their discipline and for women in STEM disciplines in general. As was the case with identifying women willing to share their stories for inclusion in *Breaking In*, garnering the participation of women in this newer, relatively less established group (even though they wouldn't be identified) was not easy. Of more than two dozen solicitations, eight responded and completed the survey.

Nevertheless, those individuals who did reply are diverse in discipline and conscientious and thoughtful in their responses. They include women in engineering, mathematics, paleontology, physics, computer science, and toxicology.

With respect to the list of possible reasons why we still see relatively few women in STEM faculty positions at research universities and in other advanced STEM careers, their selection of items and the relative importance they assigned to them are similar to those of the eight women we interviewed. And that, in and of itself, is rather discouraging.

Four of the seven academics we surveyed identified every single reason on the list as pertinent. The remaining three either did not consider media representation of female scientists as relevant to the question or had no opinion on the topic. Two others didn't see the lack of math skills as a problem, and one made no mention of a lack of confidence on the part of girls or women. The nonacademic scientist believed the lack of math skills posed a barrier but didn't comment on media representation of women scientists.

Where items such as mentoring and role models were listed multiple times or stated in slightly different ways, the women we surveyed often considered the item more relevant at one life stage than another but nevertheless noted its importance somewhere along the timeline. In addition, four women added items—one item (added by two women) was related to the lack of coverage of many STEM disciplines in high school curricula, which means girls and boys are not exposed to the discipline, particularly earth and computer sciences. Another suggested that the math skills debate is overemphasized.

The third distinct addition to the list of factors deals with the amount of time it requires an individual to go into an advanced STEM career, something we also heard from some of the women we interviewed. "Many fields require as much or more education as it takes to become a medical doctor, and the perception is you can make more money as a doctor." The implication here is that the combination of time and lack of money is an important barrier.

Of the items listed, our anonymous responders focused heavily on work-life balance issues and feelings of isolation. As one woman put it,

Women don't want careers perceived as so demanding, hard, and stressful because of home, family, and other interests. The situation is worse in computer science because of the dominance of computer science as a hobby as well as a career for many [men]. We don't want to do it 24/7 and can't keep up with those who do.

The lack of mentoring and the limited number of role models also drew comments. The young mathematics professor suggested her discipline lies at the far extreme and touches on two other issues as well. "In math, role models are fewer, the back and forth between academia and industry rarer [isolating], and it is legitimately more abstract than other STEM fields." A computer scientist added, "Most of the women I know in this field are here *despite* [respondent's emphasis] lack of encouragement from peers and role models, although parents and families are usually at least supportive."

The nonacademic scientist expanded on this theme by suggesting that not only the lack of mentoring and role modeling but also insufficient funding dissuades men and women, but particularly women, from entering these fields.

There are fewer grants and scholarships and less research and development money being spent in the U.S. It trickles down to the K–12 level where science programs along with art, music, and physical education are being cut. There's a reverse "brain drain" occurring and the U.S. is poised to lose its edge in the STEM fields if it hasn't already.

These issues were followed closely by concerns about misperceptions harbored by many about STEM fields. One woman noted, "The perception that STEM is unfeminine will never go away." She referred to this as "gender role pressure." A related comment suggested that the constant message sent to girls and women is "it's how we look that matters most."

Perceptions of STEM disciplines as geeky or irrelevant when it comes to solving societal problems and helping people seem to play havoc with computer science in particular.

Computer science has an added kicker. Most computer science labs in high schools are male dominated geek places. To make matters worse, there's the hacker in the corner who is unable to communicate with the general public and it's a real turn-off. Fields like biology and certain types of engineering have an obvious potential to help people; computer science doesn't have that identifiable link. Working at Facebook could help starving children in Africa, but it's not clear how that might happen.

The lack of respect on the part of male colleagues and subtle discounting of credibility also drew specific remarks from all the women we surveyed. One woman spoke of "condescending attitudes" and explained, "When men meet at conferences they talk about research. When they encounter women they ask about kids." The young physicist, who has now moved into another somewhat more "woman friendly" STEM field, said, "Condescension is worse in physics than in my current field and there are far fewer female colleagues and role models," which probably compounds the problem.

Finally, several of the women noted a lack of confidence as potentially problematic for women. One young academic clarified the issue in a manner that sounds reminiscent of the experiences of women featured earlier in the book. "I've heard quite a few women express anxiety about not being good enough to do these disciplines. Even if they are doing better than their peers, their personal perception is they aren't as good. Guys don't seem to have this problem."

Women in both groups (our eight more experienced and eight relatively new) acknowledged the impact of some of these forces on men as well as women, namely, dealing with the STEM image and misperceptions about STEM disciplines, better pay options outside academia, and work-life balance, in particular when dual academic careers come into play. They qualified this concession, however, by suggesting the detrimental effect is not as severe for men as it is for women.

It appears that issues relevant thirty years ago still hold sway today. The lived experiences of Cindy Barnhart, Linda Birnbaum, Susan Blessing, Teresa Golden, Sharon Hays, Angela Hessler, Bonnie Jacobs, and Radia Perlman do reflect the realities faced by our anonymous women now pursuing academic careers. In 2014, for them and we suspect many others, the past is indeed the present.

twelve

HIDDEN CHOICES

CONSCIOUS BIAS PURPOSEFULLY demeans the individual who is targeted. It's disrespectful. It's nasty. And we usually know it when we see it. In October 2013, when a post-doctoral biologist at Oklahoma State University, Danielle Lee, declined a request to donate her time and expertise as a contributor to Biology-Online, a forum affiliated with *Scientific American*, the editor's question in response—"Are you an urban scientist or an urban whore?"—clearly exemplifies conscious bias. The journal fired the blog editor in response to public outcry. When it removed the ensuing blog posts that discussed the incident in an attempt to sweep it under the proverbial rug, the journal reinforced the bias by belittling its importance to the blog's readers. *Scientific American's* actions reflected a much more subtle form of bias—unintentional and unconscious.

Unconscious bias refers to implicit preferences informed by our socialization, experiences, and exposure to others' opinions about a particular group. Teresa Golden noted that men often prefer to work and talk with other men. Such actions constitute unconscious bias that reduces women's access to information essential to their careers, not because men are consciously keeping information from women, but because they leave women out of the networking that organically occurs among male colleagues. The men in this example may be entirely unaware of these behaviors, which seem natural and normal to them. And women may harbor only vague notions of how such preferential inclinations shape their choices. More often than not, these hidden choices bubble unconsciously to the surface.

Unlike conscious bias, which results in the prejudicial treatment of or beliefs about individuals or groups of individuals based on faulty perceptions and a refusal to revise our opinions, hidden choices are made instinctively. The impact unconscious biases have on the choices we make, however, can be just as influential.

Unconscious biases permeate society at three fundamental levels—individual, institutional, and societal. Each of the women we interviewed experienced bias at one or more of these levels. However, because of the very nature of unconscious bias, its impact on women's career choices often goes unacknowledged and undiscussed.

Individual or person-specific bias refers to attitudes and actions we engage in as individuals that are based on "unintentional categorization-related judgment errors" (Krieger, 1995). Because information collection is often a costly endeavor, we sometimes rely on heuristics or already established relationships (as in the previous example, men tend to interact with other men) based on prior experience to lower these costs.

If a manager interviews several job candidates for a highly technical position and needs to quickly assess which candidates are most qualified, he or she might base the assessment on the attributes of those who have been successful in a similar position or on their personal past experiences. Radia Perlman mentions a hiring manager who asks during interviews about childhood hobbies and suggests that if he doesn't hear that you built computers out of spare parts when you were twelve that you are not a real engineer. If very few women have occupied a particular position or if those who apply have never been interested in building machines, the manager tends to confuse skill or similarity in experience with gender and hires the male job candidate, even when the candidates have similar qualifications (see, e.g., Moss-Racusina, Dovidio, Brescoll, Graham, & Handelsman, 2012; Steinpreis, Anders, & Ritzke, 1999). (Moss-Racusina et al. found that faculty ranked male applicants with identical characteristics and qualifications to their female counterparts as substantially more qualified, offered them higher starting salaries, and gave them more career mentoring opportunities. Interestingly, the gender of the faculty member evaluating the candidates made no difference in the magnitude of the bias.) Because prior experience does not include relevant examples, the heuristic used by the manager results in choices that reinforce stereotypes: we predominantly hire men for these technical positions; therefore, they must be better at them.

Barnhart, Blessing, Golden, and Jacobs all mention job search issues in their academic units that suggest gender-based selection bias. For instance, Susan Blessing recalls,

> We interviewed a woman in high-energy physics several years ago. We didn't offer her the job because two members of the group claimed they couldn't work with her. One of the two was a young guy, and I really regret not saying, "Well, then I guess you'll have to leave."

Early in Linda Birnbaum's career, she encountered a similar situation.

> When I first enrolled at the University of Illinois, I wanted to work in a specific lab, but I was quickly informed that the lab's director didn't like women in his lab because if they weren't married, they might get married, and if they were married, they might have children.

Here, stereotypical assumptions were clearly voiced by the lab director.

Angela Hessler notes unconscious bias at play in how women are recognized for their achievements.

> I do see instances where women have to work harder to get noticed professionally. . . . Women get overlooked for technical awards or consultation, in hiring, or just presenting a good idea. It's hard to put a finger on because it's not a fixed glass ceiling but more about subtle dismissiveness.

The Association for Women in Science (2012a) describes this as a more general phenomenon: "Women receive fewer scholarly awards than would be expected based on the proportion of female PhDs and full professors in [STEM] fields."

Even in relating her college experiences, which she categorized as good, Hessler recounts unconscious bias on the part of a professor who described one of her papers as "cute." Ironically, his reaction irritated her but at the time passed by her as normal and perhaps expected behavior. In contrast, one of the women we interviewed who withdrew from the book clearly recognized similar biased behavior on the part of her adviser when she spoke about his ignoring an idea she suggested but later giving credit to a male colleague for essentially the same idea.

Institutional bias surfaces when policies and procedures at academic institutions and in the workplace sustain practices that put women at a disadvantage. Institutional biases can affect men as well, but in many instances these practices disproportionately affect women. Even policies designed to alleviate bias and rectify a prejudicial situation can have unexpected consequences. The same holds true for ingrained the-way-we've-always-done-it procedures. Linda Birnbaum observes, "The woman still has to be better than the man, at least at the higher levels. But the glass ceiling now has holes in it. We have broken through; nonetheless, the career advancement system in place continues to hamper our progress."

Universities seem particularly susceptible to institutional bias, perhaps because policies tend to be arbitrary rather than universally practiced, and although procedures bear a resemblance to those of other universities, they are quite often institution specific. Two of the more common university policies (parental leave and the tenure clock) and two policy-procedure permutations (the manner in which we define faculty and spousal accommodation) illustrate the impact of institutional bias on women as they strive to establish their careers.

Birnbaum contends that many women delay having children until they've finished their education and started their careers. This delay poses a dilemma. It superimposes some of the most time-consuming years of child rearing into the period in their careers when they should be intensely engaged in the research and publishing demanded by tenure requirements.

In the past two decades, numerous universities, businesses, and government agencies have instituted maternal leave policies intended to provide time for new mothers to nurture their newborns and recuperate any lost strength incurred during birth or in the first few months of a baby's life without jeopardizing their careers. But as Hessler mentions, not every university provides such accommodations. Friends of hers who had babies before gaining tenure often went back to the classroom (and their research agendas) the same semester. Even when universities offer leave benefits, they can have unintended consequences. As Jacobs notes, there is a need for an environment that "makes life more tolerable for people who want to choose both family and work." She continues, "Institutional policies and culture often work against creating [such an] environment."

Maternity leave policies, because of protests about the preferential treatment of women, have morphed into parental leave policies similar to the one in place at the Massachusetts Institute of Technology, which applies to a newborn or adopted child's primary caregiver (male or female). It releases the caregiver for one semester from teaching and service obligations. The intent is good. But rather than leveling the playing field for new mothers, the outcome digs the furrows to career advancement deeper because the majority of faculty taking advantage of the policy (at least initially) are men, some of whom are not primary caregivers. When women take the leave, they care for the baby. When men take it, they often use the time to further their research agendas, which gives them a competitive advantage that exacerbates existing inequities between men and women on faculty. As Cynthia Barnhart commented, "Now we have to figure out how to change the policy or the way in which it is implemented."

Lengthening the tenure clock, another well-intended policy designed to help parents (in particular, mothers of young children), also has an unanticipated and subsequently unaddressed consequence—the potential loss of credibility concerning field-specific research because productivity and publishing slows among university members who do not necessarily take child rearing into account when they make decisions about whether to grant tenure. Birnbaum, Blessing, and Jacobs all note this possibility. Seeking to reduce the number of hours worked by going part-time or stopping the tenure clock completely during child-rearing years often brings about similar unforeseen results. In an effort to ease their workload, Birnbaum suggests that new mothers she employs work part-time. But she notes, "Many of them are afraid to go part-time because they believe doing so will hurt them [careerwise]."

Along these same lines, the manner in which we define tenure worthiness can also bode poorly for women. It's what Birnbaum's young mothers fear. Barnhart states bluntly, "We cling to the notion that if you are not full-time, you're not a real faculty member. . . . You aren't serious about your career." And even if a faculty member works full-time on contract or as an adjunct, her (or his) value as a department member and credibility as a researcher (with or without an active research agenda) diminishes. If you are a newborn's primary caregiver and you've slowed or stopped the tenure clock, you might have reason to worry.

The way we define the appropriateness of work further complicates the issue. Higher education institutions apportion expected faculty responsibilities in concert with their missions. The mission of a research university is threefold—research, teaching, and service—with the least emphasis placed on service, particularly in tenure-granting decisions. Yet, women seem drawn toward service, whether by virtue of a natural affinity for it or an externally driven expectation. Barnhart is quite frank about why she's an administrator: "When I'm given a task, I follow through, and I'm willing to be a good citizen."

Bonnie Jacobs and Teresa Golden took on the very time-consuming job of developing a new program. Golden, in particular, is quite open about the price she paid. Setting up the forensic program is "one reason it took me so long to get promoted to full rank." She explains, "Program devlopment hurt my annual evaluations. Although I'd started a nationally recognized forensic program . . . my external evaluations also suffered. . . . I couldn't publish or bring in [grant] monies at the expected rate." She concludes, "Quite honestly, sometimes I wonder why I did it." The real crux of the matter reveals itself when she justifies her continued involvement: "No one else wants to do it because it won't help with getting promoted."

Finally, spousal accommodation, or what is more commonly referred to in the vernacular as the *trailing spouse handicap*, illustrates how institutional bias toward business-as-usual policies and procedures can hamstring careers. As previously mentioned, female scientists interested in academic positions often marry fellow scientists, but as Blessing observes, because there are so few women in STEM disciplines, "the dual-career issue is more problematic for women." Jacobs and Hessler married fellow geoscientists they met when enrolled in the same PhD programs. Spouses in the same discipline understand its demands, which in their case involved extensive fieldwork requirements.

Several of the women we interviewed point out the difficulties faced by dual-career academics who have overlapping expertise. Usually only one position exists for a given specialization in an academic department, which can mean that a couple may have to live apart so they can both pursue tenure-track positions in academia, one person takes a non-tenure-track or part-time position, or one person does not go into academia at all. Hessler and Jacobs understood the need to establish themselves as researchers in their own right, choosing to do little, if any, collaborative work with their spouses. Even so, the career of the woman in the couple often takes a backseat.

Jacobs, perhaps, presents the most illustrative example of the detrimental impact a reliance on ignore-it-and-it-will-go-away procedures and nonexistent policies can have on academic careers. She spent seventeen years in a part-time position and was not offered a full-time position until the department discovered that her husband was serious about leaving so that she too could find a full-time tenure-track position.

While her discipline is different from her husband's, Birnbaum faced similar struggles balancing two careers. After graduate school, her husband was employed at Hamilton College in upstate New York. She states, "The Hamilton faculty could not accept the idea that a Hamilton wife—me—could also be a Hamilton faculty member. They wouldn't even consider me for a regular faculty appointment. So after that first year, I was on the job market again."

The dual-career challenge is not unique to academia for highly specialized individuals. Hessler admits that although Chevron had no qualms about hiring her and her husband, even though their areas of expertise overlap, eventually either her career or that of her husband will advance at the expense of the other because "it will be difficult for both of us to land international assignments, which can be big career boosters."

Although person-specific and institutional biases explain a great deal about why the number of women in STEM disciplines remains small, societal bias often underlies both of these biases. The Association for Women in Science (2012b) mentions four reasons women drop out of the STEM fields, which echo what we heard from the women we interviewed. Two are person specific, and the others surface at the institution level: "stereotypes of women as scientists; an 'old boys' club' culture in science and engineering departments . . .; unequal promotion, salaries, grants and benefits packages for women; [and] under-recognition of women for research and scholarship" (p. 1).

Societal bias has to do with ingrained beliefs and assumptions about preferences and abilities (those based on gender in this instance) that govern a society's norms and help shape its culture. They are systemic in nature and as such can have a powerful influence on behavior. For instance, Thoman, White, Yamawaki, and Koishi (2008) found that undergraduate women performed worse on a standardized mathematics exam when informed before the exam that men score better because they have more natural ability. When they were told nothing or that men score better because they work harder, the women in the study fared better. This study points out that simply conveying a commonly held stereotype can significantly affect performance.

We contend that social norms affect the interaction of the women we interviewed with male counterparts and their views about what they can accomplish. Sheryl Sandberg (2013) suggests that these tendencies are the product of ingrained cultural norms, which presuppose particular gender-based roles and abilities. She advises women to "lean out," to not limit options by deciding before trying that they are not capable.

Jacobs notes that when she was hired as the director of the environmental science program, she was told she was getting a course release for taking on the extra burden. "I found out later that my teaching load was identical to everyone else's in the department. . . . I thought, 'This is just another one of those things women do. We don't negotiate.'" Blessing describes dressing a certain way to fit in with the men at Fermilab. "I definitely did not want to look like a secretary. I dressed less femininely—the jeans and shirts."

Bias also affects confidence. Golden and Hessler mention that women were pretty quiet in graduate school classes for fear of being seen as stupid or less competent. Sharon Hays recalls confiding her trepidation in taking a high-level government position to a female colleague and her colleague's response.

> She looked at me and said, "Do you think [a male colleague of ours who was in a very similar role to the one I'd be taking on] worried about whether he was ready for it? He just went for it. You are absolutely prepared. . . . Why do we agonize over this stuff? Guys don't, or if they do, they hide it well." This ingrained lack of confidence and

fear of failure (which I still sometimes have) . . . contributes to my reticence when it comes to risk taking.

Radia Perlman recalls feeling panicked and intimidated when she entered her first computer programming class, wondering if she was cut out for it. Bonnie Jacobs expresses similar feelings. Blessing also observes that the culture of science may not match up well with the ways women tend to communicate.

As physicists, we're expected to work independently, without a significant amount of direction, and at the same time function within a group. We're expected to compete on the one hand and cooperate on the other. People attack you, and you must be able to stand there, defend your work, and not collapse. Guys tend to be much more challenging, and their communication style differs. It's not so much meanness as it is about socialization into the culture of being in science. It's an odd combination that school does not prepare us for.

Unlike personal or institutional biases, which remain somewhat localized and concentrated around an individual or unit, the systemic nature of societal bias pushes it into everyday living and infiltrates our broader and generally accepted knowledge base. "We have failed miserably in marketing," contends Cynthia Barnhart. "When I talk with my daughters' friends about engineering, most of them don't know what it is."

Hays and Blessing provide striking examples suggesting not only that information is missing but that what's out there is misconstrued and inaccurate. Hays observes, "Think about what's on television. How many programs are there about doctors and lawyers? Many, and the professions are glamorized. They make these professions exciting. You rarely see glamorized depictions of research scientists."

Blessing adds,

We, as a society, also send messages about "proper" women's roles. [My graduate assistant] mentioned a study about the depiction of women in TV shows. The study concluded that women today are represented by behavioral models that harken to the 1950s and 1960s— Harriet Nelson [on The Adventures of *Ozzie and Harriet*] and Jane Wyatt's Margaret Anderson on *Father Knows Best*. In contrast, TV shows in the 1970s and early 1980s portrayed women in traditional male roles, strong and more independent—*Cagney and Lacy, Laverne and Shirley*. Today? Take *The Big Bang Theory*. We've attracted more male physics majors since its first airing but not women. I think it's because girls and young women look at these nerdy guys and think, "I'm not like that.". . . And, of course, the neighbor is this beautiful blonde woman who is a waitress/actress. One female character, a neurobiologist, is so nerdy, she's not "normal."

Women have made gains. The workplace has changed. Ironically, however, most of the gains women have made appear to have occurred at the personal level, which in turn should bring about change at the professional level. Women have much more freedom in who they choose as partners (individuals often in the same or a related discipline). Doing so likely provides some familiarity with, and thus understanding of, the rigors of being a researcher. But it also might mean women are selecting men who will treat them as partners and equals.

Ideally, these same ideals should translate into a professional setting. However, what works in a personal relationship is not as easy to implement in a professional one. Equitable treatment is much harder to negotiate with colleagues than with a significant other. Even though a department is a unit, it is in reality a collection of individuals rather than a partnership. Each individual has his or her own goals and perspectives on what the workplace environment should entail.

Institutional policies, such as family leave and spousal accommodation, attempt to mitigate some of the issues women face by providing a forum for dialogue, specifically about work-life issues. In academic departments, the chair is a particularly important agent of change, since he or she has the power to set the tone and lead by example. However, the degree to which a department is women-friendly depends on individual faculty members' personal perspectives, and a faculty member's history of interactions with women, which emanate from culturally acceptable norms and expected behaviors, plays a role in how he or she relates to women colleagues.

In many ways, relationships with colleagues are more akin to arranged marriages. Some colleagues are like-minded, more similar to a partner, while others are more comfortable with traditional, societally determined gender roles. It is much easier to discuss concerns with the former than the latter. For these reasons, negotiating and navigating professional relationships is often challenging, particularly if women have little power to open up a dialogue for change. So, where do we go from here?

REFERENCES

Association for Women in Science. (2012a). *AWIS in Action! August 2012 Awards*. Retrieved from http://www.awis.org/?page=620

Association for Women in Science. (2012b). *Underrepresented groups in STEM [Factsheet]*. Retrieved from http://c.ymcdn.com/sites/www.awis.org/resource/resmgr/imported/Underrepresented_Facsheet.pdf

Krieger, L. (1995). The content of our categories: A cognitive bias approach to discrimination and equal employment opportunity. *Stanford Law Review*, *47*(6), 1161–1248.

Moss-Racusina, C., Dovidio, J., Brescoll, V., Graham, M., and Handelsman, J. (2012). Science faculty's subtle gender biases favor male students. *Proceedings of the National Academy of Sciences*, *109*(41), 16474–16479.

Sandberg, S. (with Scovell, N.). (2013). *Lean in: Women, work, and the will to lead*. New York, NY: Knopf.

Steinpreis, R. E., Anders, K. A., & Ritzke, D. (1999). The impact of gender on the review of the curricula vitae of job applicants and tenure candidates: A national empirical study. *Sex Roles*, *41*(7/8), 509–528.

Thoman, D. B, White, P. H., Yamawaki, N., & Koishi, H. (2008). Variations of gender-math stereotype content affect women's vulnerability to stereotype threat. *Sex Roles*, *58*(9–10), 702–712.

thirteen

CHOICES

Is the Past the Future?

HARVARD FACULTY MEMBER Rosabeth Moss Kanter, a prominent expert on women in leadership in corporate settings, once said, "Confidence is the expectation of a positive outcome. If you think you will be criticized and attacked . . . you hold back" (McGinn, 2005, para. 5). When girls and women encounter bias and that bias continually sends the message "You can't do it"—often the case in math and science—or they try but doing so tells them it's not worth the effort, they follow other avenues. Combine such overt and subliminal signals with the substantially higher level of angst many women associate with math and other technical skills, and we find ourselves as a nation leaving the creative talents and abilities of the vast majority of women with an affinity for STEM fields essentially untapped.

The widening disconnect between the skill sets of many high school and college graduates and STEM job growth in the United States reveals the implications of not effectively tapping into this potential. Although experts project 2.4 million STEM job openings in the United States in the next five years, only one in ten high school students (girls and boys) taking the ACT college entrance exam between 2010 and 2012 reported an interest in majoring in or developing a career in a STEM field ("Who Says Math Has to Be Boring?," 2013).

We will never eliminate bias in STEM fields, but we can mitigate it. We can help women develop the skill sets and confidence needed to pursue advanced research degrees and careers in the STEM disciplines in and outside academia. Birnbaum notes, "Today, there just isn't room in academia for the number of PhDs we're graduating. But there are many other professions that require advanced knowledge. . . . One doesn't need to go into academia to do interesting, intellectually satisfying work."

We can talk about STEM disciplines and the value of advanced degrees in these fields. Hays offers a key observation,

> People generally respect those three letters behind your name. It opens doors. It lends credibility. Having earned a PhD also instills in you a way of looking at a problem—a way of breaking a seemingly unsolvable quandary down into answerable questions. That's an extremely useful skill.

When we promote STEM in this way, we begin to bridge the gulf between the small numbers of young people pursuing STEM careers and the growing need for them.

The women in this study had a great deal to say about marketing STEM fields to create interest and energy; ensuring adequate academic preparation coming out of high school, particularly in mathematics; providing mentoring to support and encourage women as they pursue their interests in male-dominated academic and work environments; ensuring flexibility in the workplace; providing role models not only in STEM positions but among leaders; and revisiting and modifying social norms that put women at a disadvantage in the workplace and in society in general. The challenge, at least in part, is not in identifying what needs doing but in effecting change through the personal tools, policies, procedures, and mechanisms already out there.

Radia Perlman and Sharon Hays observe that the sciences are often viewed as esoteric, removed from reality, boring, or isolating. They believe we must reshape this perception so young people understand that science can open doors to many exciting opportunities. Hays goes to the heart of the issue: "Young kids need to understand that getting a degree in a technical field doesn't mean they have to wear a white lab coat and spend their entire career at a lab bench, looking at and interacting with test tubes. Science gives you options." One of the young anonymous respondents we surveyed echoes this thought. "We need to let them see how cool and fun computer science is and how many different directions it can take you."

Susan Blessing notes, "Women often gravitate to helping occupations. But they think of helping individuals one at a time. I try to get the point across that science allows you to help whole populations." Cynthia Barnhart agrees,

> Engineering certainly can find and is at the heart of developing solutions to some of society's most challenging problems. . . . When I talk with my daughters' friends about engineering, most of them don't know what it is. . . . It's important that we get the message out to kids at the grade school and high school levels that math and science hold the solutions to societal problems.

Sixty percent of high school students surveyed by Intel were more likely to consider engineering as a possible career when provided with information on what engineers actually do and how much they earn (Intel PR, 2011). Similarly, Angela Hessler focuses on the bigger picture: the need to communicate how all science affects society: "I've noticed that the girls ask more questions about how my job helps people. Not that boys don't care about helping others, but girls are much more interested in how what I do contributes directly to society."

Programs that target young people and illustrate how the STEM disciplines change the world can build interest. For instance, Barnhart highlights programs at the Massachusetts Institute of Technology (MIT) designed to

> excite school-age girls about engineering. The [MIT] STEM program targets middle school girls and boys [through] a five-week summer institute; a nine-month mentoring program that pairs middle school students with MIT undergraduates pursuing degrees in math, science, and engineering; and a series of seminars that focus on succeeding in an academic environment and applying to private high schools and colleges.

Hessler conducts Take Your Daughters to Work Days at Chevron to expose young girls to career choices in the sciences. Perlman mentions a colleague who mentors a high school girls' team for robotic competitions: "She has no trouble recruiting team members, and they often win."

Intel's chief executive officer, Diane Bryant, suggests, "We need to offer teens real-world, hands-on engineering experience and interaction with engineers, like that found in robotics programs and science competitions, to improve the likelihood that they'll get hooked on the subject and pursue it in college" (Intel PR, 2011).

As president of the operations research (OR) professional society INFORMS, Barnhart started a competition for college students called Doing Good With Good OR to raise awareness of how technologies can be used to benefit society.

> Students . . . apply OR to different important societal problems. They work in health care on problems such as designing radiation treatments for cancer patients or matching kidneys or livers with patients. They design logistical responses to natural disasters. They develop ways to provide clean water to people in third world and developing countries. The experience broadens their perspectives and piques their interest.

In addition to marketing STEM better, it is essential for young people graduating from high school to be equipped with the basic skill set required to advance in these fields. Indeed, a *New York Times* editorial points out that most jobs in STEM fields require critical thinking and problem solving skills ("Who Says Math Boring?," 2013).

Changing the approach to curricular delivery and content, as Blessing suggests, by focusing on project-based, real-life, open-ended problems keeps young women in the classroom. Florida State University's Women in Math, Science, and Engineering (WIMSE) introduces women to open-ended Fermi problems (e.g., How many piano tuners are there in the city of Chicago?) in their freshman year of college. Although they initially struggle, Blessing says, "Kids need to face situations in which multiple or even no answers exist, and they need to do it when they are young."

Blessing, Hays, Barnhart, Perlman, and Hessler single out mathematics as a fundamental building block. As Blessing puts it, "If you know math, I can teach you physics; but if you're weak in math, I can't teach you physics." Hays comments,

> We need to catch young girls early if we want more women to go into science. We don't necessarily want to convince young people they want to be scientists at age five or seven or ten or whatever the magic number is. But science is one of those fields that if you don't have the right foundation, it's extremely hard to catch up.

The mathematics professor who responded to our survey advises, "Mentoring should start no later than eleven—that's the critical age for me." A study by Geary, Hoard, Nugent, and Bailey (2013) emphasizes the need to start even earlier. They found the best predictor of success in mathematics in middle and high school is exposure to numbers before entering the first grade.

Blessing wonders

> if elementary school teachers are afraid of science and math and transfer this fear to their students. In middle and high school, we find an overabundance of biology teachers who are told to teach chemistry or physics. They don't like it, and they don't understand it. They simply keep a chapter ahead of the students. Such attitudes and actions don't kindle interest in the sciences.

In fact, the majority of high school students are taught science by teachers who did not major in the subject. This reality underscores a recent national call for more adequately trained STEM teachers at the high school level. (The White House set a goal of training 100,000 new math and science teachers by 2020. The National Math + Science Initiative, supported by the likes of the Bill and Melinda Gates Foundation and several corporations, started the UTeach program to improve the quality of STEM teaching, [Office of Science and Technology Policy, 2013].)

The academic preparation needed to successfully pursue STEM-related careers also suggests the essentiality of providing young women with role models and mentors all along the pipeline. Former secretary of state Madeleine Albright once commented, "I think it's important for women to help one another. There's a special place in hell for women who don't" ("10 Questions for Madeleine Albright," 2008). Strong words, but the women in this study make clear the significance of their meaning. Linda Birnbaum believes "it helps when women see women in positions of responsibility." Bonnie Jacobs thinks it is important for women in the STEM disciplines to be visible to young people, to convince them "that 'normal' girls can grow up to be scientists." Hays observes, "Young women entering academia have a limited set of female role models. We need to change that dynamic if we're going to get more women in senior tenure-track research positions." Susan Blessing contends that programs that offer intensive mentoring "keep women in science."

Indeed, successful female role models demonstrate for young women what is possible and provide them with proof that women can be scientists, mothers, and wives simultaneously. Many of the women we interviewed had role models growing up who encouraged their interest in math and science. Birnbaum recalls that she felt it was okay to like science in junior high school "because I could be like my biology teacher, who was well liked and exuded all the characteristics teenage girls need to feel comfortable about."

Perlman remembers,

> When we didn't understand a homework problem, we'd come to class the next day and argue about whose parent was right. Someone would say, "My father says it should be done this way," and someone else would counter that his father knew the correct approach. And I'd chime in, "My mother said it should be done this way." Our teacher thought it was funny [that my mother, not my father, made the suggestion] and called it to my attention. Breaking the stereotype, I suppose.

Hessler says, "The key is to find those examples of a lifestyle you want, consider it possible, and trust that even though many women seem to be scaling back their careers, it doesn't necessarily mean they are making the better decision."

WIMSE at Florida State University is one example of a program designed to provide intense mentoring and ready access to role models for women interested in STEM fields. As Blessing puts it, "The program fosters team building, STEM learning, and hands-on experiences.

Faculty partners open their research labs to our students. Guest speakers share their experiences in STEM careers."

The need for mentoring and role models continues throughout a woman's career. Birnbaum advocates a different kind of post-doc experience.

> Some scientists have post-docs and want them tied to the bench, doing what they (the scientists) want them (the students) to do, as opposed to trying to expand their students' horizons. . . . Such an experience can be isolating. I like post-docs to spread their wings and fly—to take a new direction, to depart from what they did as graduate students. We're working very hard at NIEHS to develop better mentoring of our students and post-docs.

All the less experienced professional women we surveyed suggested that mentoring is essential. A remark made by one of the young professionals on her survey reinforces the efficacy of the need for continued advice and mentoring.

> Mid-career mentoring/advice and information on advancement or even on pursuing new opportunities with the skills and knowledge learned is nonexistent. I would like to stay in a STEM field and am not happy with what I am currently doing but see no one to reach out to or discuss this with.

Golden and Barnhart both stress the value of mentoring in the STEM disciplines, especially in the faculty ranks. Golden points out,

> Good mentoring can be about passing on information about applying for a grant, or something to do with institutional politics, or how to handle situation X, or why it's important to apply for Y, or when to talk to the chair about a particular issue. Good administrators help, and programs that advance your summer pay until a grant becomes active do wonders to reduce stress and promote healthy work environments.

Although the anonymous young academics we surveyed advocate mentoring and having sufficient role models at all life-cycle stages, they stressed its particular importance in the workplace.

Some of our women note the necessity of much more fundamental change in the workplace, maintaining that women are different from men in the way they interact with colleagues. Golden suggests, "If you value certain characteristics, then those values drive institutional decision making. . . . If we don't value women's ways, then there's no way women are going to enter the academic job market." Along similar lines, Perlman argues,

> We can make sure people feel safe enough to ask questions, ask for help. . . . We assume getting enough women in senior roles, as professors or in top management, will help. But it isn't so much that leaders must be female as that they must be the right people—approachable, nurturing, generous with credit, collaborative.

Policy and procedural adjustments can ameliorate institutional bias. Adopting a universally consistent approach to parental leave, reconceptualizing faculty positions and refining what tenure entails, and accommodating spouses and dual careers might all go a long way toward not only demystifying faculty life but making it more attainable and attractive. But Bird (2011) notes that administrators and faculty at universities "have been slow to recognize that systemically gendered barriers will have to be reduced or eliminated in order for women faculty to advance in their careers"(p. 202).

To a woman, our anonymous survey respondents stressed the need to address work-family balance issues as a top priority, calling particular attention to the need for affordable, on-campus child care. Their comments, however, were all qualified with a note similar to this one: "These [policies] should be equally available to men. Otherwise there is a huge perception problem of [any of these policies] being a 'girl's thing.'"

Birnbaum suggests we look to Scandinavia for examples of how to handle parental leave. Barnhart questions, "What about a three-quarter time, tenure-track position?" She suggests job sharing, a recommendation made in a study conducted by the University of California system, and asks, "Wouldn't it be great if an academic could have a part-time appointment when family priorities are at their peak?" Likewise, Hessler mentions part-time and telecommunicating options as ways to help women balance work and family. She also advises hiring for overlap (a common practice in industry) because "you can focus on hiring the best candidate, . . . ease some of the research isolation felt by department personnel," and accommodate dual-career couples.

Grants that specifically target those who have interrupted their academic careers, such as the one Jacobs received from the National Science Foundation (NSF), can also play an important role in increasing the options available to women (and men) who are starting families at the same time they leave graduate school or those who have dropped out to raise families. Today's NSF Increasing the Participation and Advancement of Women in Academic Science and Engineering Careers grants aim to encourage longer-term changes in STEM fields with regard to representation and advancement of women. (Ninety-three percent of the principal investigators and 8 percent of the coprincipal investigators for these grants are women.) The program focuses on changing the institutional work environment by improving work-family policies and the organizational climate (De Welde & Stepnick, 2014).

None of the women we interviewed mentioned a more fundamental first step than bringing bias out in the open so it can be dealt with at the personal and institutional levels through more effective communication and training. Bird (2011) points to dissemination of research and training to university administrators and faculty on "how systemic barriers operate and why these barriers disproportionately disadvantage women" (p. 202) as a particularly important tool for improving career advancement of women, particularly in STEM disciplines.

Our survey of the eight anonymous respondents asked whether training programs to educate administrators on issues women faculty care about or face might be useful. Five of the women believed they would be. We did not, however, ask about programs targeting young men who populate STEM programs as students, faculty, and nonacademic professionals. But De Welde and Stepnick (2014) did. One of their participants, a young graduate student in a STEM field, commented on how male graduate students in her particular program made life difficult and ultimately contributed to her decision to leave the program. She spoke of one young man telling her she was lucky, that it is easier for women to get into graduate school because they receive preferential treatment. In fact, she was as or more qualified to be in the program than the young man. Her contention is that sensitivity training should start early because many of these young men become faculty and should know how to treat their female graduate students.

The challenge with this approach lies in our natural desire to not intrude on others' privacy. We often make these types of programs voluntary and short in duration. In contrast, if we mandate training at the institution level, it helps. If such efforts systematically address bias over time, it works; one-shot, cure-all programs do not.

Barnhart points out that institutional avenues for two-way communication between female faculty and the administration can also give women a voice and provide an avenue for change. She contrasts Georgia Tech, where the female faculty "did not have a high level of confidence that the administration was on their side," to MIT, where

> the administration's reaction [to the institution's Status of Women Report in 1999] created a very positive atmosphere for women at MIT. We identified issues—low numbers, high attrition rates, little representation in administrative and senior committee positions. We clearly articulated what we wanted and why. And the administrators—the president and deans—supported us. They gave us the resources we needed to fix the problem.

The ideas these women have suggested can soften or even eliminate many biases that occur at the personal and institutional levels, but some bias originates at a societal level. In this country, we underestimate the value of mathematics and its importance to our country's future viability as a global leader. We pay cursory lip service to the notion of mentoring and role modeling. We adhere to images and perceptions of women as less capable than men when it comes to science and engineering. We live in a society that has radically changed over time but has somehow left women mired in culturally prescribed roles that discourage STEM careers. Biological or "nature" explanations still hold sway, identifying differences between men and women as genetic and thus unalterable: Women are just hardwired to be different than men. The logical extension of this argument is that nothing can be done to change the situation.

In reality, although some gender differences exist, variability within genders and overlap between genders also occur. Perlman and Jacobs mention that they are quite different from their sisters. Jacobs observes, "I always joke about our differences—artsy versus science." Likewise, Perlman notes, "Even though my sister and I are the offspring of the same mother, we are very different people."

The nature-nurture debate often surfaces as a contentious line of research when directed at gender differences because of perceptions about what biological differences mean. Psychologists, particularly those specializing in couples' therapy, often describe differences in communication styles or processing of emotions. Several of the women we interviewed sensed this difference between men and women. Perlman observes,

> I always thought the reason for any difference between girls and boys had to do with sexist parents bringing up their children to conform to certain expectations, until I had my own. Then I rethought my position. It is amazing how much of one's personality and skills are inbred, that come with the DNA or the mixture of chemicals you were steeped in while you grew inside your mother. . . . And my kids [a boy and a girl] couldn't be more different from each other.

Communication styles are deeply ingrained and very likely relate, at least in part, to the ways we process information. But culture or environment can reinforce, override, or provide alternatives to innate behaviors. For example, women tend to be risk averse, a behavior often linked anthropologically to women's role as caretakers for the next generation of the species. In contrast, risky behavior in men might relate to sexual selection (see Bertrand, 2010; Kolb, 2009; Schmitt, Realo, Voracek, & Allik, 2008). Innate behaviors? Perhaps. But they are also likely cultural in origin.

One way to reduce societal bias is suggested by Goffee and Jones (2009) and Goldsmith (2007): change personal habits in order to interface more effectively with other people, which builds on the old adage "I might not be able to change my neighbor, but I can change me."

For women in STEM the logical extension of this one-person-at-a-time approach to shifting cultural mainstays translates into more effective networking with other women in these fields. Blessing emphasizes that one of the most important aspects of WIMSE is

> ensuring that students bond, that they know people, even if they don't work in exactly the same discipline. They're all on the same career timeline. Every student will be able to talk to somebody she knew when she was eighteen who's also now in graduate school. And she can talk to another woman who's also looking for a job as an assistant professor.

Likewise, Birnbaum emphasizes, "Professional organizations also provide great opportunities to network and interact with people you might otherwise not regularly see." Throughout her career she has been very active in various societies, and she says, "All those connections work for me."

A more fundamental way to address societal bias is to embrace and accommodate gender differences while recognizing that women are just as smart and capable as men, thus creating a better work environment for everyone. Golden suggests, "The problem's not with women; the problem's the culture. . . . If you have to be a male to get ahead, then none of the women are ever going to get ahead. . . . Personally, I'm not going to spend all my time strategizing about how to 'be a man.' It's too much work."

Perlman prefers a positive tactic but admits reality gets in the way. "We lose women (and men) because of the unpleasantness of dealing with aggressive, overbearing, condescending individuals. . . . I'd rather we focus on building and sustaining cultures that foster creativity and productivity than concentrate solely on gender." Blessing and Golden succinctly sum up the situation. As Blessing puts it, "I'm bucking the 'fit in to get along' norm in favor of 'girls can be girls.'" Golden states even more bluntly, "I want the default to be 'I can figure this out,' not 'I'm dumb.'"

Over the past fifty years, we have seen changes in the role of women in society and in relationships between men and women that arose out of the women's movement. Sexual divisions of labor have diminished, and power dynamics in relationships and households have become more equitable. These changes have had a favorable influence on STEM women. Men have become more concerned about understanding women's perspectives because they have daughters, sisters, and significant others they want to encourage in the pursuit of STEM careers.

Golden mentions a male colleague concerned about his female students. "The issue hits close to home for him. He has daughters. He worries about them. He wants them to do well." Likewise, male colleagues ask Barnhart about how she balances work and family: "These men often [have] daughters who [are] trying to manage careers and families simultaneously. [They are] aware of the inherent challenges and supportive of women who [are] trying to make it work."

Individually centered initiatives, such as networking and the shifting views of fathers with daughters, represent agonizingly slow paths to cultural change. But they do represent a start. Whether differences between men and women are innate or cultural, social change can provide inroads to acceptance and understanding of these differences. Change perceptions, you change beliefs. Change beliefs, you change cultures.

The success of other movements has relied on many people becoming invested in their success and working actively together to solve the underlying problems. The issue of women in the STEM fields, however, is still often pigeonholed as a women's issue.

Golden participated in a program called COACh, which she says was useful, but

> they're trying to train us how to be more like men—how to interject like a man so you get noticed, how to negotiate salary like your male colleagues do. I ask myself, 'Why can't I do it like a woman would?' I like guys, I work with them every day, but I have no desire to act like they do. I've always felt that those types of workshops don't address the real issue.

Similarly, Perlman cautions, although women-only events "can be fun and even inspiring . . . making [an event] exclusionary to one gender perpetuates the myth that women are always getting favorable treatment or are incapable and need help."

In effect, these gender-based programs attempt to fix the woman, not the problem, which is perceptions, image, and the environment. And we should remember, at least one aspect of the environment—the struggle for work-life balance—touches both women and men. One study concludes, "Lack of flexibility in the workplace, dissatisfaction with career development opportunities, and low salaries are driving both men and women to re-consider their [academic] profession" (Association for Women in Science, 2012).

Today, we are a wired community. Media greatly influence our perceptions and over time modifies our beliefs and cultural predispositions about reality and women. In spite of evidence that girls have more extensive vocabularies and use longer sentences than boys at a young age, parents are two and an half times more likely to ask if their son is gifted rather than ask if their daughter is gifted (an intelligence issue). And they are twice as likely to ask whether a daughter is overweight than to ask the same about a son (an issue of public perception and acceptable image) (Eriksson et al., 2012; Stephens-Davidowitz, 2014).

Stereotyping of toys for boys and girls also seems to have increased, with a pink explosion in the toy aisles. A *Huffington Post* article contrasts the pink Lego sets aimed at girls today with a 1981 advertisement in which a little girl in pigtails and overalls proudly holds up something she has built from a traditional set of red, blue, and yellow Legos (Samakow, 2014). Lego did, however, add a female scientist to its set of characters for the first time in 2013, and companies such as GoldieBlox have as an explicit aim to inspire future female engineers at an early age with its toys. (For an active conversation on this subject, see Miller [2013] and Waldman [2013]).

Jacobs is optimistic: "Girls today have a lot more going for them if they are interested in STEM disciplines than we had as children. Despite the presence of stereotypes out there, people overall are more open to women being scientists than they were in the past." Blessing contends,

> The culture has and will continue to gradually change as more women enter the field. . . . I never expected that so much of my career would be devoted to working to improve the work climate for women and confronting environmental culture issues. I truly believe if we improve the climate for women, we improve the climate for everybody.

Hessler claims, "It's hard to change the landscape if [women are] not there." Her departure from the corporate setting, however, echoes an ominous theme (see Steele, 2013), which she discussed in some detail in her interview.

> Although women seem to be entering geology PhD programs at increasing rates, they are not pursuing academic careers, and in industry more women work part-time or quit their jobs than do men. When I started at GVSU, there were three women tenure-track faculty, none of us married or with children. Every male faculty member had a spouse at home. . . . A female undergraduate geology major

paying any attention would get the message that a woman needs to choose between having a tenure-track job and having a family.

At Chevron it's not quite so clear-cut, but women are the only ones with part-time positions, and at the time of this interview, my husband [was] one of only two people on his all-male team with young children and a spouse working full-time.

Media have muddied the waters by inadvertently and sometimes overtly reinforcing gender-based stereotypes. We see women leaving the professional ranks. We confront ingrained behaviors, some so subtle that they fail to register as biased actions deeply steeped in a patriarchal culture. All the young, anonymous academics listed changing the culture as one of their top recommendations, but none of them had any idea how to go about it.

We arguably have an uphill battle ahead of us. Can we overcome the mixed messages sent to young girls and women through television, magazines, and the Internet, and perhaps even their own parents at home and, later, colleagues in the workplace? Most societies resist change. Force, revolutionary or governmental, often becomes the tipping point because we are comfortable with inertia and like the way things have always been done. Those in power want to remain in power.

We in the United States push back against mandated change. And we push back hard. The women's suffrage movement began in 1848. It wasn't until thirty years later that the 19th Amendment to the Constitution, which grants women the right to vote, was written and introduced to Congress by Susan B. Anthony. It took an additional forty-one years for it to be enacted into law.

Likewise, Executive Order 10925 was signed into law by John Kennedy in 1961, followed in 1965 by Executive Order 11246 under Lyndon Johnson, to outlaw discrimination based on race, creed, or nationality. Gender wasn't added as a protected class until 1967. Forty-nine years after it had been first proposed, the Equal Rights Amendment, which grants women fair treatment under the law, passed in Congress in 1972 but was never ratified (Francis, n.d.). It has been reintroduced every year since 1982. Another example, the Supreme Court ruling in *Roe v. Wade* (1973), which guaranteed women the right to abort an unwanted pregnancy, also deals explicitly with women's rights. Like the Equal Rights Amendment, *Roe v. Wade* is under almost constant siege, as is the Patient Protection and Affordable Care Act of 2010, both of which greatly affect the well-being of women. The Lily Ledbetter Fair Pay Act (2009), one of the government's latest attempts to force change, targets unfair pay practices based on gender.

Despite this long history of fighting unfair and inequitable treatment of women in the United States, as of March 2014, women still earn on average 77 cents on the dollar compared to their male counterparts (Hill, 2014). A meager 16.6 percent of people serving on Fortune 500 corporate boards are women (Soares, Mulligan-Ferry, Fendler, & Kun, 2013) and a scant 4.6 percent of CEOs of Fortune 500 and 1000 corporations are women ("Women CEOs of the Fortune 1000," 2014). Only 19 percent of Congress's members are women ("Facts on Women in Congress," 2014). Less than a quarter of the presidents of doctorate-granting universities in the United States are women (Kim & Cook, 2014), and women remain underrepresented in almost all STEM PhD programs and advanced careers.

Large-scale national efforts have moved women forward in this country. We no longer argue about a woman's right to vote. We have looked (and will continue to look) at women as viable presidential candidates. But each workplace forms a subculture, and those in the majority typically hold sway. Within each subculture, polices designed to confront women's issues are sometimes summarily ignored, bypassed, or worked around to benefit the greatest voice. For instance, Claire Cain Miller (2014) writes,

> Sexism exists in many places, but start-up companies have particular qualities that allow problems to go unchecked. The lines between work and social life are often blurry because people tend to be young and to work long hours, and the founders and first employees are often friends. And start-ups pride themselves on a lack of bureaucracy, forgoing big-company layers like human resources departments. They say they can move faster because they aren't bogged down in protocol. But a result can be an anything-goes atmosphere . . . and a culture of intimidation and disrespect of women.

Maternity leave—now parental leave—is a prime example.

Even when rigorously supported, progressive policies cannot completely remove bias at all levels of society because they do not necessarily alter how people interface at the subcultural or interpersonal levels. We tend to interact with people who look and act like us. Ethnic neighborhoods pop up independent of any segregation policy. The proverbial "good old boys' club" still exists in many workplaces despite efforts to eliminate it. For instance, articles in the *New York Times* and the *Economist* point to a rampant boys-only culture in information technology, reporting depressing statistics, such as only 5 percent of venture capital investments in the United States go to firms owned by women (see Miller, 2014; "The Dark Side," 2014).

The Internet has enabled a host of subcultures to flourish across international boundaries. Emily Bell (2014) in *The Guardian* highlights the irony that surrounds some of the borderless enterprises spawned in this environment. She asserts that Internet journalism startups illustrate how self-identification influences our ability to be inclusive. These startups claim to be cutting-edge because they are breaking free of the corporate journalism structure that stifles diversity in news reporting. She challenges this claim and reprimands them for not hiring enough women or minorities. In effect she asks: How cutting-edge can they be when they maintain the same White male-dominated work structure?

Nate Silver, a statistician best known for his statistical projections of national elections and sports analysis, in his response to Bell (2014) illustrates some of the challenges of integrating women into a male-dominated culture. Bell chided Silver because only 30 percent of hires at his new company were women. As a statistician, Silver could have simply responded that this proportion of women is actually sizable given how few women possess the requisite qualifications—a statistics/journalism combination. Instead, he responded emotionally, claiming that as a stats and Internet geek he is an outsider and as a consequence his "clubhouse" could not possibly be biased in its hiring procedures.

People are often unwilling to admit they have blind spots or misconceptions about what equity means to other people. Indeed, we all cling to biases, misconceptions, and inappropriate stereotypes. We put people into categories to simplify the complexity of the world. It is part of what makes us human. But categories hide unconscious biases.

We have moved forward in our attempts at making racism and sexism culturally unacceptable. An unintended consequence, however, hampers our progress. Our advances have had a chilling effect that hinders our ability to engage in frank discussions about the hidden choices we make and their impact on others. They put us on the defensive. For example, if the statement "I really don't think having a baby will affect the quality of her research" was simply taken as an attempt to educate someone with a misperception rather than as an accusation of sexism by someone with a feminist perspective, change might occur more rapidly.

We as a society refuse to change without external pressure, and when that pressure is applied, *we push back*. That's the reality. And it's a reality that plays out daily in the lives of many STEM women, particularly those who work in environments in which they are either the lone woman or, at best, greatly outnumbered.

The overall tenor of the stories in this book illustrates how small-scale interactions influence women. At the national level, discussions of women in science are forceful and critical; at the individual level, women tell more nuanced stories and learn to work within the system in which they find themselves. The tone these women use to tell their stories reflects a more pragmatic perspective given the realities of being different and the danger of having their message misconstrued.

As a society we can benefit greatly from the inclusion and full participation of women in STEM. But we need comprehensive action and a shift in our understanding of the role and value of women's participation in the workplace. Will we undertake it, or will we continue to patch together piecemeal approaches to attracting more girls into STEM disciplines and moving them through the pipeline into industry, government, and faculty positions at research universities? The question remains: Is the past the future?

REFERENCES

Association for Women in Science. (2012). *The work-life integration overload.* Retrieved from http://c.ymcdn.com/sites/www.awis.org/resource/resmgr/imported/AWIS_Work_Life_Balance_Executive_Summary.pdf

Bell, E. (2014, March 12). Journalism startups aren't a revolution if they're filled with all these White men. *The Guardian.* Retrieved from http://www.theguardian.com/commentisfree/2014/mar/12/journalism-startups-diversity-ezra-klein-nate-silver

Bertrand, M. (2010). New perspectives on gender. In D. Card & O. Ashenfelter (Eds.), *Handbook of Labor Economics* (Vol. 4B, pp. 1546–1592). New York, NY: Elsevier.

Bird, S. (2011). Unsettling universities' incongruous, gendered bureaucratic structures: A case-study approach. *Gender, Work, and Organization, 18*(2), 202–230.

The dark side: Founder's blues. (2014, January 18). *The Economist.* Retrieved from http://media.economist.com/sites/default/files/sponsorships/%5BKY 56b%5DHuawei/180114_SR.pdf

De Welde, K., & Stepnick, A. (Eds.). (2014). *Disrupting the culture of silence: Confronting gender inequality and making change in higher education.* Sterling, VA: Stylus.

Eriksson, M., Marschik, P. B., Tulviste, T., Almgren, M., Pereira, M, P., Wehberg, S., . . . Gallego, C. (2012). Differences between girls and boys in emerging language skills: Evidence from 10 language communities. *British Journal of Developmental Psychology, 30*(2), 326–343. Retreived from http://onlinelibrary.wiley.com/doi/10.1111/j.2044-835X.2011.02042.x/ abstract

Exec. Order No. 10925, 26 C.F.R. 1977 (1961).

Exec. Order No. 11246, 30 C.F.R. 12319 (1965).

Facts on women in Congress 2014. (2014). Retrieved from Rutgers Center for American Women in Politics website: http://www.cawp.rutgers.edu/ fast_facts/levels_of_office/Congress-CurrentFacts.php

Francis, R. W. (n.d.). *The equal rights amendment: Unfinished business of the Constitution.* Retrieved from http://www.equalrightsamendment.org/ history.htm

Geary, D. C., Hoard, M. K., Nugent, L., & Bailey, D. H. (2013). Adolescents' functional numeracy is predicted by their school entry number system. *PLOS One.* Retrieved from http://www.plosone.org/article/ info:doi/10.1371/journal.pone.0054651

Goffee, R., & Jones, G. (2009). *Clever: Leading your smartest, most creative people.* Cambridge, MA: Harvard Business Review Press.

Goldsmith, M. (2007). *What got you here won't keep you there: How successful people become even more successful.* New York, NY: Hyperion.

Hill, C. (2014). *The simple truth about the gender pay gap.* (2014). Retrieved from http://www.aauw.org/research/the-simple-truth-about-the-gender-pay-gap/

IntelPR. (2011). Exposure to engineering doubles teens' career interest etrieved from http://newsroom.intel.com/community/intel_newsroom/ blog/2011/12/06/exposure-to-engineering-doubles-teens-career-interest

Kantrowitz, B. (2005, October 24). When women lead. Vote of confidence. *Newsweek*, 67.

Kim, Y. M., & Cook, B. J. (2014). *Diversity at the top: The American college president 2012*. Retrieved from https://www.aacu.org/ocww/volume41_1/data.cfm

Kolb, D. M. (2009). Too bad for the women or does it have to be? Gender and negotiation research over the past twenty-five years. *Negotiation Journal*, *25*, 515–531.

Lilly Ledbetter Fair Pay Act, S. 181, 111th Cong. (2009).

McGinn, D. (2005, October 23). Vote of confidence. *Newsweek*. Retrieved from http://www.newsweek.com/vote-confidence-120879

Miller, C. C. (2013, November 20). Ad takes off online: Less doll, more awl [Web log post]. Retrieved from http://bits.blogs.nytimes.com/2013/11/20/a-viral-video-encourages-girls-to-become-engineers/

Miller, C. C. (2014, April 5). Technology's man problem. *New York Times*. Retrieved from http://www.nytimes.com/2014/04/06/technology/technologys-man-problem.html

Office of Science and Technology Policy. (2013). Obama announces new steps to meet president's goal of preparing 100,000 STEM teachers [Press release]. Retrieved from http://www.whitehouse.gov/sites/default/files/docs/stem_teachers_release_3-18-13_doc.pdf

Patient Protection and Affordable Care Act, 42 U.S.C. § 18001 et seq. (2010).

Roe v. Wade, 410 U.S. 113 (1973).

Samakow, J. (2014, January 17). Lego add from 1981 should be required reading for everyone who makes, buys or sells toys. *Huffington Post*. Retrieved from http://www.huffingtonpost.com/2014/01/17/lego-ad-1981_n_4617704.html

Schmitt, D. P., Realo, A., Voracek, M., & Allik, J. (2008). Can't a man be more like a woman? Sex differences in big five personality traits across 55 cultures. *Journal of Personality and Social Psychology*, *94*(1), 168–182.

Soares, R., Mulligan-Ferry, L., Fendler, E., & Kun, E. W. C. (2013). *2013 catalyst census: Fortune 500 women board directors*. Retrieved from http://www.catalyst.org/knowledge/2013-catalyst-census-fortune-500-women-board-directors

Steele, B. (2013). *Something about STEM drives women out*. Retrieved from http://phys.org/news/2013-11-stem-women.html

Stephens-Davidowitz, S. (2014). Google, tell me. Is my son a genius? *New York Times*. Retrieved from http://www.nytimes.com/2014/01/19/opinion/sunday/google-tell-me-is-my-son-a-genius.html

10 questions for Madeleine Albright. (2008, January 21). *Time*, 8.

Waldman, K. (2013, November 19). This awesome ad, set to the Beastie Boys, is how to get girls to become engineers [Web log post]. Retrieved from http://www.slate.com/blogs/xx_factor/2013/11/19/goldieblox_commercial_rewrites_the_beastie_boys_urges_young_girls_to_pursue.html

Who says math has to be boring? [Editorial]. (2013, December 7). *New York Times*. Retrieved from http://www.nytimes.com/2013/12/08/opinion/sunday/who-says-math-has-to-be-boring.html?hp&rref=opinion&_r=2&

Women CEOs of the Fortune 1000. (2014). Retrieved from http://www.catalyst.org/knowledge/women-ceos-fortune-1000

appendix

WEB-BASED STEM-RELATED RESOURCES FOR GIRLS AND WOMEN

THIS APPENDIX PROVIDES a sampling of STEM-related online resources targeted to the interests and needs of K–12 girls and college age and professional women. We've organized this document into two main sections—websites related to K–12 and those geared toward college students and professional women. In addition, we've included two fairly extensive reading lists of books and articles specific to women in science and engineering, and a short list of books about women and leadership.

K–12 RESOURCES

The Internet provides a wealth of information about programs designed to encourage girls' interest in STEM-related fields. Following are several examples we found especially informative. The name of the organization, its Web address, and a brief description of each are provided. To make it easier for the reader, we divided the material into four subsections: comprehensive websites; program-specific websites; college- and university-sponsored program websites; and research, media outlets, and other related materials. All lists are arranged alphabetically.

Career Cornerstone Center

www.careercornerstone.org/women.htm

The Career Cornerstone Center, which is part of the Alfred P. Sloan Foundation, provides support for girls and women who are interested in exploring career paths in STEM, computing, and health care. The site offers ideas for networking, exploring STEM via summer projects, and scouting and providing teacher resources. Viewers can search this site by discipline.

Engineering Education Service Center

www.engineeringedu.com

The Engineering Education Service Center specializes in providing products for K–12 schools to teach and share the fun of engineering. The site provides a list of pre-engineering summer camps by state (some gender specific).

Girl Geeks

www.girlgeeks.org/education/resources.shtml

This website provides a list of resources and outreach programs for girls and technology.

Iowa State University Resources

www.pwse.iastate.edu/resources.html

The Iowa State University Program for Women in Science and Engineering offers an extensive list of websites for girls, teachers, and parents of female students in elementary, middle, and high school and at the undergraduate level.

Advocates for Women in Science, Engineering and Mathematics

www.awsem.com

This group provides mentorship programs and workshops to encourage and support women and girls with science, engineering, and mathematics.

Aspire

http://aspire.swe.org

This K–12 outreach program, sponsored by the Society of Women Engineers, has information about scholarships, events, chapter locations, and role models.

Association of Women in Mathematics Mentor Network

https://sites.google.com/site/awmmath/programs/mentor-network

The network matches mentors with girls and women who are interested in mathematics or are pursuing careers in mathematics. Grade school and high school students can apply. Mentors may be women or men, but students have the option of indicating a strong preference for a female mentor on the application.

Brain Cake

www.braincake.org

This site is sponsored by the Girls, Math and Science Partnership of the Carnegie Science Center, whose mission is to engage, educate, and embrace girls, ages seven to eleven, as architects of change. The program works with girls, parents, and the community to encourage middle school girls to pursue STEM careers.

DigiGirlz

www.microsoft.com/en-us/diversity/programs/digigirlz/default.aspx

Microsoft's DigiGirlz gives high school girls the opportunity to learn about careers in technology. The company hosts DigiGirlz Days so that students interact with Microsoft employees and see what it's like to work there. Microsoft also sponsors a multiday High Tech Camp for girls at no cost.

Engineer Girl

www.engineergirl.org

The Engineer Girl website is designed to bring national attention to the exciting opportunities engineering offers girls and women. The website is a service of the National Academy of Engineering and grew out of the work of the academy's Committee on the Diversity of the Engineering Workforce.

Engineer Your Life
www.engineeryourlife.org
This website provides a guide to engineering for high school girls. Major funding for Engineer Your Life is provided by the National Science Foundation and the Northrop Grumman Foundation.

Expanding Your Horizons Network
www.expandingyourhorizons.org
This network encourages middle and high school girls to pursue STEM careers by providing role models and hands-on activities.

Figure This!
www.figurethis.org
This website targets junior high school girls by presenting math challenges for families by the National Science Foundation and the U.S. Department of Education.

First LEGO League Robotics Program
www.usfirst.org/roboticsprograms/fll
The program exposes Lego robotics teams, K–12, to the values of teamwork and cooperation in science and engineering in a fun and supportive environment. Teams can be gender specific.

For Women in Science
http://www.loreal.com/Foundation/Article.aspx?topcode=Foundation _AccessibleScience_WomenExcellence_W
In partnership with UNESCO, the For Women in Science program provides support for women researchers on all continents and at different points in their careers. This may come in the early stages of a young researcher's vocation or be in celebration of a full career committed to scientific advancement. A world-wide programmatic offshoot is For Girls in Science, which offers summer camps and opportunities for girls to experience STEM options.

GEMS: Girls Excelling in Math and Science
www.gemsclub.org
The GEMS club exposes fifth and sixth grade girls to the fun and wonder of math, science, and technology. The website provides instructions for starting a club and for club activities.

Girl Scouts
www.girlscouts.org/program/basics/science
See also http://forgirls.girlscouts.org
Through its programs, Girl Scouts introduces girls of every age to STEM experiences relevant to everyday life. Whether they're discovering how a car engine runs, learning how to manage finances, or exploring careers in STEM fields, girls are fast-forwarding into the future. The Scouts' approach to STEM is unique because the experiences are framed within the context of leadership. The activities are led by girls and are hands-on and cooperation based. Girl Scouts partners with organizations like Microsoft, Lego (robotics), and Lockheed Martin (field trips and shadowing opportunities) to provide some of its programs.

Girl Up
www.girlup.org
Girl Up is an innovative campaign of the United Nations Foundation. We give American girls the opportunity to become global leaders and channel their energy and compassion to raise awareness and funds for United Nations programs that help some of the world's hardest-to-reach adolescent girls.

Girls Inc. Operation SMART
www.girlsinc.org/resources/programs/girls-inc-operation-smart.html
This website develops girls' enthusiasm for and skills in STEM through hands-on activities and interactions with women and men pursuing STEM careers. Girls Inc. has developed an approach organizations can apply to their own single events or to their multiyear programming.

Girls Rock Math
www.girlsrockmathematics.com
Based in Seattle, Washington, this program offers summer and after-school activities and classes using its unique, art-based curriculum for girls in grades K–8. The program strives to boost interest and confidence in mathematics by emphasizing collaboration, persistence, strategy building, and mathematical thinking.

Girlstart
www.girlstart.org
Girlstart's mission is to empower girls in STEM. Founded in Austin, Texas, in 1997, Girlstart is one of the few community-based informal education programs in the nation specifically dedicated to empowering and equipping K–12 girls in STEM. The organization offers after-school programs, Saturday camps, and summer camps.

Inspiring Girls Now in Technology Evolution (IGNITE)
www.igniteworldwide.org
IGNITE is a nonprofit based in Seattle, Washington, sponsored by the Seattle Public School District, Microsoft, and Synapse Product Development. It offers an affordable, community-based, multifaceted approach to STEM education, providing tool kits and curricula that allow educators across the globe to replicate the successful model that thrives in Seattle public schools.

Inspiring Girls in Cyber Security
www.lockheedmartin.com/us/isgs/connect/cyber-stem-11-27-12.html
Lockheed Martin's program introduces girls to career options in the industry. The company is partners with Girl Scouts and the National Science Foundation, among others. It participates in the Annual Cool Careers in Cyber Security for Girls Summit for middle-school-age girls.

My Gifted Girl
www.mygiftedgirl.com
My Gifted Girl is a community for gifted girls and women in all subjects, including STEM fields. Organization members serve as a resource for parents, educators, mentors, and other organizations that support talented girls and women.

National Center for Women and Information Technology
www.ncwit.org
The NCWIT Award for Aspirations in Computing recognizes high school girls for their computing-related achievements and interests.

National Engineers Week Foundation
http://discovere.org
This site offers programs, activities, and guidelines for starting programs for girls interested in engineering.

National Girls Collaborative Project
www.ngcproject.org/program/wise-women-interested-science-and-engineering
Funded in part by the National Science Foundation, this project is designed to reach girl-serving STEM organizations across the United States. Organizations host local collaboratives that take diverse approaches, but they all work to increase gender equity in STEM fields. The project currently has twenty-eight collaboratives serving thirty-eight states and plans to expand to at least an additional three states in upcoming years. To find a collaborative in your area, click your state on the website's map. The site also features a list of programs and contacts.

Sally Ride Science
https://sallyridescience.com
Sally Ride Science maintains a strong focus on STEM education among elementary and middle school students and the real-world applications of STEM concepts. The science books, student programs, and professional development programs place a strong emphasis on gender and racial equality in the classroom and provide role models of working scientists, engineers, and mathematicians who exemplify this diversity in their fields. Partnerships with EducationUnlimited to offer summer camps and ExxonMobil to conduct professional development programs for elementary and middle school math and science teachers, specialists, and administrators are two of its numerous collaborations with other foundations and corporations.

Science Club for Girls

www.scienceclubforgirls.org

The mission of this organization is to increase the self-confidence and literacy in STEM in K–12 girls belonging to groups that are underrepresented in these fields through free programs that include hands-on learning, mentorship, and leadership opportunities.

Techbridge

www.techbridgegirls.org

Techbridge is funded by the National Science Foundation and hosted by Chabot Space and Science Center, Oakland, California, in collaboration with Chevron to encourage girls' interests in technology, science, and engineering.

COLLEGE- AND UNIVERSITY-SPONSORED WEBSITES

Colleges and universities across the country also offer STEM-related programs during the year and as summer experiences specifically for girls. We provide links to a few of these but suggest that you investigate the websites of the community colleges, colleges, and universities in your area for more examples of exciting outreach efforts. A school-based program is also included in this section.

Arizona State University
Compugirls

http://sustainability.asu.edu/research/project/618/compugirls%3A-a-culturally-relevant-technology-program-for-girls

Prime the Pipeline Project

https://prime.asu.edu/content/p3

Boise State University
e-Girls (grades 9–11)

http://coen.boisestate.edu/k-12/files/2011/06/E-Girls-Flyer2014.pdf

Clemson University
Camp Voyager (South Carolina)

www.clemson.edu/yli/pages/voyager.php

Embry-Riddle Aeronautical University
Girls Exploring Math
http://daytonabeach.erau.edu/degrees/summer-camps

Fox Valley Technical College (Wisconsin)
GirlTech Summer Camp
http://www.fvtc.edu/news/Home/girltech-summer-camp-126029

Grand Valley State University
Regional Math and Science Center (Allendale, Micigan)
www.gvsu.edu/rmsc

Kansas State University
Girls Researching Our World
www.k-state.edu/grow

Massachusetts Institute of Technology
Office of Engineering Outreach Programs
http://web.mit.edu/stem/STEM_Home.html

MIT Women's Technology Program
http://wtp.mit.edu

Northern Illinois University
STEM Outreach
www.niu.edu/stem/resources/k_12_Student_Resources.shtml

Pollard Middle School (Cambridge, Massachusetts)
Science Club for Girls
http://scienceclubforgirls.org
www.girlsangle.org

Temple University
Girls and Mathematics Program
https://math.temple.edu/girlsandmath

University of California, Berkeley
Mathematical Science Research Institute
www.msri.org/web/msri;jsessionid=848C5533EFE0D0853BEE24790
B43C9D7

University of Kansas
Society of Women Engineers Weekend of Engineering
www.engr.ku.edu/prospective/undergraduate/events.html

University of Nebraska, Lincoln
All Girls All Math
www.math.unl.edu/programs/agam

Vermont Technical College Women in Technology
http://web.vtc.edu/WIT

RESEARCH, MEDIA OUTLETS, AND OTHER RELATED MATERIALS

Center for Children and Technology
http://cct.edc.org
This center conducts research and designs, develops, and evaluates curricula that integrate technology with education and after-school programs.

Exploring Gender and Technology
www.gse.harvard.edu/~wit/exploring/index.htm
The goal of this website-based instructional resource is to engage learners in an interactive environment that allows them to use existing research and explore innovative models to construct gender-equitable technology programs and polices. This site presents current research, perspectives, and innovative approaches to the gender gap in technology collected from secondary research. It offers statistics, case studies, videos, online discussion, an annotated bibliography, and links for educators and girls.

National Women's History Project
www.nwhp.org
This educational nonprofit organization celebrates the diverse and historic accomplishments of women by providing educational resources and programs.

Appendix

Science, Gender, and Afterschool
www.afterschool.org
http://edequity.org/programs/science-and-math-programs
http://edequity.org/programs/gender-equity
These sites are for researchers, education professionals, policy makers, parents, and others interested in strengthening the role of after-school education by increasing girls' participation in STEM education and careers.

Smart Girl
www.smartgirl.org
This site offers a chat space for girls interested in computers to discuss all sorts of issues including games, movies, social issues, and websites.

Tech Up
www.techup.org/media/media_main.html
The goal of this Web page is to encourage women and girls, and the organizations that serve them, to use technology to share ideas, opinions, support, creativity, and political action. Discussions focus heavily on media imaging of women. The project is cosponsored by the Women's Foundation and the Electronic Frontier Foundation and is funded by Pacific Bell.

Whyville
www.whyville.net/smmk/top/gates
Whyville is designed to help elementary, middle, and high school students understand and enjoy science. It uses avatars, games, computer simulation and modeling, a Whyville newspaper, and interactivity among Whyville participants.

Women@NASA
women.nasa.gov/about-nasa-girls
This site allows students to meet, interact with, and read biographies of inspiring women who have math, science, and technology careers at NASA. Teaching guides are provided to incorporate this material into classroom curricula.

Women in Science, Technology, Engineering, and Mathematics on the Air!

www.womeninscience.org

This radio series broadcast by WAMC/Northeast Public Radio airs stories of women working in STEM fields to increase participation of women in science and provides information about programs and practices throughout the United States in an attempt to broaden the participation of women in STEM. The National Science Foundation is a primary sponsor of the program.

RESOURCES FOR COLLEGE AND PROFESSIONAL WOMEN

The Internet provides a wealth of information about programs designed to encourage college women's interests in STEM-related fields and resources for professionals in these fields. Any search engine will yield multiple listings. We provide several examples we found especially informative. We've listed the name of the organization, the Web address, and a brief description of each. To make it easier for the reader, the material is divided into four sections: comprehensive websites, discipline-specific websites, websites for undergraduates, and scholarships and fellowships at the doctoral and career levels. All lists are arranged alphabetically.

COMPREHENSIVE WEBSITES

ADVANCE Portal

www.portal.advance.vt.edu/index.php

This is a clearinghouse for materials produced through National Science Foundation grants in the Increasing the Participation and Advancement of Women in Academic Science and Engineering Careers program.

American Association for Women in Community Colleges

www.aawccnatl.org

According to its website, AAWCC has a "commitment to equity and excellence in education and employment for women in community, junior and technical colleges."

American Association of University Women

www.aauw.org

AAUW has a broad mission of empowering women that includes advocacy, research, leadership opportunities, and scholarships. Women in STEM disciplines make up one major area in its mission. It has published numerous research reports on girls and women in science.

Association for Women in Science

http://awis.org

The umbrella organization for women in science and technology fields, AWIS has regional and university chapters. Like the American Association of University Women, it provides advocacy, research, leadership opportunities, and scholarships.

National Research Council's Committee on Women in Science, Engineering, and Medicine

http://sites.nationalacademies.org/pga/cwsem/index.htm

The goal of this committee is to increase the participation of women in the sciences through research and advocacy.

Women in Science, Technology, Engineering, and Mathematics on the Air!

www.womeninscience.org

This radio series broadcast by WAMC/Northeast Public Radio airs stories of women working in STEM fields to increase participation of women in science and provides information about programs and practices throughout the United States in an attempt to broaden the participation of women in STEM. The National Science Foundation is a primary sponsor of the program.

DISCIPLINE-SPECIFIC WEBSITES

Each website highlights career, mentoring, and networking opportunities.

American Astronomical Society Committee on the Status of Women in Astronomy

www.aas.org/cswa

American Chemical Society Women Chemists Committee
http://womenchemists.sites.acs.org

American Physical Society Committee on the Status of Women in Physics
www.aps.org/programs/women/index.cfm

Anita Borg Institute (women in technology)
http://anitaborg.org

Association for Women in Computing
www.awc-hq.org/home.html

Association for Women Geoscientists
www.awg.org

Association for Women in Mathematics
https://sites.google.com/site/awmmath

Computing Research Association Committee on the Status of Women in Computing Research
www.cra-w.org

Institute of Electrical and Electronics Engineers Women in Engineering
www.ieee.org/membership_services/membership/women/index.html

National Center for Women and Information Technology
www.ncwit.org

National Institute for Women in Trades, Technology and Science
www.iwitts.org

Society of Women Engineers
http://societyofwomenengineers.swe.org

Women in Bio
www.womeninbio.org

Appendix

Women in Engineering Proactive Network
www.wepan.org

Women in Technology International
www.witi.com/center/aboutwiti

WEBSITES FOR UNDERGRADUATES

Career Cornerstone Center
www.careercornerstone.org/women.htm
We've included this website here, even though it appears in the "Comprehensive Websites" section under "K–12 Resources," to make sure young college women also take advantage of this great resource. The Career Cornerstone Center is a clearinghouse for multiple age groups of students, parents, and educators interested in careers in STEM fields. The site provides an extensive list of resources for girls and women as well as underrepresented minorities, which include scholarship opportunities, discipline-specific organizations, and summer programs.

Girl Geeks
www.girlgeeks.org
This site is aimed at encouraging girls and women to pursue careers in technology by providing information on education, careers, and running a tech business.

MentorNet
www.mentornet.net
This is an online mentoring network for women and minorities in science and technology.

National Science Foundation Research Experiences for Undergraduates
www.nsf.gov/crssprgm/reu/index.jsp
The National Science Foundation funds research sites that focus on training undergraduates in STEM fields. Students work closely with faculty on specific research projects.

American Association for the Advancement of Science International Funding Opportunities for Women in Science, Technology and Engineering
www.aaas.org/programs/international/wist/fundwomen.shtml
www.aaas.org/search/gss/Funding%20Opportunities%20for%20Women%20in%20Science%2C%20Technology%20and%20Engineering
These sites provide lists of funding sources for work and study in the United States and abroad.

Association for Women in Science Educational and Professional Development Awards
www.awis.org/displaycommon.cfm?an=1&subarticlenbr=510
AWIS gives awards for professional development for women in STEM fields, graduate students, and scientists in their early careers.

L'Oréal USA Fellowships for Women in Science Program
www.aaas.org/programs/education/loreal.shtml
This is the U.S. version of the UNESCO fellowship that funds five researchers beginning their careers.

Scholarships for Women
www.scholarshipsforwomen.net
This independently run website contains a list of scholarships available in different STEM fields.

UNESCO Fellowships Programmes
www.unesco.org/new/en/fellowships
Funding is provided to support 15 doctoral or post-doctoral women in life sciences fields to conduct research.

BOOKS ON WOMEN IN SCIENCE AND ENGINEERING

Ambrose, S. A., Dunkle, K. L., Lazarus, B. B., Nair, I., & Harkus, D. A. (2004). *Journeys of women in science and engineering: No universal constants.* Philadelphia, PA: Temple University Press.

Appendix

American Association of University Women Educational Foundation. (2004). *Under the microscope: A decade of gender equity projects in the sciences.* Washington DC: Author.

Bilimoria, D., & Liang, X. (2012). *Gender equity in science and engineering.* New York, NY: Routledge.

Bystydzienski, J. M., & Bird, S. R. (Eds.). 2006. *Removing barriers: Women in academic science, technology, engineering, and mathematics.* Bloomington IN: Indiana University Press.

Ceci, S. J., & Williams, W. M. (2007). *Why aren't more women in science? Top researchers debate the evidence.* Washington DC: American Psychological Association.

Ceci, S. J., & Williams, W. M. (2010). *The mathematics of sex: How biology and society conspire to limit talented women and girls.* Oxford, UK: Oxford University Press.

Committee on Gender Differences in the Careers of Science, Engineering, and Mathematics Faculty; Committee on Women in Science, Engineering, and Medicine; Committee on National Statistics; & National Research Council. (2010). *Gender differences at critical transitions in the careers of science, engineering, and mathematics faculty.* Washington DC: National Academies Press.

Committee on Maximizing the Potential of Women in Academic Science and Engineering, National Academy of Sciences, National Academy of Engineering, & Institute of Medicine. (2006). *Biological, social, organizational components of success for women in academic science and engineering: Report of a workshop.* Washington DC: National Academies Press.

Committee on Maximizing the Potential of Women in Academic Science and Engineering, National Academy of Sciences, National Academy of Engineering, & Institute of Medicine. (2007). *Beyond bias and barriers: Fulfilling the potential of women in academic science and engineering.* Washington DC: National Academies Press.

Committee on the Guide to Recruiting and Advancing Women Scientists and Engineers in Academia, Committee on Women in Science and Engineering, & National Research Council. (2006). *To recruit and advance: Women students and faculty in U.S. science and engineering.* Washington DC: National Academies Press.

Daniell, E. (2006). *Every other Thursday: Stories and strategies from successful women scientists.* New Haven, CT: Yale University Press.

Davis, C.-S., Ginorio, A. B., Hollenshead, C. S., Lazarus, B. B., & Rayman, P. M. (Eds.). (1996). *The equity equation: Fostering the advancement of women in science, math, and engineering.* San Francisco, CA: Jossey-Bass.

Dean, D. J. (2009). *Getting the most out of your mentoring relationships: A handbook for women in STEM.* New York, NY: Springer.

Didion, C. J., Guenther, R. S., Gunderson, V.; Rapporteurs; Committee on Women in Science, Engineering, and Medicine; Policy and Global Affairs; & National Research Council. (2012). *From science to business: Preparing female scientists and engineers for successful transitions into entrepreneurship: Summary of a workshop.* Washington DC: National Academies Press.

Etzkowitz, H., Kemelgor, C., & Uzzi, B. (2000). *Athena unbound: The advancement of women in science and technology.* Cambridge, UK: Cambridge University Press.

Fisher, R. L. (2007). *Making science fair: How can we achieve equal opportunity for men and women in science?* Lanham, MD: University Press of America.

Hall, L. E. (2007). *Who's afraid of Marie Curie?: The challenges facing women in science.* Emeryville, CA: Seal Press.

Hill, C., Corbett, C., & St. Rose, A. (2010). *Why so few women in science, technology, and mathematics?* Washington DC: American Association of University Women.

Huyer, S., & Westholm, G. (2007). *Gender indicators in science, engineering and technology: An information toolkit.* Paris, France: UNESCO Publishing.

Karnes, F. A., & Stephens, K. R. (2002). *Young women of achievement: A resource for girls in science, math and technology.* Amherst, NY: Prometheus Books.

Long, J. S. (Ed.). (2001). *From scarcity to visibility: Gender differences in the careers of doctoral scientists and engineers.* Washington DC: National Academies Press.

Monosson, E. (2008). *Motherhood, the elephant in the laboratory: Women scientists speak out.* Ithaca, NY: Cornell University Press.

Preston, A. E. (2004). *Leaving science: Occupational exit from scientific careers.* New York, NY: Russell Sage Foundation.

Purcell, K. (2012). *Unlocking your brilliance: Smart strategies for women to thrive in science, technology, engineering, and math.* Austin, TX: Greenleaf Book Group Press.

Rosser, S. V. (2004). *The science glass ceiling: Academic women scientists and the struggle to succeed.* New York, NY: Routledge.

Rosser, S. V. (2012). *Breaking into the lab: Engineering progress for women in science.* New York, NY: New York University Press.

Selby, C. C. (Ed.). (1999). *Women in science and engineering: Choices for success* (Annals of the New York Academy of Sciences). New York, NY: New York Academy of Sciences.

Smith-Doerr, L. (2004). *Women's work: Gender equality vs. hierarchy in the life sciences.* Boulder, CO: Lynne Rienner.

Stewart, A. J., Malley, J. E., & LaVaque-Manty, D. (2007). *Transforming science and engineering: Advancing academic women.* Ann Arbor, MI: University of Michigan Press.

Appendix

Wyer, M., Barbercheck, M., Geisman, D., Örün Öztürk, H., & Wayne, M. (Eds.). (2001). *Women, science and technology: A reader in feminist science studies.* New York, NY: Routledge.

Xie, Y., & Shauman, K. A. 2003. *Women in science: Career processes and outcomes.* Cambridge, MA: Harvard University Press.

ARTICLES ON WOMEN IN SCIENCE AND ENGINEERING

Adamo, S. A. (2013). Attrition of women in the biological sciences: Workload, motherhood, and other explanations revisited. *BioScience, 63*(1), 43–48.

Addessi, E., Borgi, M., & Palagi, E. (2012). Is primatology an equal-opportunity discipline? *PLOS One, 7*(1), e30458.

Ampaw, F. D., & Jaeger, A, J. (2011). Understanding the factors affecting degree completion of doctoral women in the science and engineering fields. *New Directions for Institutional Research, 2011*(152), 59–73.

Amrein, K., Langmann, A., Fahrleitner-Pammer, A., Pieber, T. R., & Zollner-Schwetz, I. (2011). Women underrepresented on editorial boards of 60 major medical journals. *Gender Medicine, 8*(6), 378–387.

Barres, B. A. (2006). Does gender matter? *Nature, 442*(13), 133–136.

Cameron, E. Z., Gray, M. E., & White, A. M. (2013). Is publication rate an equal opportunity metric? *Trends in Ecology & Evolution, 28*(1), 7–8.

Ceci, S. J., & Williams, W. M. (2011). Understanding current causes of women's underrepresentation in science. *Proceedings of the National Academy of Sciences, 108*(8), 3157–3162.

Ceci, S. J., Williams, W. M., & Barnett, S. M. (2009). Women's underrepresentation in science: Sociocultural and biological considerations. *Psychological bulletin, 135*(2), 218.

Fara, P. (2013). Women in science: Weird sisters? *Nature, 495*(7439), 43–44.

Fox, M. F., Sonnert, G., & Nikiforova, I. (2009). Successful programs for undergraduate women in science and engineering: Adapting versus adopting the institutional environment. *Research in Higher Education, 50*(4), 333–353.

Fox, M. F., Sonnert, G., & Nikiforova, I. (2011). Programs for undergraduate women in science and engineering: Issues, problems, and solutions. *Gender & Society, 25*(5), 589–615.

Guiso, L., Monte, F., Sapienza, P., & Zingales, L. (2008). Culture, gender, and math. *Science, 320,* 1164–1165.

Hyde, J. S., Lindberg, S. M., Linn, M. C., Ellis, A. B., & Williams, C. C. (2008). Gender similarities characterize math performance. *Science, 321,* 494–495.

Karukstis, K. K., Gourley, B. L., Wright, L. L., & Rossi, M. (2010). Mentoring strategies to recruit and advance women in science and engineering. *Journal of Chemical Education, 87*(4), 355–356.

Ledford, H., Petherick, A., Abbott, A., & Nordling, L. (2013). From the frontline: 30 something science. *Nature, 495*(7439), 28.

Martin, L. J. (2012). Where are the women in ecology? *Frontiers in Ecology and the Environment, 10*(4), 177–178.

McCook, A. (2013). Women in biotechnology: Barred from the boardroom. *Nature, 495*(7439), 25.

McGuire, K. L., Primack, R. B., & Losos, E. C. (2012). Dramatic improvements and persistent challenges for women ecologists. *BioScience, 62*(2), 189–196.

Monroe, K., Ozyurt, S., Wrigley, T., & Alexander, A. (2008). Gender equality in academia: Bad news from the trenches, and some possible solutions. *Perspectives in Politics, 6*(2), 215–233.

Moss-Racusin, C. A., Dovidio, J. F., Brescoll, V. L., Graham, M. J., & Handelsman, J. (2012). Science faculty's subtle gender biases favor male students. *Proceedings of the National Academy of Sciences, 109*(41): 16474–16479.

Nelson, D. J., & Brammer, C. N. (2008). Women in science: A top-down approach. *Science, 320*, 1159–1160.

Petersen, A. M., Riccaboni, M., Stanley, H. E., & Pammolli, F. (2012). Persistence and uncertainty in the academic career. *Proceedings of the National Academy of Sciences, 109*(14), 5213–5218.

Raymond, J. (2013). Sexist attitudes: Most of us are biased. *Nature, 495*(7439), 33–34.

Rosser, S. V., & Zieseniss, M. (2000). Career issues and laboratory climates: Different challenges and opportunities for women engineers and scientists (Survey of Fiscal Year 1997 POWRE Awardees). *Journal of Women and Minorities in Science and Engineering, 6*, 95–114.

Schilt, K., & Wiswall, M. (2008). Before and after: Gender transitions, human capital and workplace experiences. *The B. E. Journal of Economic Analysis & Policy, 8*(1), 1–26.

Shen, H. (2013). Inequality quantified: Mind the gender gap. *Nature, 495*(7439), 22.

Spelke, E. S. (2005). Sex differences in intrinsic aptitude for mathematics and science? *American Psychologist, 60*, 950–958.

Symonds, M. R. E., Gemmell, N. J., Braisher, T. L., Gorringe, K. L., & Elgar, M. A. (2006). Gender differences in publication output: Towards an unbiased metric of research performance. *PLOS One, 1*(1), e127.

Williams, W. M., & Ceci, S. J. (2012). When scientists choose motherhood. *American Scientist, 100*, 138–146.

Xu, Y. J. (2008). Gender disparity in STEM disciplines: A study of faculty attrition and turnover intentions. *Research in Higher Education, 49*, 607–624.

See also the National Academy of Engineering, *Women in Engineering at* http://www.nae.edu/Publications/Bridge/WomeninEngineering7332.aspx

and the *University of Venus* blog at http://www.insidehighered.com/blogs/
university-venus/taking-time-think-about-expectations-women-under-
graduate-science. This blog features commentary on women with careers
in higher education and frequently focuses attention on women in science.

BOOKS ON WOMEN AND LEADERSHIP

American Association of University Women Educational Foundation. (2001).
Beyond the gender wars. Washington DC: Author.

Babcock, L., & Laschever, S. (2007). *Women don't ask: The high cost of avoiding
negotiation and positive strategies for change.* New York, NY: Bantam.

Bronson, P., & Merryman, A. (2013). *Top dog: The science of winning and losing.* New York, NY: Hachette.

Corbett, C., & Hill, C. (2012). *Graduating to a pay gap: The earnings of women
and men one year after college graduation.* Washington DC: American Association of University Women.

Corbett, C., Hill, C., & St. Rose, A. (2008). *Where the girls are: The facts
about gender equity in education.* Washington DC: American Association of
University Women.

Dey, J. G., & Hill, C. 2007. *Behind the pay gap.* Washington DC: American
Association of University Women.

Mason, M. A., & Ekman, E. M. (2007). *Mothers on the fast track: How a new
generation can balance family and careers.* Oxford, UK: Oxford University
Press.

Sandberg, S. (2013). *Lean in: Women, work and the will to lead.* New York, NY:
Knopf. See also http://www.leanin.org, a nonprofit foundation that forms
partnerships with corporate sponsors to offer online seminars and guidelines for establishing support circles (mentoring groups in the workplace).

Tannen, D. (1990). *You just don't understand: Women and men in conversation.*
New York, NY: HarperCollins.

Index

AAAS. *See* American Association for the Advancement of Science
academia
    Barnhart choosing, 14, 24–25, 155, 156, 159
    Blessing on jobs in, 52, 53, 154–55
    Hays, S., on, 83, 85
    Hessler on, 106, 107–8, 113–15, 155
    industry compared to, 113–15, 157, 159
    Perlman on, 139–40
    STEM and, 2, 154–55
ADVANCE Portal, 212
advisors
    Blessing on, 49
    Golden on Wang as, 68
    Hays, S., on thesis, 83–84
    Hessler on Lowe as, 105
Advocates for Women in Science, Engineering and Mathematics, 202
Africa
    Jacobs, B., on Kenya and husband in, 124–25, 154

Jacobs, B., on lab in, 125
Jacobs, B., research in Ethiopia, 119–20
National Museum of Kenya, 125
air and water pollution issues, 35
Albright, Madeleine, 183–84
"Algorhyme," 137–38
American Aging Association, 42
American Association for the Advancement of Science (AAAS) Congressional Fellowship, 86, 86n2
American Association for the Advancement of Science International Funding Opportunities for Women in Science, Technology and Engineering, 216
American Association for Women in Community Colleges, 212
American Association of University Women, 132, 213
American Astronomical Society Committee on the Status of Women in Astronomy, 213

Department of Civil and
Environmental
Engineering, MIT, 17
De Welde, K., 187–88
Digigirlz, 203
Digital Equipment Corporation,
135–36
Digital Equipment Corporation
Network (DECnet), 137
discipline-specific websites, college
and professional women,
213–15
D Magazine, 132
'Doing Good With OR,' 27, 182
Drug Enforcement Administration
(DEA), 74
D'Souza, Nandika, 72
dual-careers
Blessing on issues of, 52–53,
156
challenges of STEM and, 156
institutional bias in, 172–73
Jacobs, B., on women and,
129–30, 158
Duke University, 36
DZero experiment, 45–46, 53

Economist, 195
education. *See also* primary and
secondary education
websites
Birnbaum and, 32–33
of Golden, 66, 67
of Hays, S., 91–92
Hessler and, 104
of Jacobs, B., 120–21
of Perlman, 144–45
Ehlers, Vernon James, 86
Embry-Riddle Aeronautical
University Girls Exploring
Math, 208

encounters, serendipitous, x. *See also*
Hays, Sharon
Energy Technology Company (ETC)
of Chevron, 112
Engineer Girl, 203
engineering, ix, 2. *See also* science,
technology, engineering,
and mathematics (STEM);
Women in Math, Science
& Engineering program
(WIMSE)
articles on women in science
and, 219–21
Barnhart on women in, 16–17
books on women in science
and, 216–19
civil, 13
mechanical, 22
operations research branch of,
27
Engineering Education Service
Center, 202
engineers, ix, 13
Engineer Your Life, 203
Environmental Protection Agency
(EPA), 35
EPA Health Effects Research
Laboratory, 35
Equal Rights Amendment, 193
ETC. *See* Energy Technology
Company of Chevron
Ethernet, 137, 141
European Organization for
Nuclear Research (CERN),
46, 49
Executive Order 10925, 193
Executive Order 11246, 193
Expanding Your Horizons Network,
204
Exploring Gender and Technology,
210

Golden on ratio of men to
women, 70
Hessler on, 109
study on male graduate, 187–88
Summers, Lawrence, 3
Sun Microsystems, 140
SUNY. *See* State University of New
York
SUNY Buffalo (UB)
Jacobs, B., on classes at, 121–22
Jacobs, B., on teaching
assistantship at, 123
Superconducting Super Collider
(SSC), 51
Superfund site, Libby, Montana, 36
Sweden, women STEM graduates
in, 2
Syracuse University, 33

teaching
Birnbaum on, molecular
genetics, 33
Blessing on, and research, 46
Hessler on GVSU, position,
109
Jacobs on, assistantship at UB,
123
need for trained, in STEM
fields, 183
Techbridge program, 102, 102n2, 208
technology, ix. *See also* Georgia
Institute of Technology;
House Science, Space, and
Technology Committee;
Illinois Institute of
Technology; Massachusetts
Institute of Technology;
Office of Science and
Technology Policy; science,
technology, engineering,

and mathematics; Women's
Technology Program
Tech Up, 211
Temple University Girls and
Mathematics Program, 209
tenure
Barnhart on, 25–26
Blessing on, track, 53
-clock policy as bias, 171–72
Texas A & M University, 67
Texas Tech University, 67
Thoman, D. B., 174
Thomas, Ruthann, 71
Thomson, Joseph John, 47
Townsend, Fran, 88
toxicology, 34
trailing spouse handicap, 172
TRansparent Interconnection of
Lots of Links (TRILL), 141
Transportation@MIT initiative,
18–19
True Colors program, 59, 60
Tsinghua University, China, 20
Turkey, women STEM graduates
in, 2
TV shows, 55–56, 98, 98n5

UB. *See* SUNY Buffalo
unconscious bias, 167
individual or person-specific,
188–70
institutional, 170–73
societal, 174–77
undergraduate websites, 215
The UNESCO Fellowships
Programme, 216
United Kingdom, women STEM
graduates in, 3
United States
STEM job openings in, 179

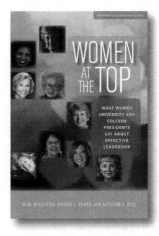

Women at the Top
What Women University and College Presidents Say About Effective Leadership
Mimi Wolverton, Beverly L. Bower, and Adrienne E. Hyle

"A book that is a truly exceptional contribution to the literature on leadership. The authors' distillation of the interviews to derive the nine tenets of effective leadership make this a must read for aspiring leaders and followers in higher education. I especially liked the fact that the tenets were tucked away in the back after the authors' thoughtful discussion of the obstacles of this 'road less traveled.' They highlight the speed bumps and crossroads that traditionally hold women and people of color from leadership positions.

Women at the Top is inspirational because most women who read it will see themselves trying to balance their competing family priorities with career paths and can say, 'I can do this too.' This deeply personal and reflective book will serve as a guidebook and resource for other women who seek leadership roles in the nation's colleges and universities."

—*Teachers College Record*

Sty/us

22883 Quicksilver Drive
Sterling, VA 20166-2102   Subscribe to our e-mail alerts: www.Styluspub.com

Also available in the Journeys to Leadership series

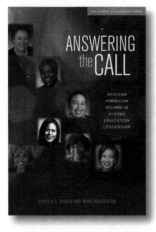

Answering the Call
African American Women in Higher Education Leadership
Beverly L. Bower and Mimi Wolverton

"The book is an excellent resource for anyone interested in the stories behind the successes of prominent African American women leaders, and contains valuable lessons about leadership in context and in general."

—On Campus with Women

This book presents the stories and the reflections on thepaths to leadership of seven African American women. Each has been the first woman, or first African American, or first African American woman in one or more of the positions of authority that she has held. Along the way, they have overcome the double bind of sexism and racism that can inhibit the professional attainment of African American women, particularly as they move toward the top of their professions.

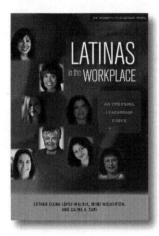

Latinas in the Workplace
An Emerging Leadership Force
Esther Elena López-Mulnix, Mimi Wolverton, and Salwa A. Zaki

"The volume is a quick but inspiring read."

—On Campus with Women

Although Latinos constitute one of the fastest growing segments of our population, these Latina leaders represent a relatively small percentage of women in leadership in the United States. They hope that their stories inspire not only their contemporaries but the next generation of Latinas as well.